MUSICAL CROSSROADS

Stories Behind the Objects of African American Music

A NIGHT-CLUB MAP OF HARLEM

The stars indicate the places that are open all night ..... The only important omission is the location of the various speakeasies but since there are about 500 of them you wont have much trouble .....

MUSICAL CROSSROADS

Stories Behind the Objects of African American Music

Edited by
Dwandalyn R. Reece

NATIONAL MUSEUM
of AFRICAN AMERICAN
HISTORY & CULTURE

National Museum of African American History and Culture
Smithsonian Institution, Washington, DC, in association with D Giles Limited

Editor: Dwandalyn R. Reece

Publication Manager: Douglas T. Remley

Essays by Dwandalyn R. Reece
Profiles and stories by Timothy Anne Burnside, Tuliza Fleming, Hannah Grantham, Steven W. Lewis, Vanessa L. Moorer, Kelly Elaine Navies, Dwandalyn R. Reece, Douglas T. Remley, Deborah Tulani Salahu-Din, Kevin M. Strait, Angela Tate, and Eric Lewis Williams
Captions by Timothy Anne Burnside, Hannah Grantham, Steven W. Lewis, Dwandalyn R. Reece, and Eric Lewis Williams

For the National Museum of African American History and Culture
Andrew W. Mellon Director: Kevin Young
Associate Director for Curatorial Affairs: Dwandalyn R. Reece
Publications Team: Timothy Anne Burnside, Hannah Grantham, Steven W. Lewis, Dwandalyn R. Reece, Douglas T. Remley

For D Giles Limited
Copyedited and proofread by Jenny Wilson
Designed by Alfonso Iacurci
Produced by GILES, an imprint of D Giles Limited
Printed and bound in Italy

First published in 2023 by GILES
An imprint of D Giles Limited
66 High Street
Lewes, BN7 1XG, UK
gilesltd.com

ISBN: 978-1-911282-87-7 (hardcover)
ISBN: 979-8-218-07599-6 (softcover)

Library of Congress Control Number: 2022915005

Front cover: Dress worn by Celia Cruz, 1970s; Gretsch G6138 "Bo Diddley" model rectangular guitar owned by Bo Diddley, 2005; Travel wardrobe trunk used by Cab Calloway, after 1927

Back cover: Poster advertising the 1973 Memphis Gospel Festival, 1973 (detail)

Frontispiece: "A Night-club Map of Harlem" by Elmer Simms Campbell, 1933 (see p. 170)

Right: Dress worn by Lena Horne in the 1943 film *Stormy Weather* (see p. 158)

For larger versions of the images on pages 21, 22, 31, 46, 65, 73, 99, 157, and 159 please see the Appendix.

Contents

Foreword 7

Introduction 11

Chapter 1
Music and the Meaning of Things 15

Chapter 2
Roots and Branches 35

Chapter 3
Music in the Community, Music of the Community 71

Chapter 4
I Wish I Knew How it Would Feel to be Free 117

Chapter 5
The Power(s) of Black Music 169

Endnotes 194

Appendix 196

Bibliography 206

Acknowledgments 209

Contributors 211

Image credits 213

Index 220

Foreword

arriet Tubman's hymnal. A flyer for the "Eighth Wonder," pianist Blind Tom. Charlie Parker's saxophone. Chuck Berry's Cadillac Eldorado. Bo Diddley's washboard and his rectangular guitar. Thomas A. Dorsey's piano. A button announcing "Dizzy Gillespie for President." Radio Raheem's boombox from *Do the Right Thing*. Janet Jackson's key earring. Sammy Davis Jr.'s childhood tap shoes. Nona Hendryx's silver spacesuit. The "Queen of Salsa" Celia Cruz's shimmery dress. Prince's purple suit with makeup still on the collar. A script for a little-known Langston Hughes radio play. And above all, the Mothership.

These remarkable and resonant items each have made their way into the nearly four thousand objects that make up the music collection stewarded by the National Museum of African American History and Culture—many of which are found across the Museum's 400,000 square feet of exhibits. These musical materials tell a story of Black innovation, survival, and ingenuity—whether that's repurposing a washboard to make music from what could be work, sewing a costume to achieve the stellar stagecraft that allowed the freedom of performance, or the enslaved and free creating handmade instruments during the antebellum period to sustain them in their daily lives and that expressed their rich afterlives. For the enslaved, their bodies could become an instrument in an oppressive system where much of their music was outlawed; their spirits undaunted, they achieved, as Tubman's hymnal testifies, a higher calling of faith and freedom.

Such stories and artifacts are central to Dwandalyn R. Reece's tremendous *Musical Crossroads: Stories Behind the Objects of African American Music*, which plumbs the material culture of the music collection. As her subtitle suggests, Reece believes—and inspires even those who find themselves already in her choir—that these objects refine meaning and redefine culture. As Timothy Anne Burnside, one of the book's contributors writes, "Objects and the moments associated with them are often what we use to shape and hold on to memories." "Costumes and props are usually only meant to be worn or used for a fleeting moment in time, but they are things that have a lasting impact on the way a song is remembered and felt," Reece writes. Anyone who finds themselves in the *Musical Crossroads* exhibit in the Museum would surely agree; holding this book in your hands, you have an unparalleled opportunity to take the exhibit or collection on the road and revisit it with Reece, the best of tour guides. "Vote Dizzy"!

Reece's scholarship and skill bring these items to life, less interpreting them than evoking their power. And, Reece reminds us, the power of Black music is found in transformation. Early instruments like African-inspired banjos crafted from gourds, or more recent fare like hand-drawn xeroxed hip-hop flyers, speak to the ways that Black musicians and fans have made a way out of no way across the centuries. They did so even when, in slavery, the drum and other forms of music were outlawed. Or when, as testified to by Chuck Berry's restored red Cadillac, segregation prevented them from playing certain clubs, for mixed audiences, and equal pay.

For generations, Black music has demanded a criticism as sophisticated and varied as it is, from W.E.B. Du Bois, James Weldon Johnson, and Zora Neale Hurston's discussion of spirituals to Angela Davis and Amiri Baraka (LeRoi Jones) and their powerful narratives of the blues. "These homemade instruments and experimentations often led to criticism that influenced musical genres of all kinds," Reece writes, tying such inventions to the criticism that interacted with it. Reece adds her powerful voice to this critical chorus, illuminating Black pride and persistence.

I feel equally inspired by my grandfather's fiddle, an instrument that he made his own with small tassels, a jerry-rigged bow, and patched-up strings—one he once used to play zydeco music. In its original worn wooden case in my living room, it is small yet sturdy, my chief inheritance. Though I never got to hear him play, even in its tattered case—like Black music more broadly and the dozens of objects featured here—it still sings.

Kevin Young
Andrew W. Mellon Director
National Museum of African American
History and Culture

The Angela Davis Legal Defense Fund produced this poster to advertise a June 29, 1972, victory celebration acknowledging Davis's recent release from prison and accompanying acquittal from charges that landed her on the FBI's "most wanted list." The benefit featured an eclectic mixture of artists lending their voices to support political prisoners.

— THE ANGELA DAVIS LEGAL DEFENSE FUND —

Presents

A VICTORY CELEBRATION

THURSDAY – JUNE 29 – 7:30 P.M.

An Evening with Angela Davis

BENEFIT FOR ALL POLITICAL PRISONERS

Rey Barretto * Jerry Butler
Carmen McCrae * Pete Seeger
* Voices of East Harlem *
Ossie Davis, M.C.

TICKET PRICES:
$12.50 $10.00 $7.50 $5.00 $3.00
PATRON SEATS $50.00
ALL PATRONS INVITED TO A
"Meet the Stars"
RECEPTION PRIOR TO THE CONCERT
—AT STATLER HILTON HOTEL—

MAIL ORDER:
PLEASE MAKE YOUR CHECK OR
MONEY ORDER PAYABLE TO:
ANGELA DAVIS LEGAL DEFENSE FUND OR
CYRIL PHILIP, TREASURER,
AND MAIL to:
EVENING, ROOM 203 LEGAL DEFENSE FUND
1 UNION SQUARE WEST, NEW YORK, N.Y. 10003

— FOR TICKET INFORMATION CALL: (212) 691-0271 —
TICKETS AVAILABLE AT THESE LOCAL OUTLETS:

NEW YORK COMMITTEE to FREE ANGELA DAVIS
150 FIFTH AVE. (20TH ST.), Room 425
JEFFERSON BOOK SHOP, 100 E. 16TH ST., MAN.
BEN DAVIS BOOK SHOP, 2717 8TH AVE., MAN.

madison square garden
Pennsylvania Plaza, 7th Ave., 31st to 33rd Sts.

NEW YORKER BOOKSTORE,
250 W. 89 ST., MANHATTAN

RECORD SHACK, 274 W. 125 ST., MAN.
BIRDEL'S, 540 NOSTRAND AV. AT FULTON B'KLYN
PEOPLES BOOK STORE,
137 WASHINGTON ST., NEWARK

The Tulsa, Oklahoma-based group The Gap Band was
formed in the late 1960s by brothers Charlie, Ronnie,
and Robert Wilson, with the "Gap" name originating as
an acronym for Greenwood, Archer, and Pine Streets in
the African American Greenwood neighborhood. The
band released a series of hit recordings in the late 1970s
and early 1980s featuring the brothers playing a variety
of instruments, including this flugelhorn used by Ronnie.
Eventually they became a popular source of samples for
hip-hop producers.

Introduction

I n 2003, President George W. Bush signed legislation authorizing the creation of the National Museum of African American History and Culture. The dream that originated over a hundred years earlier was now on the precipice of becoming a reality. Lonnie G. Bunch III, 15th Secretary of the Smithsonian Institution, was the Museum's founding director. When he assumed the position in 2005, the Museum had a staff of two people, no building, no location for a building, and most importantly, no collection. In the middle of fundraising, securing approval for a site on the National Mall, and selecting an architect, curators joined the staff. Their primary tasks included building a collection of national significance that spoke to diverse experiences of African Americans across the United States and abroad. These stories would be included in the Museum's permanent exhibitions and made easily accessible to the public online through detailed cataloging records, digitized images, and the Museum's other interpretive programming and materials.

In building the music collection, I based my strategy on the Museum's mission. It should be inclusive and reflect a history of African American music and music-making that incorporates the experiences, perspectives, values, and personal and professional choices that encompass a broad time period, as well as diverse geographical regions, cultural and gender identities, sexual orientations, racial identifications, ethnicities, and classes. The collection would include celebrated artists, popular music genres, high-profile professionals, institutions, and historical events. Still, it would also have artifacts that reflected the role music played in the day-to-day lives of individuals in their homes, churches, schools, and local communities. African American music and music-making originated with the forced migration and enslavement of Africans in the Americas. The newly formed community of people of many cultures,

German-born photographer Clemens Kalischer took this photograph of blues musician John Lee Hooker (1917–2001) in September 1951 at the Music Inn in Lenox, Massachusetts. Hooker, along with Mahalia Jackson and several other musicians, scholars, and dancers, was a panelist on jazz scholar Marshall Stearns's third roundtable on the history of jazz and Black folk music. Stearns's summertime roundtable series extended from 1950 through 1956.

John Birks "Dizzy" Gillespie (1917–1993) hosted staged presidential rallies in 1963 and sold buttons like this one to support the Congress of Racial Equality (CORE) during the Civil Rights Movement. Vocalist Jon Hendricks supported Gillespie's campaign by re-working Gillespie's 1943 bebop piece "Salt Peanuts" into the campaign song "Vote Dizzy."

created from this traumatic event, adapted the musical and performance traditions of their ancestors to the musical languages of their new home to become an essential means of survival, protest, and triumph, despite the barriers imposed by a culture of oppression and systemic racism in the United States.

Today there are over four thousand music-related objects in the Museum's collection. These objects are tangible evidence of music's existence or, more simply, music's material culture. This material culture, along with the methodologies employed to study it, is commonly used by curators, scholars, and students in anthropology, archaeology, art history, folklore studies, and history. The growing number of music exhibitions, museums, and historical sites that are popping up in countries around the world—and the increasing public interest in acquiring albums, photographs, instruments, clothing, and other music-related objects—illustrate the historical, cultural, and educational value these collections hold for audiences worldwide.

Musical Crossroads: Stories Behind the Objects of African American Music highlights objects from the Museum's collection through the lens of material culture studies. A material culture approach sees an object as a primary source that functions as an agent and mediator between the past and present. Material culture research in music can push the boundaries of

historical analysis and contemporary interpretation by destabilizing the primacy and power of the written word and letting objects guide us to the multiple stories that are still waiting to be unearthed.

This book is divided into five chapters. In Chapter 1, "Music and the Meaning of Things," the process of conceptualizing a framework to identify the objects that constitute a material culture of music is discussed; and the rest of the chapter provides an overview of the different methodologies that demonstrate how to apply and interpret findings. The remaining four chapters are organized by narratives commonly found in research on African American music. Each chapter integrates methodological approaches with different case studies presented in an introductory essay, short profiles that focus on one or two objects, and longer stories that interpret a group of objects under a particular topic or theme.

Dwandalyn R. Reece

With its rows of sequins staggered in undulating bands of purple, red, and gold, this dress would have gleamed underneath stage lights as its wearer, Cuban-born vocalist Celia Cruz (1925–2003), danced her way through performances. The "Queen of Salsa" was renowned for her warm contralto, vocal dexterity, and wardrobe of brightly colored gowns that accentuated her exuberant spins and hip movements.

1813 - 1883

Oct. 11, 1960   Wagner - Compositional devices:

    1. pedal - point {10-60 measures - usually dom.
                sometimes ✗
    2. suspension
    3. appoggiaturas
    4. Deceptive Cadences (deceptive motion)
    5. Chromaticism °chrom. bassline - one -needs not to worry
    6. Sequences
    7. Modulations
    8. ½ Dim. Sevenths (chords) - used as leading to to maj. key.

Constant - continuous motion in Wagner. Why did Wagner modulate?
    ans.: For sake of modulation + to express thoughts

Favorite harmonic relationships}   IV chord relationships

If strong $\underline{V} - \underline{I}$ chords - I will have appoggiatura.

Oct. 14, 1960 - Comparisons of music - Composers
look up score Corelli - Baroque - interested in
    instrumental music, trio sonata.
what music keyboard music - Concerti grossi
looked like figured bass -
harpsichord, violins, viola, trumpets,
oboe, tympani, celli, organ -

what music}
looks like} groupings: 'E' solo   contrapuntal texture melody -
    2[large   rhythm - motor tempo - running tempo.

    violins
    closely related keys - 5th usually
    violin
    celli

Chapter 1

MUSIC AND THE MEANING OF THINGS

Music is at the center of an eco-system that lives and thrives through a network of connections and encounters among people, communities, places, organizations, and institutions. The material culture of music is both a description and a research methodology. The description applies to the evidence that music activity leaves behind. As a research tool, an object requires different analytical questions when it is used as a primary source rather than an illustration.

The objects of African American music history embody the stories of individual and community perspectives and experiences. Some objects speak to the obstacles, challenges, and injustices African Americans encounter due to systemic racism and personal bias. Others speak to accomplishments and achievements against the odds, and capture people's emotional, spiritual, and bodily experiences with music alone and with others.

Material culture has been a growing field of interest for decades, and scholarship on the topic continues to inform the work of academics, museum curators, archivists, and others who are interested in the tangible objects that humans create, use, and keep. Dr. E. McClung Fleming's "Artifact Study: A Proposed Model" (1974) was one of the early texts on the topic. Fleming breaks down his approach into four categories: Identification, Evaluation, Cultural Analysis, and Interpretation. These steps are basic museum identification procedures that can be used by anyone interested in deepening their understanding of music and the role it plays in society.

Objects make their journeys to museums like the NMAAHC in myriad ways. Some artifacts arrive well-documented with pages of descriptive historical background pre-established for museum staff to work from as they strive to make information publicly available. Others come as rare or recently discovered items with murky provenance histories that leave something to be desired in the object's story. Museum professionals have for decades honed systems of recordkeeping informed by registration, conservation, collections, and curatorial staff that contribute to catalog records describing an object's history, physical makeup, appearance, state of preservation, and cultural significance. Fleming's model invites other academic disciplines less often engaged with museum collections to approach artifacts as museum staff would, to explore lines of questioning elicited from object examination.

Fleming's model begins with essential primary identifications that unpack an object's factual, material, construction, design, and functional elements. In this step, his model encourages viewers to engage with artifacts by asking questions. What is

Shirley Verrett (1931–2010) entered Juilliard in 1955, to study vocal music. The pages of this Manuscript Music Book from autumn 1960 to early 1961 include her handwritten comments on works by Wagner, Mahler, Brahms, and others. Her detailed notes also examine music theory and vocal exercises. Verrett went on to become an internationally renowned opera singer.

DeFord Bailey, Black Opry Pioneer

Like other American music traditions, country music is a hybrid idiom that reflects a combination of European and African musical influences. The segregation of the 1920s recording industry—"hillbilly" music for rural white audiences, "race" music for Black audiences—obscured the contributions of Black country pioneers and discouraged the participation of later Black artists. Despite the exclusionary country music industry, Black artists have continued the fight to have their voices heard.

This Hohner harmonica, from the 1970s, belonged to DeFord Bailey (1899-1982), the most prominent Black artist in the early country music industry. Bailey, pictured here in the 1970s at the Grand Ole Opry, was a harmonica virtuoso and one of the first stars of the Grand Ole Opry. He was born in Smith County, Tennessee, in 1899 and learned to play the harmonica while bedridden with polio as a small child, teaching himself to mimic sounds he heard in his community. Bailey's introduction to the instrument was common among children in those years. Because harmonicas cost about five cents at the turn of the century, they were frequently given to children as gifts. The affordability of mass-produced harmonicas helped make them prevalent in turn-of-the-century Black folk music, replacing earlier instruments like reed panpipes.

Bailey moved to Nashville as a young man and made his radio debut in 1925, after honing his skills in local harmonica competitions and impressing Grand Ole Opry founder George D. Hay. He performed and toured with the Opry from 1926 to 1941, helping to establish the radio show's popularity and becoming famous for a style that blended the blues with imitations of trains and animal sounds. Despite his success, however, Bailey endured Jim Crow segregation during his many tours of the South. Hay often belittled Bailey on air as the show's "mascot," and Bailey was paid less than his white Opry co-stars. After Bailey's departure in 1941, no other Black artist would appear on country music's flagship show until Charley Pride's Opry debut in 1967. In the 2010s and '20s, a new generation of Black artists, including Mickey Guyton and Jimmie Allen, have made their mark on country music, building on Bailey's early efforts. SWL

the object made of? Where was the object created? Who used the object before it arrived in its current location? These are the initial questions museum professionals start with when completing accession records that travel and grow with an object's use. Information gathered during the identification process feeds the evaluation and cultural analysis stages where classifications or networks of themes further inform an object's broader contextual background. Preliminary conclusions drawn during this interrogation open up different avenues for interpreting artifacts. These can be incredibly narrow in exploring a particular event or wide enough to speak to general cultural phenomena during a period of years. The narratives that bubble to the surface using Fleming's model demonstrate the transient qualities of objects as primary resources.

In studying material culture, examinations of the physical qualities of the object, the context of its original use and purpose, and how that context changes over time are equally important—this type of information informs the object's biography. Like a person's life story, an object's biography is told and shaped by the people, places, and events it encounters over its life span. This biography should also place the object within the context of its original purpose and mark how that has shifted over time. When we engage with an object in any given moment, questioning it helps to uncover the multiple stories that resonate inside and around it. Jules Prown perhaps captured the value of this type of approach best when he

In 1971, Charley Pride (1934–2020) was named Male Vocalist of the Year and Entertainer of the Year by the Country Music Association, and became the first Black artist to win in either category. This award for the former category, a carved piece of walnut on a marble and brass base, signifies country music's strength, durability, and warmth. Pride's presence in country music connected audiences to the genre's roots in Black music and opened doors for the next generation.

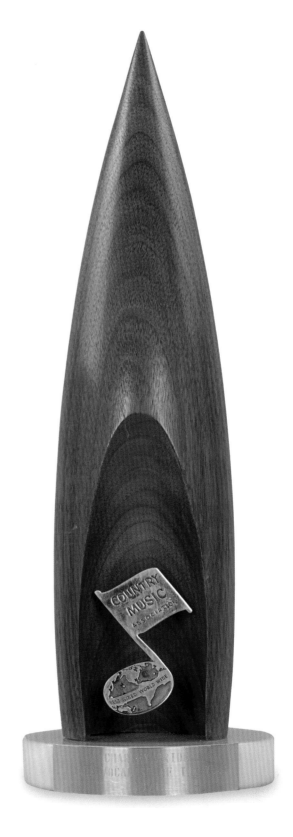

Cab Calloway Travels the World

Bandleader Cab Calloway (1907-1994) used this Herkert & Meisel trunk to store his clothing and belongings while on tour for much of his career, beginning perhaps as early as the late 1920s. Calloway owned it until his death in 1994, but likely stopped using it at some point in the 1960s. Trunks of this style fell out of favor in the 1960s and '70s as airplanes replaced older modes of long-distance transportation like trains and ships. Calloway possibly used this trunk during various domestic and international tours, including his 1934 European tour with his orchestra and his 1952-56 world tour as Sportin' Life in a revival of George Gershwin's *Porgy and Bess*. When standing upright, the trunk's

left compartment has space for hanging dress clothes, while its right compartment contains a set of six drawers. The trunk came into the NMAAHC's possession with an array of small items in the drawers, representing the everyday objects Calloway would have carried on his travels: socks, ties, business cards, receipts, bottle openers, and wash cloths, among other things.

Objects like Cab Calloway's steamer trunk tell us about the realities of musicians' lives on the road. Even a famous and well-paid musician like Calloway would have dealt with the discomfort of living out of a trunk during long tours. Black groups on domestic tours faced the additional struggle of finding decent

lodgings and restaurants that were open to Black clientele. Although Calloway's success meant that his band could use private rail cars to avoid the indignity of Jim Crow travel, trunks like this one would still have been important lifelines in the uncertain conditions facing traveling Black musicians for much of the twentieth century.

Calloway's trunk is a notable illustration of the mobility of Black musicians, which began in the latter half of the nineteenth century. As early as the 1870s, with the famous European tours of the Fisk Jubilee Singers (see p. 169), and expanding around 1900 with the growth of vaudeville, Black musicians were key figures in the rapidly expanding global network of entertainment venues. With their regular travel to reach audiences overseas, they spread African American musical innovations around the world. This movement of music and musicians across international borders would make Black art forms like ragtime, jazz, blues, and hip-hop into truly global phenomena. SWL

Hall Johnson (1888–1970) was a violinist, composer, arranger, and choral director. He is most well-known for interpreting spirituals and directing the Hall Johnson Choir, which had a successful concert, recording, and film career for over thirty years (see p. 64). Johnson was also an avid photographer. His archive includes numerous photographs, including this group portrait of Paul Robeson (back center), Jester Hairston (center, in front of Robeson), and three unidentified men.

wrote, "The underlying premise is that human-made objects reflect, consciously or unconsciously, directly or indirectly, the beliefs of the individuals who commissioned, fabricated, purchased, or used them and by extension the beliefs of the larger society to which these individuals belonged."[1]

Material culture studies spell out how artifacts can expand our understanding of music's value and place within everyday life. Traditionally, the various music disciplines—musicology, ethnomusicology, historical musicology, and music education—have been significantly, if not entirely, reliant on written text, recordings, fieldwork, and performances. Predictably, the outcome of this work replicates the processes—historical narratives firmly shaped by a fixed set of aesthetic values, musical canons, and hierarchies that assign value based on essentialist notions of authenticity, skill, and interpretation—that

favor Western European models. Consequently, the whole culture of non-Western music and the way it functions in society, along with the way people experience it in their daily lives, are omitted or distorted in music discussions and scholarship in ways that hamper a complete understanding of the vibrant musical life happening globally. The Fleming model's utility for musicological investigations is evident when applied to musical material culture within the NMAAHC's collection.

A careful study of these artifacts as texts reveals how material culture can enrich our understanding of African American music-making and the impact it has had on American culture, within the African diaspora, and on the musical traditions and cultural expressions of communities around the world. Questioning objects leads to information supporting the continuity of African traditions within a developing African

You Are My Sunshine

State of Louisiana
EXECUTIVE DEPARTMENT
Baton Rouge

JIMMIE H. DAVIS
GOVERNOR

December 3, 1962

Mr. Charles Sullivan
Sullivan's Enterprises
919 Grove Street
San Francisco, California

Dear Mr. Sullivan:

Of course, the Ray Charles version of "YOU ARE MY SUNSHINE" is far different to my version; and, incidentally, my version is more or less on the "cornfed" side. But, nevertheless, the tune itself is well established and planted in the minds of the people throughout the world.

But, now to the Ray Charles version -- I had a feeling when I heard his recording that it would be a nation-wide hit and perhaps go to the No. 1 position. I had always felt that if it got the right kind of what I call the "wild treatment", by the right artist, it couldn't miss. And, frankly, I do not know of a person who is in a better position to give it this "wild treatment", or the modern touch, or whatever you want to call it, than Ray Charles because he is a person that knows pretty much what to do with any song that he records, and when he sings one, it's had the works. "SUNSHINE" is one of the "naturals" that lends itself to various background support, and this group that Ray Charles had on this number really worked it over.

I don't care how they sing it -- just so they sing it!

Very truly yours,

Jimmie Davis
JIMMIE DAVIS

JHD/A

The pioneering career of Ray Charles (1930–2004), pictured above in 1965, was at its peak in the late 1950s and early 1960s. His crossover triumph had been crowned in 1959 with a lucrative ABC-Paramount Records contract that gave him ownership of his master recordings. Charles scored an unlikely hit in 1962 with a recording of his soulful arrangement of "You Are My Sunshine." His success prompted unexpected accolades from Jimmie Davis, a Louisiana politician and staunch segregationist who was serving his second term as governor of the state. Davis, a former country musician who had copyrighted and published the song, had recorded his own influential version of "You Are My Sunshine" in 1940. His music would earn him a place in the Country Music Hall of Fame in 1972.

On December 2, 1962, Davis composed this letter praising Charles's version of "You Are My Sunshine" on official State of Louisiana letterhead. While Davis is complimentary of Charles's performance, his references to Charles's "wild" interpretation lean into racial stereotypes. By the early 1700s, white spectators were commenting on the "savage wildness" of Black music,[2] while stereotyping Black people as innately or instinctively musical.[3] Demeaning ideas of Black music as "wild"—and potentially dangerous to white listeners—persisted well into the twentieth century, as demonstrated by the controversies that surrounded ragtime, jazz, rhythm and blues, rock and roll, rap, and hip-hop in turn.

Davis's letter inadvertently highlights the close though underacknowledged connection between country music and genres like R&B, jazz, and blues. Although Davis emphasizes the distance between his "cornfed" performance of "You Are My Sunshine" and Charles's "wild treatment" of the song, country music and R&B have common roots in the blues. Indeed, at the time of Davis's writing, Charles had reestablished the connection between the two genres with his hit April 1962 album *Modern Sounds in Country and Western Music*. This proved to be one of the most acclaimed albums in twentieth-century popular music, permanently altering the landscape of country music while also bridging the racial divide established by the segregated music industry decades earlier. SWL

In 1983, a fan of vocalist Maxine Sullivan (1911–1987) wrote a letter sharing his appreciation for her "very soft voice." In the letter he asked about the vocalist's race, writing, "I would like to know if she is a colored person? On the cover she looks colored but her singing doesn't." The fan's question highlights how voices are racialized and how mainstream society perceives Black musical voices.

American population. Musical items used and made by African Americans also facilitate conversations about hybridization, since African American music also includes influences from European and Indigenous populations.

Objects can point us to information that the written record of newspapers, magazines, or historical documents often does not provide by complete omission or racially biased interpretation that marginalizes African Americans. The results of these investigations prove to be a practice of recovery that transforms knowledge through its reporting of what extant artifacts tell us about African American music-making and its role within American society.

For example, at first glance, *Gospel Hymns No. 2*, published by P.P. Bliss and Ira D. Sankey in 1876, is simply a nineteenth-century book with a hard cover and black printing (see opposite). However, asking a question about the provenance record of ownership will dramatically alter the meaning and significance of this particular hymnal. The book was included in a collection of items belonging to Harriet Tubman (ca. 1822–1913), donated to the Museum in 2011 by historian Charles L. Blockson, founder of the Charles L. Blockson Afro-American Collection at Temple University, Philadelphia. Tubman's great-niece, Eva Stewart Northrup, was raised by Tubman and inherited the items from her. The collection was eventually passed on to Northrup's daughter, Meriline Wilkins, who bequeathed it to Blockson in her will.

Inside the hymnal are 112 pages of hymn lyrics. No musical notation is included, which was a common practice with hymnbooks published during this time. According to Kate Clifford Larson, author of the book *Bound for the Promised Land: Harriet Tubman, Portrait of an American Hero* (2004), this hymnbook most likely came from one of the churches Tubman attended, and Northrup or Wilkins probably wrote the inscription of Tubman's name inside, since

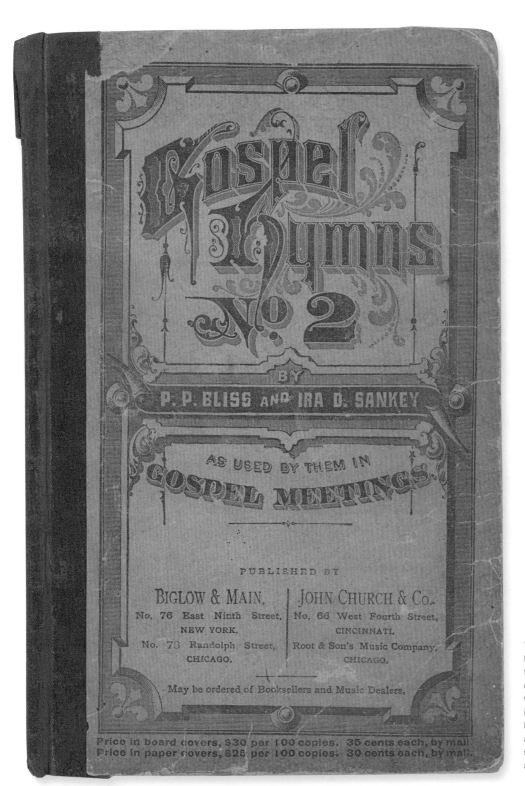

Though scholars of Harriet Tubman have long noted her inability to read or write, the fact that she would hold within her most cherished possessions Bliss and Sankey's widely circulated *Gospel Hymns No. 2* (1876) illustrates both her longing for literacy and her love of sacred music. Enslaved Africans and their descendants, in addition to creating sacred music of their own, often adopted and adapted European hymnody.

Lena and Edouard

Edouard Plummer (1928–2018) met Lena Horne (1917–2010) in the 1950s, when he visited her backstage after a performance. The two had an instant rapport and maintained a friendship that would last until Horne's death in May 2010. In 2011, Plummer donated his Lena Horne Archive to the Museum.

Plummer grew up in West Virginia and attended West Virginia University. After four years in the Army, he moved to Paris in 1952. During this time, he became friends with several expatriates, including James Baldwin, Richard Wright, and Josephine Baker. In 1959, he returned to the United States and accepted a teaching position at Wadleigh Junior High School in New York City. Five years later, he established the Wadleigh Scholars Program, which has since prepared over six hundred disadvantaged students to enroll in elite boarding schools, colleges, and universities across the country.

Plummer's Archive is both a record of Lena Horne's professional career and the history of their friendship. It includes posters, personal photographs, publicity stills, press kits, newspaper clippings, scrapbooks, albums, personal correspondence, and other memorabilia. Much of the material once hung on the walls of his apartment, alongside personally autographed photographs and memorabilia featuring such artists as Chita Rivera, Martina Arroyo, Mattiwilda Dobbs, and Josephine Baker.

Plummer attended many of Horne's performances and frequently served as a sounding board and sometimes advisor on a variety of things. He was at the center of a network of friendships among some of the most important artists of the period.

Horne, in turn, supported Plummer's community projects and his work with the Wadleigh Scholars Program. She would often speak to the students during special events and lend additional support whenever she could. The black and white photograph of Plummer gazing at Horne captures the pride and admiration he had for his friend. Horne's handwritten note to Plummer was sent shortly after the death of her dear friend, composer Billy Strayhorn, in May 1967. It offers an intimate glimpse of the relationship between the two friends, as one carefully holds the weight of the grief and sense of loss that is experienced by the other, while the turbulence of violence, bigotry, anger, class warfare, and social and economic injustice continues to bubble up around her. DRR

In his quest for finding the right guitar sound, Bo Diddley frequently modified his instrument to get distinctive effects that influenced rock and roll and electric guitar manufacturing. This 2005 Gretsch, owned by Diddley and modeled after the iconic rectangular guitar he invented in the 1950s, was part of a partnership that led to three Bo Diddley-designed guitars.

Tubman could neither read nor write. But even this is a fact that perhaps reflects what Tubman wanted the public to believe. Tubman's retention of the hymnal challenges the historical record by forcing us to consider what we know about her as a historical figure versus the more intimate side of her life and her family relationships.

The connection established between Tubman and this hymnal during the identification stage raises questions about what special significance it held for her. How did she acquire it, and how did she use it at home? Did keeping this book reflect her aspirations for literacy? What kind of engagement did she have, flipping through these pages containing words she could not read, but to songs she knew so well? Tubman was a deeply religious woman who drew strength and comfort from spirituals and hymns. It is easy to see how this one small book became one of her most cherished items.

In working with objects, finding ways to discern their meaning is a critical part of the process. Sense transforms an object into a multidimensional repository of stories, people, and events. These stories and connections offer much more than a simple description can. In material culture methodologies, objects are not in service to historical scholarship but act as agents of their own. This becomes apparent when approaching the manufacturing and design identifications for objects such as this red Gretsch G6138 Bo Diddley model rectangle guitar made in 2005. Documenting the instrument's design leads researchers further back in time to contextualize the decades of tinkering that went into making the final model.

The rectangular guitar is a trademark of Bo Diddley (1928–2008). Born Ellas Otha Bates, Diddley was one of the key architects of rock and roll, and asserted the music's subversive attitude with his inventive mind and the rectangular guitar of his own making. The famous Bo Diddley beat, a five-accent clave rhythm, is his sonic signature, and can be heard in rock and popular music. Diddley was also an innovative guitarist who used distortion, feedback, and a complex, aggressive strumming style to emphasize the sharp signature rhythms in his music. Needing a smaller instrument that was less restrictive to give him more freedom to jump around the stage, he made his first rectangular guitar in 1945 as an experiment. By 1958, he had built more than two dozen iterations, with various modifications. At that point, Diddley struck a deal with Gretsch's guitar company to build a custom-made guitar based on his design.

This partnership between Diddley and Gretsch was the outcome of Diddley's ingenuity and creativity, working with everyday materials and technologies to build instruments and experiment with new sounds. Diddley did not need to pay Gretsch to come up with the concept. That innovation was all his own. Diddley's inspiration to develop a new guitar model prompts a reconsideration of rock and roll's history, and how African Americans' musical and technological innovations are situated within the popular narrative.

One can apply this type of investigation to other objects, like clothing. Diana Ross (b. 1944) wore this costume playing Billie Holiday in the 1972 film *Lady Sings the Blues*. The film was Motown Records founder Berry Gordy's first big venture after he had moved the Motown headquarters from Detroit to Los Angeles to pursue other opportunities in the entertainment industry. Gordy's ambition and reach in developing projects that featured Black content and told relevant stories helped shape the model that

In 1972, Motown Productions released its first feature-length film, *Lady Sings the Blues*, starring Diana Ross as Billie Holiday. This twill dress-vest ensemble (with an accompanying hat) was designed by California-based costumer Bob Mackie, renowned for elaborate clothing worn by entertainers like Diahann Carroll and Whitney Houston. Mackie's costumes for the film captured Holiday's sense of elegance and secured him (and his fellow costume designers Ray Aghayan and Norma Koch) an Academy Award nomination.

today's hip-hop moguls embrace. The film earned several Academy Award nominations, including one for Bob Mackie, Ray Aghayan, and Norma Koch for costume design and a Best Actress nomination for Diana Ross.

Proceeding to descriptions of materials and physical appearance, Fleming's model facilitates conversations about performance and the things that musicians use to communicate their messages. Flavor Flav's clock, used by the artist during Public Enemy's rise in the 1980s, presents an opportunity to pause and reflect on the concept of an artist's iconic accessory. William Drayton Jr. (b. 1959), known by the stage name Flavor Flav, wore the clock suspended from a thick rope, which starkly contrasts with the ubiquitous metal chains generally associated with hip-hop. The plastic surface of the clock has scuffs and nicks that document the wear it saw when it hung from Flav's neck as he bounced, grooved, and moved about the stage during his duties as Public Enemy's hype man. While the group delved into serious content addressing themes of racism, corruption, and violent oppression, Flavor Flav provided a comedic foil to his bandmate Chuck D's "lyrical protest." His clock was a visual reminder to his audiences that, despite the hijinks he might pull, he was serious about the urgency needed to address issues harming the African

Responding to a dare from rapper Son of Bazerk in the 1980s, Public Enemy hype man Flavor Flav replaced his usual stopwatch props with an actual clock. Clocks like this one, which he wore during performances in the 1980s and '90s, became integral to his public persona and conveyed his message that time is "the most important element in our life."

Janet's Treasured Earring

A simple key hangs from a hoop earring. The silver tones are a little tarnished, but the key—with its onyx center—still shines in the light despite the slight dullness. This makeshift piece of jewelry was worn by one of the world's most influential music superstars. It is nowhere near the most flashy or expensive piece of jewelry she has ever worn, but it is, undeniably, the most recognizable.

Janet Jackson (b. 1966), the youngest member of the Jackson family, started performing professionally at a very young age. Even though she was part of a famous family, she, like most children, still had chores to do around the house, including taking care of the family's many animals. She fed them and cleaned their cages. The cages had to be opened with a key, and since Janet didn't use a keychain, she put the key on her earring so that she wouldn't lose it.

After many years of performing with her brothers and acting on television, in the early 1980s Jackson started focusing on her own music career. Her debut album, *Janet Jackson*, was released in 1982. When Jackson attended the 10th American Music Awards in 1983, she wore a pair of hoop earrings, one of which had a small gold key attached. After her second album, *Control*, was released in 1986, Jackson wore the same key earring when she performed at the 14th American Music Awards. By the time she released *Janet Jackson's Rhythm Nation 1814* in 1989, the key earring had become her visual signature.

Jackson is pictured on the album's cover wearing a military-style uniform and hat. The key earring is prominently visible hanging from her right ear. *Rhythm Nation 1814* marked her growth since the coming-of-age era of *Control* and cemented her status as a social and musical icon for people all over the world. Jackson wore this key earring throughout the next year of public appearances, award shows, and the incredibly successful Rhythm Nation World Tour 1990. The earring is a connection to her childhood, and perhaps a representation of her finally unlocking the many facets of her creativity and personal agency. TAB

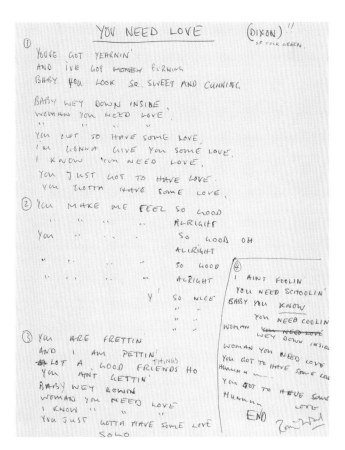

Willie Dixon handwrote these lyrics for his 1962 song "You Need Love." Soon after its first recording by Muddy Waters later that year, the song became popular with British rock bands, including Led Zeppelin, the Rolling Stones, the Animals, and the Yardbirds. In 1985, Dixon sued Led Zeppelin for allegedly plagiarizing "You Need Love" in their recording of "Whole Lotta Love," eventually settling out of court.

clock helps us get to Flav's message that time waits for no one, and his call for listeners to be actively involved in social justice and fighting the powers that be.

In the cultural analysis stage, artifact study situates material culture within broader contexts that lead us to explore how an item fits within a subject's career and overall cultural legacy. These handwritten lyrics for "You Need Love" are among songwriter and bassist Willie Dixon's most famous. Dixon (1915–1992) wrote some of the best-known songs associated with Chicago blues in the 1950s and '60s. Like his contemporaries—Muddy Waters and Howlin' Wolf, among others—Dixon migrated from Mississippi to Chicago to become a key player on the urban blues scene. The lyrics include several lines that were later interpolated into songs by the blues-influenced British rock bands of the 1960s. The most famous of these groups was the Rolling Stones; longtime Stones guitarist Ron Wood's signature on these lyrics in the bottom right-hand corner highlights the connection. Although Dixon originally signed to Chess Records as a recording artist in 1948, he served as a talent scout, producer, session musician, and staff songwriter by 1951. In light of this background, materials like this sometimes raise more questions than they answer. When were these lyrics written? Why did Ron Wood sign them? Despite—or because of—these unanswerable questions, handwritten lyrics offer a uniquely intimate look at a musician's creative process.

In the final stage of interpretation of Fleming's model, all of the information gathered about an object is used to contextualize it and establish its significance as material culture. As objects within the NMAAHC collection demonstrate, this process has the power to uplift musicians whose careers have rarely been included in historical examinations. A poster in the collection advertising an appearance

This poster advertises a performance by Ernie Fields (1904–1997) and his orchestra in Tulsa, Oklahoma, during the late 1950s to early 1960s. Fields, a Tulsa-based musician who began his career in the 1930s in the network of Black theaters commonly known as the "chitlin circuit," successfully adapted his swing band to new trends in post-World War II popular music. The biggest hit of his career was a 1959 recording of his arrangement of "In the Mood."

of the Ernie Fields Orchestra, for example, opens up the conversation of the tremendous impact of territory bands, who toured around a large geographic "territory" of cities and towns centered around a home base. From their base in Tulsa, Oklahoma, Fields's group was one of the leading Black bands in the region. Unlike other territory bands—like the Jay McShann and Count Basie orchestras, who were heavily blues-influenced and catered mainly to African American audiences—Fields's group played in a pop-inflected "sweet" style that was popular with Black and white audiences alike. Perhaps this crossover appeal allowed them to break barriers in the era of segregation, becoming one of the first African American ensembles to perform at Tulsa's historic Cain's Ballroom. Through further analysis, the poster could expand on the aspects of Fields's band and its little-known featured soloists that made them "fun to watch," "easy to dance to, and really enjoyable to hear."

From these few brief examinations, it is abundantly clear that there are nearly endless ways to look at artifacts to inspire research. These things are left behind to act as trails to the stories. New and different conclusions can be drawn about how African Americans engage with and shape American musical life by going beyond the written record to focus on objects, correspondence, and personal archives. But, perhaps most excitingly, the material culture of music centers music at the heart of the African American experience.

Eubie's Century

Bobbiegita Walker (b. 1942) created this portrait bust sculpture of James Hubert "Eubie" Blake (1887–1983) in 1981. Walker had met the nonagenarian Blake earlier that year and, impressed with his lively personality, requested to make a sculpture of him. This photograph shows one of the four resulting three-hour-long modeling sessions, in which Blake passed the time by telling stories from his long career. Walker made two castings of the sculpture: the original, which he kept for himself and eventually donated to the NMAAHC, and a second copy he presented to Blake during his "99th birthday" celebration at the Songwriters Hall of Fame in New York City.[4] Walker also made life casts of Blake's hands about two months before his death in February 1983.

By the time Blake sat for Walker's sculpture, he was revered as a living link to the history of ragtime and early jazz. Born in Baltimore, Blake wrote his first composition, "Charleston Rag," in 1899. He wrote the hit musical *Shuffle Along* (see also p. 140) with his longtime collaborator Noble Sissle in 1921. *Shuffle Along* was one of the first major musical productions to be written, produced, and performed entirely by African Americans, and its success opened the door for Black talent on Broadway. The show launched stars such as Paul Robeson and Josephine Baker and featured two of Blake's best-known songs, "I'm Just Wild About Harry" and "Love Will Find a Way."

Blake retired in 1946 but returned to the stage during the ragtime revival of the 1950s. As a veteran artist who had met legends like Scott Joplin, he experienced a career renaissance as a concert soloist and lecturer. In the 1970s he received a string of honorary degrees and was the subject of a Broadway musical before receiving the Presidential Medal of Freedom in 1981.

Blake's life underscores the incredible amount of change and growth that occurred within Black music in only a century. Blake, who spent his adolescence playing ragtime in the sporting houses of nineteenth-century Baltimore, lived long enough to witness the birth of hip-hop culture in 1970s and '80s New York City. Within one lifetime—albeit an unusually long one—Black music had blossomed, fueled by twentieth-century transportation and mass-media technologies. SWL

Chapter 2

ROOTS AND BRANCHES

Studying the material culture of African American music opens the door to a broad network of encounters, relationships, community structures, and activities that bring music to life. As source material, objects pose and invite questions that, when answered, have the potential to unearth hidden figures, additional narratives, and new possibilities. They can challenge or affirm established paradigms, uncover the voices and experiences of those who have been unheard or overlooked, and have the potential to expand historical narratives in new directions.

The musical and cultural practices that enslaved Africans carried with them often blurred the line between the sacred and secular worlds. This alignment, or tension, comes up in discussions about the appropriateness of playing certain musical styles in religious settings or performing religious music in secular arenas for commercial purposes. This chapter draws upon objects from different time periods to explore the roots of African American music through traditional narratives and overarching themes.

In many African cultural traditions, the line between the sacred and secular is not clearly defined; at times, both realms are seen as one. In the history of African American music, the alignment or tension between the sacred and secular world has played out in numerous ways over the last four centuries. Discussions about the appropriateness of musical styles, genres, or types of instruments in religious settings; lyrical content, and intended purpose of the music—in church or as a profession in the commercial marketplace; sacred music in the public sphere as a social protest or public education on African American history and culture; and the foundation of American popular music being rooted in African American sacred music and performance traditions: all have formed some of the frameworks under which the music has evolved.

Ira Tucker Sr. (1925–2008) and the Dixie Hummingbirds won their first Grammy for the 1973 recording of Paul Simon's song "Loves Me Like a Rock" in the Best Soul Gospel Performance category (see next page).[5] When Tucker, who sang lead vocal, joined the group in 1938, his blues sensibilities and intricate harmonizing catapulted the Dixie Hummingbirds to becoming one of the most prominent and influential gospel groups of the era. The group had retired from the music business in 1966 and were only performing in the church when they recorded "Loves Me Like a Rock." The record's success brought new attention to the group and to gospel's influence on popular music.

Tucker's showmanship added another unique element to the group's appeal. Instead of performing standing still in front of a microphone, his running

Since the early days of slavery until now, dance has remained a dynamic feature of the African American worship experience. Here, dancers from the Liturgical Dance Ministry of Metropolitan Baptist Church in Largo, Maryland, reclaim their bodies in worship as they leap in "sanctified air" during a ceremonial groundbreaking service in 2004. Within the religious cultures that sustain such practices, dance can be performed both individually and communally.

through the aisles and leaps off the stage excited audiences and influenced many of the R&B artists that would come on the scene in the 1950s and '60s. Movement and dance is another element of African American musical expression and, like the blurry lines between sacred and secular music, is performed and embodied in the same contested spaces. Whether it is staged or improvised, choreography expresses or responds to current moods and circumstances. In religious settings, it can take the form of silent meditation or an energetic explosion of emotion as the body deepens the focus on prayer and worship. The detail of a photograph by Jason Miccolo Johnson

on page 34 was taken as part of his "Soul Sanctuary" project. Traveling across the country, Johnson visited small rural and urban store-front churches and large inner-city and suburban churches to capture the essence and rhythms of the Black Christian worship experience.

Dance also has a significant role in community and social life. It is a collaborative experience of creativity and ingenuity that serves as a collective response or intervention that is transmitted over geographical borders or re-imagined over time. Through social commentary, gamesmanship, celebrations, and demonstrations of power, authority, and solidarity,

The Dixie Hummingbirds gospel quartet grew out of a Black church in South Carolina in 1928 and introduced the highly percussive and melodic sounds of African American religious traditions to the American soundscape. This 1973 Grammy Award for Best Soul Gospel Performance is indicative of the tremendous influence the Hummingbirds and traditional Black sacred musical forms had on American music and world music culture.

Memphis Gospel Festival

This large poster advertises the 1973 Memphis Gospel Festival, which was held in Memphis, Tennessee's Mid-South Coliseum. It was printed by the Globe Poster Printing Corporation, a Baltimore-based company known for using fluorescent Day-Glo ink and large, bold type on its posters. Globe is well-known for its posters for Black jazz, gospel, R&B, and blues artists. The festival featured leading gospel artists and groups, including Rev. James Cleveland, Inez Andrews, the Swan Silvertones, and the "World Famous" Soul Stirrers, among others. Ford Nelson, from the influential Memphis R&B and gospel radio station WDIA, served as Master of Ceremonies.

The artists featured at the Festival demonstrate the blend of sacred and secular expressions that has long characterized gospel. For example, despite James Cleveland's stature as a leading guardian of the gospel tradition—he co-founded the Gospel Music Workshop of America in 1968—he also found success with gospel adaptations of secular songs. Two years after the Memphis Gospel Festival, Cleveland's reinterpretation of Gladys Knight and the Pips's 1973 "You're the Best Thing That Ever Happened to Me" quickly rose to the top of the Billboard gospel charts. Two of the other groups featured on the poster, The Soul Stirrers and The Violinaires, were training grounds for leading soul singers of the 1960s, featuring Sam Cooke and Wilson Pickett, respectively.

The 1973 Festival demonstrates gospel music's spread from its traditional place within the church to a variety of secular venues as its influence on popular culture solidified. Beginning in the 1940s and '50s, with crossover artists such as Sister Rosetta Tharpe and the Ward Singers, gospel artists found commercial success in nightclubs, theaters, music festivals, and other venues. In 1969, just a few years before the 1973 festival, Edwin Hawkins's R&B-influenced hit recording of "Oh Happy Day" re-emphasized gospel's crossover potential, unofficially marking the move from traditional to contemporary gospel. If this change concerned conservative church members, it also reflected the music's success in bringing its message to a broad swath of the American public. SWL

Mr. Cameron's Violin

Clarence P. Cameron donated his childhood violin to the NMAAHC to highlight a story he believed connected the violin to an enslaved maker. Modifications and scattered traces of repaired cracks on the instrument's soundboard provide visual evidence of the two centuries of playing this instrument withstood. The physical marks illustrate the care its owners took to keep the instrument playable for many years and help to unravel its history.

Cameron received the violin from Alice L. Austin Allen, a family friend, when he was a fifth-grade student and needed an instrument to play. The violin had belonged to Allen's late father, W.L. Austin. Accompanying the instrument was a yellowed note card created by Austin that listed the violin's Black owners, going back over two hundred years to its first documented owner, Joseph Fox, whom Austin was told made the instrument. On the card, Austin dated the instrument to ca. 1809 and recorded its former owners as: "W.L. Austin, Richard Burton, Henry Kole, Clark of Ellisville, Henry Buckley, and Joseph Fox."

When the violin arrived at the NMAAHC, staff examined the instrument and explored genealogical records for the former owners documented on the note card. The violin's physical markers, like its double-lined purfling, aided in dating the instrument. However, they also conflictingly suggested that the instrument was made in Central Europe between the 1820s and 1870s for the international commercial export market. The modest price of these violins made them popular in places like the United States where musicians, including enslaved Black violinists, played them at home or for events like social dances.

Genealogical records indicate that some former owners had advanced carpentry skills. W.L. Austin, a carriagemaker, or Henry Kole, a chairmaker, could have been responsible for repairs and fill-ins found on the soundboard. Perhaps, then, the story of the enslaved maker grew from the real actions of the owners who cared for the instrument. Cameron's violin raises many questions that are not easily answered, but it provides researchers with an opportunity to investigate the history of Black violinists maintaining and passing down instruments from one generation to the next. HG

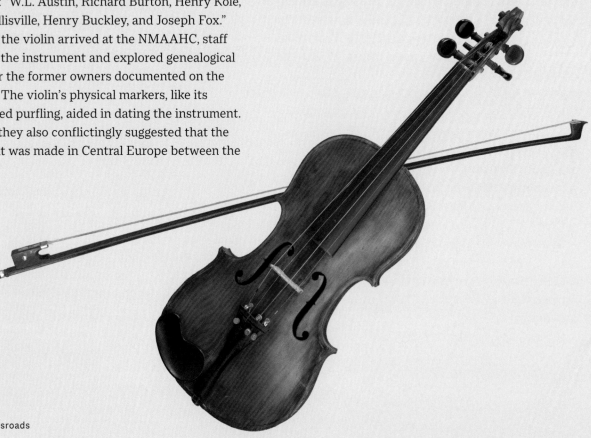

the impact of African American culture on American dance forms is recognized across the world.

This unopened package of View-Master slides belonged to Michael Holman (b. 1955), founder, manager, and choreographer for the New York City Breakers, an influential b-boy dance crew established in the early 1980s. It provides evidence of the way hip-hop was marketed in its early years. Elements of hip-hop culture grew out of the experiences and innovations of the Black and Brown communities in the Bronx. As hip-hop's popularity grew and spread throughout the United States, it was not long before corporations and the music industry realized that the genre had commercial appeal. The instructional guide incorporated into this nostalgic novelty toy signals that anyone can "learn how to breakdance with the New York City Breakers," but it also shows that mastery requires skill, practice, and discipline. Hip-hop-themed merchandise of this period played a significant role in hip-hop's global dominance in the marketplace and cultural sphere.

Dance required music, and music-making often required instruments. Most of the enslaved who arrived directly from Africa did not come with musical instruments. What they did have was the skill and knowledge to build and play an instrument. Replicating the musical sounds of their homeland required resourcefulness, experimentation, and innovation to produce the rhythmic melodies and pulses that would accompany dancing. Creativity and improvisation would not just be a process but a necessity. Access to the right materials to construct a drum or banjo was not openly available, so common objects were taken apart and pieced together into new instruments of sound, turning everyday objects into musical instruments. For centuries, this practice was commonly used by African Americans who had an interest in music but lacked the financial resources or access to buy a device. Making instruments

Long after nineteenth-century stereoscopes but decades before Instagram, there was the View-Master. With every click of the View-Master's plastic lever, the slide reel advances to the next 3D transparent photograph. This set of slides— *How to Breakdance* (1984)—features dancers from the New York City Breakers, a breakdancing or b-boy crew established in the early 1980s. As hip-hop's popularity grew, the dance element gained attention, and ephemeral instructional materials were marketed to those who wanted to learn.

The concept of the washboard as a musical instrument originated in the South. They were played as accompaniment to the folk and blues music of the region. This washboard belonged to rock pioneer Bo Diddley, who often worked with singer and musician Bobby Hebb (1938–2010), who would play the washboard with his band. Hebb got his start playing washboard for his family band before playing with Diddley and Roy Acuff's Pap's Jug Band.

out of materials found around the home or in the neighborhood was an example of ingenuity and a source of inspiration. These homemade instruments and experimentations often led to innovations that influenced musical genres of all kinds.

Bo Diddley experimented with materials and music technologies to build instruments and create new sound effects. This wooden-framed "Brass King" washboard was just one of many tools that Diddley kept at his disposal. At some point, musicians discovered washboards could be used as an instrument. By being held in the crook of the arm, or positioned on the lap, while the brass ridges were scraped down with thimbles, spoons, or other household objects, a washboard could be turned into a percussion instrument. Washboards are played in various musical genres, including blues, jazz, zydeco, and gospel. Bo Diddley used this washboard to push his music and rock and roll in new directions.

Many African American musicians also incorporate traditional African instruments in their performances, sometimes making modifications to achieve a particular sound or effect. Musician Pete Cosey (1943–2012) played this hand-held lamellophone (known as a *mbira* in Zimbabwe, a *kalimba* in Malawi and Zambia, and more colloquially as a "thumb piano"; see above) while a member of Miles Davis's

Felton Williams's Steel Guitar

In the *Musical Crossroads* exhibition, a table steel guitar sits quietly in a case next to the piano that gospel legend Thomas A. Dorsey played as music director at Pilgrim Baptist Church in Chicago (see p. 94). Its worn appearance, featuring hand-painted fret markers and hand-wound pick-ups, looks humble compared to other electric guitars displayed nearby and made by ubiquitous manufacturers. Still, in the hands of its maker, Felton Williams Jr. (1934–2012), it was equally captivating, with its impressive loudness that united worshippers in song on Sunday mornings.

Williams spent most of his life within the tight-knit community of The House of God, Jewell Dominion, established by Bishop Mattie Lou Jewell in the 1930s.[6] Within these Pentecostal worship practices, guitars are a focal point, raising the energy by riffing off of sermons and playing short melodies that grow with each repetition. Williams took to guitars as a young child in Mississippi and was a principal guitarist for his family's church in the Detroit area by his teenage years after migrating north.

As with other Detroiters, such as John Lee Hooker and Berry Gordy, Williams's musical creativity benefited from working in automotive factories. However, Williams honed his manufacturing skills there, rather than his songwriting skills. He started out as an apprentice at Ford, and during his 37-year career with the company, worked in roles ranging from building repair to machine maintenance. His experience as an electrician, along with his childhood hobby of electrifying instruments using scrap materials, informed his design and construction of what he called the "white guitar."

Upon being plugged into an amplifier he had built years earlier, the white guitar became a dominating force in speaker battles between Detroit-based House of God musicians. During these battles, Williams garnered attention for his set-up and playing style that fused the country, jazz, R&B, and sacred music that influenced him. He amazed young people and exemplified music's relevance in The House of God, as it continually grew to reflect changing tastes and technical capabilities. HG

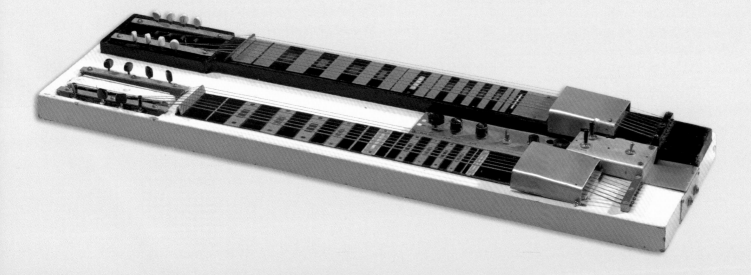

Sub-Saharan lamellophones like the *mbira* go by various names that refer to the handheld instrument with metal tongues that sound in response to a player depressing them. Pete Cosey used this *mbira*, manufactured by the African Musical Instrument Company, while he toured Japan as a member of Miles Davis's band in the 1970s. It exemplifies the instrument's increased appearance in funk music during the Black Power era.

band in the 1970s. Cosey made frequent use of the *mbira*, remembering that he had "at least two...with different tunings,"[7] which he would apply to different songs. Cosey, a Jimi Hendrix-influenced guitarist and member of the avant-garde jazz collective known as the Association for the Advancement of Creative Musicians, significantly influenced Davis's electric sound in the 1970s. His unique approach to the guitar included synth effects, alternative tunings, and restringing in unusual ways. He would also apply this experimental approach to sound with the *mbira*, adding electric amplification to the traditional African instrument.

Inspiration is drawn from all forms of African American cultural expressions. African American oral traditions are rich in poetry, including spirituals, gospel music, blues, and rap. This oral poetry also

appears in the African American tradition of Christian sermons, which uses deliberate repetition, cadence, and alliteration. African American literature—primarily written poetry and prose—has a strong practice of incorporating these forms of oral poetry, often mimicking the rhythms, rests, and accents of speech and song.

James Baldwin (1924–1987), writer, activist, and public intellectual, also had a strong affinity for poetry. His verses reflected his appreciation of the blues, rhythms, and silences when improvisation and imagination could take flight. Baldwin's poem "Some Days" appeared in *Jimmy's Blues and other Poems* in 1983 (see p. 44). When composer and musician Steve Marzullo was working on the musical *Once on This Island*, an adaptation of Rosa Guy's novel *My Love, My Love: Or, The Peasant Girl*, a cast member suggested he read some works by James

Rakim's Mic

For William Michael Griffin Jr., better known as Rakim (b. 1968), this Shure Beta 58A microphone is a symbol that is integral to his identity as a hip-hop artist. Rakim used this mic in 1997 to record his first solo album, *The 18th Letter*. The cordless mic proved exceptionally efficient. Within the context of hip-hop culture, the mic is an iconic symbol of rap and spoken word—poetry set to beats or music, and explicitly created for vocalization before audiences—exemplifying the rich and enduring oral traditions of African Americans that evolved from slavery as survival mechanisms and cultural expressions. In the title track "The 18th Letter," Rakim uses Biblical and Qur'anic allusions to convey a present-day need to acknowledge the oral traditions and styles of all geographic regions and to encourage constructive responses to regional and stylistic differences within hip-hop culture.

With themes such as self-exploration and self-empowerment, Rakim's lyrics generally reflect his fervent belief that the message is the central focus of rap. Although Rakim is known for his mastery of rhythm, rhyme, and flow, he purposefully refrains from focusing on form alone. This artistic impulse is consistent with his familial roots in the jazz and R&B crafted to inspire and uplift the oppressed. It also aligns with the cultural beliefs of his proto-Islamic affiliations—the Nation of Islam and Five Percenters. Indeed, the influence of his religious faith has guided and pushed his thinking and broadened the scope of his art. Rakim is pictured above during a 1988 performance at the Apollo Theater in Harlem. DTS

Some days

worry

Some days

glad

Some days

more than drive you

mad.

Some days

some days

more than shine :

see what's coming

on down the line!

Some days

you say,

oh, not me, never!

Some days

you say

Bless God forever.

Some days

you say

Curse God, and die :

then the day comes

when you wrestle

with that lie.

2

Some days

tussle

some days

groan.

Some days

don't even leave

a bone.

Some days

you hassle

all alone.

I don't know,

sister,

what I'm saying :

nor do no man

if he don't be praying.

I know that love

is the only answer

and the tight-rope lover

is the only dancer.

When the lover comes off the rope,

Today,

The net which holds him

is how we pray.

When the tight-rope lover

hits the air

our love is supposed

to meet him there.

3

Some days

leave

some days

grieve

Some days

you almost don't

believe.

Some days

like you

some days

don't

Some days

believe you

(and you won't)

Some days

worry

some days

mad

some days

more than make you

glad

Some days,

some days

more than shine,

making it, baby,

on down the line !

love,
Jimmy

July 28, 6:50 A.M.
St. Paul

James Baldwin sent this poem to his youngest sister, Paula, from his home in St. Paul de Vence in France. Baldwin and Paula were extremely close. He was nineteen when her father, Baldwin's stepfather, died of tuberculosis a few hours before she was born. Baldwin was Paula's surrogate father and wrote "Some Days" as a gesture of love and support during a difficult time in her life.

Baldwin. While flipping through a copy of *Jimmy's Blues*, Marzullo landed on "Some Days." In reading the poem, Marzullo said, "There was something very rhythmic about the verse.... It felt like it should be a song."[8] He went to his piano and put the poem to music. The song eventually made its way to singer and actress Audra McDonald and appears on her 2013 album, *Go Back Home*.

Objects that point to the history of African Americans in Western European classical music traditions offer an opportunity to position this genre within the larger context of African American history. Part of the difficulty of accepting African Americans as full and equal participants in this musical art form is the erasure of the history of their involvement. The invisibility is a by-product of racism that rendered Black people as commodities whose value solely rested in their ability to provide free labor. As such, any evidence of their learned experiences had little value to the dominant culture, which is illustrated in how difficult it is to find or identify material culture from this period that one can easily associate with African Americans. This underscores why a piece of sheet music composed and published by a Black composer in 1824 is an essential resource. It is a clear demonstration and historical record of a man who had the ability, talent, skills, and accomplishments to engage in classical musical traditions successfully—something that many would find difficult to imagine or even believe. This lack of awareness and perceived absence feeds the bias and the constant tug of war around race and classical music.

Francis Johnson (1792–1844) was a composer, bandleader, and instrumentalist who played the keyed bugle and violin, and published over three hundred pieces of music. He developed his skills as a composer and multi-instrumentalist while working in Mathew Black's brass band. Brass bands comprised of bugles, French horns, fifes, and drums were quite

In the 1820s, instrumentalist and composer Francis Johnson organized his first band by recruiting other musically trained free men of color living in Philadelphia. He composed the "General La Fayette Bugle Waltz" in 1824 for a special performance at a ball hosted during the Revolutionary War hero's visit to Philadelphia.

popular in the wake of the War of 1812, when many professional bands assembled for military duties. In part because of this demand for band music, Johnson successfully established himself as a professional musician in Philadelphia, where he started publishing his compositions in 1818.

The sheet music for the "General La Fayette Bugle Waltz" transports us to an era of elegant balls where American high society gathered to eat, mingle, and perform the quadrille or other social dances to the accompaniment of hired musicians. Johnson's band of African American free men trained in military, dance, and sacred music repertoire had a busy schedule performing at fashionable functions around Philadelphia, and even touring Europe. This

Thomas Greene Wiggins

Printed around 1877 in New York, this broadside produced by the team supporting Thomas Greene Wiggins (1849-1908) hails the multi-instrumentalist, familiarly called Blind Tom by his fans, as "the Eighth Wonder of the World." Curiously, the broadside also announces Wiggins's emancipation and describes him as "The Last Slave Set Free by order of the Supreme Court of the United States." The blocks of text below lay out a manipulative biography of Wiggins that Amiri Baraka referred to as "the ugly jumble of white supremacist mumbo-jumbo."[9] Mixing fact with fiction, the broadside mentions Wiggins's origins in Georgia, where he was born blind to enslaved "field hands." The emphasis on his "rare natural ability" and "mind clouded from infancy" persuaded audiences into believing Wiggins was what is now referred to as an autistic savant and obscured the years of study he had put into his musicianship since his enslavers discovered his talents.

The broadside was distributed on the heels of an 1887 dispute which saw Wiggins, by order of a federal judge, released from his enslaver General James Neil Bethune and placed in the custody of the general's estranged daughter-in-law, Eliza Bethune, as his legal guardian. After the judge's ruling, Wiggins was released, as the *New York Times* reported, with only his wardrobe and a cherished silver flute. The lone flute Wiggins managed to hold on to has an engraved oval nameplate documenting that it was made for him by New York-based flute maker William R. Meinell. The two head joints and the

silver body with its Boehm key system lie nestled in a case lined with burgundy-colored velvet. The elegant bands of vegetal designs and the dark buildup on the keys marking wear from repeated use are evidence of Wiggins's musicianship that did not get included in the PR-friendly narratives of his life crafted by his oppressors, which focused on the novelty of his untrained genius. What more could we learn about the American music industry's close connections to enslavement from the study of extant instruments? HG

Singer and actress Mattie Wilkes began her career performing in the Black vaudeville circuit. This advertisement for her performance at the Holliday Street Theatre in Baltimore is made of two pieces: the poster features a color illustration of Wilkes, and the brown paper attachment at the bottom includes information about the performance.

piece of sheet music is a tangible piece of evidence of Johnson's accomplishments and musical legacy. The existence of his published work opens a window on the multiple ways in which music reflects the tensions and complexities in navigating freedom within the constraints that society at large imposes every day.

Take, for example, a poster advertising a performance by soprano Mattie Wilkes (1875-1927), which points to different classical music questions about African Americans. Narratives can go in various directions when gender, skin color, class, ethnicity, geographical region, or period come into play. As with many of her generation, Wilkes's story is woefully incomplete, and her work straddling classical music and early American musical theater is an area ripe for further research. Like other Black female classical vocalists of her era, Wilkes did not have the same access to concert hall venues as white performers, so she often performed with Black minstrels such as Bert Williams (1874-1922), George Walker (1872/73-1911), and her husband Ernest Hogan (1865-1909).

A painted illustration captures Wilkes looking wistfully out. A pink rose in her hair is paired with a romantic off-the-shoulder dress with gathered ruffles receding into the background. Her idealized visage suggests an intriguing sonic and visual juxtaposition, with "the beautiful" Wilkes's "phenomenal soprano" programmed alongside Williams's and Walker's blackface routines. The poster joins the reported record in teasing out further opportunities to pursue more information regarding Wilkes and early twentieth-century classically trained vocalists.

Another standard narrative around how music translates to people's lived experiences is through autonomy, freedom, and the power of self-determination. This is a struggle played out in various ways and will be discussed in greater depth in Chapter 4 (see p. 117). For performers, attire becomes a powerful statement. It could be as a sign of respectability, a reflection of one's cultural heritage, a projection of identity formation, or a celebration of individual authenticity. It also serves as a sign of resistance from classification or the values and belief systems suppressing difference over assimilation.

Pushing boundaries and exercising personal freedom are the easiest ways to describe music, personal values, and public image. Prince Rogers Nelson (1958–2016)—known by his stage name, Prince—used clothing to express his aesthetic sensibilities and his identity. Prince's clothing was an expressive outlet to tie other elements of his aesthetic ideas into his onstage persona. He constantly challenged traditional concepts of masculinity, with glamorous androgynous styles that confronted stereotypes of gender and sexuality. The power of his public persona emanated from a confidence that served him well in multiple aspects of his career.

This lavender suit, designed by Domenico Serio, with matching custom-made boots, is emblematic of the fashion style that many people associated with Prince in the 1990s (see opposite). The top's sculpted collar, with a bit of residual makeup left behind, and the arranged gathered folds down the center are reminiscent of his ruffled white shirts paired with long purple jackets that made him a cultural icon. The heeled boots have a dangling gold "Love Symbol" that stylishly reminds the onlooker of Prince's move to rename himself using a design based on the Roman symbols for Mars and Venus. As a whole, the ensemble calls to mind the creative project that Prince embarked on, which blended his artistic vision with his political stances on sexuality and racial justice. Clothing was only a tiny aspect of his legacy, but it significantly transformed American popular culture in the twentieth and twenty-first centuries.

Famous artists are not the only people who make public statements about their identity and values through music. Record collecting is another popular way for an individual to make a public statement about their own values. Although some people may base their collections on the monetary value of rare one-of-a-kind items, any albums that one saves or collects form part of one's autobiography. Records, like other treasured items, are repositories of memories and chapters of an individual's story, while also allowing people to display their personal aesthetic taste (via cover art) to others. Albums in the NMAAHC's collection serve a similar purpose. The music, the cover art, the liner notes, and the other information that can be read on the jacket or label, capture a moment in time, bringing a sense of nostalgia for some visitors and offering a gateway to historical and cultural moments for others. As with any other object, in peeling back the layers from the cover art to the studio recording the album, the lists of artists, designers, musicians, producers, and songwriters are all ripe for further exploration. Albums that belonged to musicians open another area of investigation, as they can present an opportunity to learn more about the artist and the album.

A 1980 LP of *Music of Many Colors* (see p. 51) brings together vibraphonist Roy Ayers's (b. 1940) fusion of R&B and new age spirituality with Fela Kuti's (1938–1997) Afrobeat—a rhythmically propulsive combination of funk, soul-jazz, and Ghanaian high life music. Recorded after a three-week concert tour in Nigeria, both musicians saw the collaboration as a symbol of pan-African solidarity. The album's ethos reflects the influence of pan-African thought on many Black musicians throughout the African diaspora during this period. *Music of Many Colors* distills centuries of hopes and dreams into a brief monument of musical resistance. The B-side of the album features the song "2000 Blacks Got To Be Free," a celebration of a utopian vision of freedom for Black people everywhere.

Staying true to his signature color, Prince wore this two-piece suit of flowy lavender satin in the late 1990s. Since Prince's performances often included a lot of movement, the heels of the custom boots were reinforced with stainless steel bars. Prince always showcased his unique style and complex identity, as seen in his iconic "Love Symbol" on the zippers of the boots.

Music of a City: Go-Go

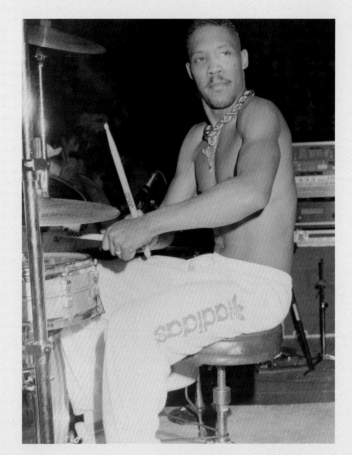

Go-go drummer William Julius House's bass drumhead features decorative painting that leaves a sense of the musician's personality on the stretched plastic. An image of Jimi Hendrix's face consumes most of the space, in a nod to the artist's creative impact on the members of House's band, Experience Unlimited (E.U.). In red and orange ombre letters, House's nickname "Ju Ju" is spelled out, with stickers applied to each "J." The drumhead is currently located on the fourth floor of the NMAAHC, in a case next to a conga highlighting E.U. and Washington, DC's homegrown go-go music scene which emerged in the twentieth century.

E.U., hailing from Southeast Washington, DC, were among several groups organized after Chuck Brown founded go-go with his band, The Soul Searchers. Blending a wide array of diasporic genres, including funk, jazz, hip-hop, acid rock, and calypso, DC's go-go

artists have bridged generational gaps and created a style that celebrates the diverse population of Black people living in DC and the contributions they have made to the district's culture. In recent years, locals have utilized the music as an empowering protest against the rapid development and rising rents that jeopardize their local cultural legacies, by blasting go-go's looping grooves from their storefronts and staging go-go parades.

House, pictured above in the 1990s, used the drumhead on display at the NMAAHC in the late 1980s as E.U. rose to national prominence in 1988, when their single "Da Butt" was featured in Spike Lee's film *School Daze*. The song was loud and funky, and featured hallmarks of go-go music such as Afro-Caribbean percussion instruments and shout-outs by frontman and bassist Gregory "Sugar Bear" Elliot, who called on DC, LA, Philly, Atlanta, and Baltimore between the background chants of "we got the butt." Lee's use of the song in his film introduced DC's entrancing corner music—which had already drawn in the residents of "Chocolate City" with its boisterous political nature—to national audiences. HG

Like many other Black men, I have a dream.... I have a vision with that dream. My dream and my vision are the coming together of Black minds within this universe we live in. —"2000 Blacks Got To Be Free"

History is shaped by the stories a culture values and wants to tell. The history of African American music does not have to be framed through one particular lens. Many things can define it at once. Objects offer a pathway in identifying the questions waiting to be asked. Studying the material culture of African American music allows us to consider how that history is being written, discussed, and defined. Music's material culture encourages us to be more expansive in defining African American music, building a foundation for future research that embraces multiple narratives that co-exist under one umbrella.

Transatlantic movements of people and sounds have influenced music in the African diaspora for four centuries. *Music of Many Colors* (1980) brought vibraphonist Roy Ayers and Afrobeat trumpeter-vocalist-bandleader Fela Kuti together to address the plights of Black people across the Atlantic. Speak-singing over polyrhythmic grooves, they dream of "the coming together of Black minds," asking people to think about "unity" and "Blackness."

Rhythm Changes

Rhythm, ranging from the flexible swing of jazz to the interlocking syncopations of funk, is one of the most immediately distinguishing characteristics of African American music. Observers as early as the seventeenth century noted the distinctive rhythmic complexity of Black music in the Caribbean and on the North American mainland. And yet this essential element of Black music history is a challenge to document through material culture. Fearful of African drummers' potential to incite slave rebellions, colonial American governments instituted prohibitions on drumming by the enslaved. The handful of transcriptions of eighteenth- and nineteenth-century Black music are problematic, as white observers often failed to accurately notate the subtleties of the unfamiliar music they heard. While this aspect of Black music's early history remains elusive in the material culture record, objects and artifacts in conjunction with written accounts help us to reconstruct the persistence and development of African rhythmic traditions in Black music. There is also extensive documentation of Black American rhythm in music from the twentieth century forward.

A pair of tap shoes associated with Sammy Davis Jr. (1925-1990) connect his early career to much earlier traditions of Black American rhythm. Tap dancing is an extension of the longstanding practice of Black body percussion. In antebellum practices like "patting juba" and "hambone," Black people used their bodies as drums in environments where white authorities forbade traditional drumming. This practice, born of necessity, has given rise to traditions ranging from tap dancing, in which dancers create intricate rhythms with their feet, to beatboxing, in which musicians use their voices to emulate drum machines and other percussion. Davis appeared as a child act in vaudeville, where he performed as part of a trio led by his godfather, Will Mastin (1878-1979), and his father, Sammy Davis Sr. (1900-1988). His vaudeville notoriety led him to become a movie star by age seven, appearing alongside Ethel Waters in the 1933 film *Rufus Jones for President*. As artifacts associated with Davis's career, his tap shoes remind us of the central role that vaudeville played in the early careers of many Black artists in the first decades of the twentieth century.

Twentieth-century objects illustrate the role that African American rhythms came to play as a unifying element in much of American music. A collection of objects donated by trailblazing drummer Terri Lyne Carrington (b. 1965) traces the career trajectory of a great percussionist in recent history. One notable item from the collection is a pair of Zildjian drumsticks stamped with Carrington's signature. Carrington, who began her career as a child prodigy, went on to lead her own award-winning groups, while also collaborating with artists including Herbie Hancock, Esperanza Spalding, and Wayne Shorter, among many others. These drumsticks point to the important contributions of women musicians to jazz,

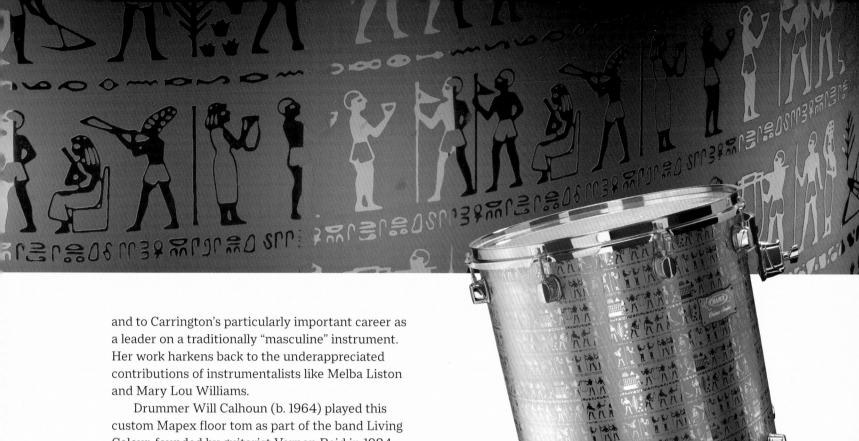

and to Carrington's particularly important career as a leader on a traditionally "masculine" instrument. Her work harkens back to the underappreciated contributions of instrumentalists like Melba Liston and Mary Lou Williams.

Drummer Will Calhoun (b. 1964) played this custom Mapex floor tom as part of the band Living Colour, founded by guitarist Vernon Reid in 1984. The drum's polished silver shell is etched with Egyptian-style hieroglyphs of musicians and other human figures in profile. With an eclectic style that mixed rock with elements of jazz fusion and Delta blues, Living Colour won Grammy Awards in 1990 and 1991 for Best Hard Rock Performance. Calhoun's drumming also won him awards from prominent publications, including *Modern Drummer Magazine*, *Number One Progressive Drummer*, and *Rolling Stone*. As a solo artist, Calhoun also worked with a variety of artists in rock, jazz, blues, and hip-hop. His drum points to the underappreciated role that Black musicians have continued to play in rock music since the 1960s. Its history contradicts the common misconception that Black musicians stopped making influential contributions to rock music after R&B was appropriated from African Americans and marketed as "rock and roll" beginning in the 1950s. Calhoun's work with Living Colour exemplifies the contributions

of more recent Black rock artists, and a survey of his work in the genres of hip-hop, blues, and jazz re-emphasizes the connections that an ostensibly "white" music like rock has to other African American musical idioms.

The work of Black drummers such as Carrington and Calhoun reminds us of the fundamental position that drums and drummers have long occupied in Black music. Despite early attempts to stamp out Black rhythm in America, their achievements exemplify how it has survived and thrived in the work of artists throughout American history. SWL

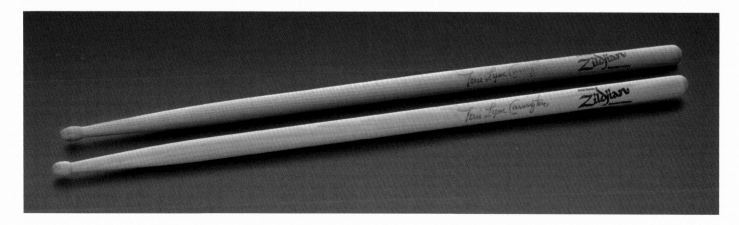

Body and Soul

Music and dance are intricately entwined. The "ring shout" is thought to be the earliest African American dance form developed in North America. This fusion of counterclockwise hypnotic movement, call-and-response singing, handclapping, and stick beating has distinct West African roots. The ring shout provided a tether to the spirit and ancestors and reinforced a sense of community—principles that were very much in line with the world from which they were taken. As Black, Indigenous, and white populations danced in front of one another, they picked up new techniques and styles that were incorporated into new social and concert dances. Over the nineteenth century, white actors appropriated African American dance movements and incorporated them into their dehumanizing performative caricatures. This wellspring of historical inspiration informed members of the budding Black concert dance movement that emerged during the era of the Harlem Renaissance.

Working to challenge widely held racist assumptions with roots in minstrels' dissemination of demeaning stereotypes, pioneers such as Edna Guy, Asadata Dafora, and Randolph Sawyer, infused their performances with authentic representations of their African American heritage in the concert hall. In the 1940s, dancers including Katherine Dunham (1909-2006) and Pearl Primus (1919-1994), both trained anthropologists, pushed the movement forward as they traveled to Africa and the Caribbean to research the roots and origins of African American dance. By the time Dunham opened her namesake dance school in 1944, the African aesthetic was a legitimate component of modern dance.

By the mid-twentieth century, a new generation of pioneers including Alvin Ailey, Dr. Chuck "Baba Chuck" Davis, and Arthur Mitchell picked up the gauntlet.

Alvin Ailey (1931-1989) received formal training with Lester Horton at the suggestion of his high school friend, dancer Carmen de Lavallade (b. 1931). After several years of performing, he founded the Alvin Ailey American Dance Theater (AAADT) in 1958. The company's twin aims were to express Black cultural heritage and to enrich American dance with a diversity of cultural voices. Ailey's choreography drew thematic material and movement vocabularies from his African American heritage and his early years growing up in Texas. He also employed vernacular dance, modern dance, and jazz dance styles. Music was a focal point in Ailey's work. His signature piece, *Revelations*, is an emotional journey through the African American experience, where moments of deep grief and great joy are choreographed into and supported by a soundtrack of spirituals, song-sermons, gospel songs, and holy blues arranged by composer Hall Johnson, singer and educator Ella Jenkins, and gospel and folk singer Brother John Sellers, among others.

From 1961 to 2004, photographer Jack Mitchell collaborated with Alvin Ailey and later Judith Jamison, who succeeded Ailey as artistic director, to document the Company's many dances, dancers, and performances. In a collection of over ten thousand photographs that are jointly owned by the NMAAHC and AAADT, images of some of Ailey's most famous dances—including a 1961 performance of *Roots of the Blues* with his friend, Carmen de Lavallade—showcase the troupe's evolution from its earliest days to an internationally recognized company steeped in African American cultural heritage.

While Alvin Ailey brought Black cultural heritage into classical dance, Dr. Chuck "Baba Chuck" Davis (1937-2017) was one of the foremost teachers and choreographers of traditional African dance in the United States. Davis saw dance as an agent for

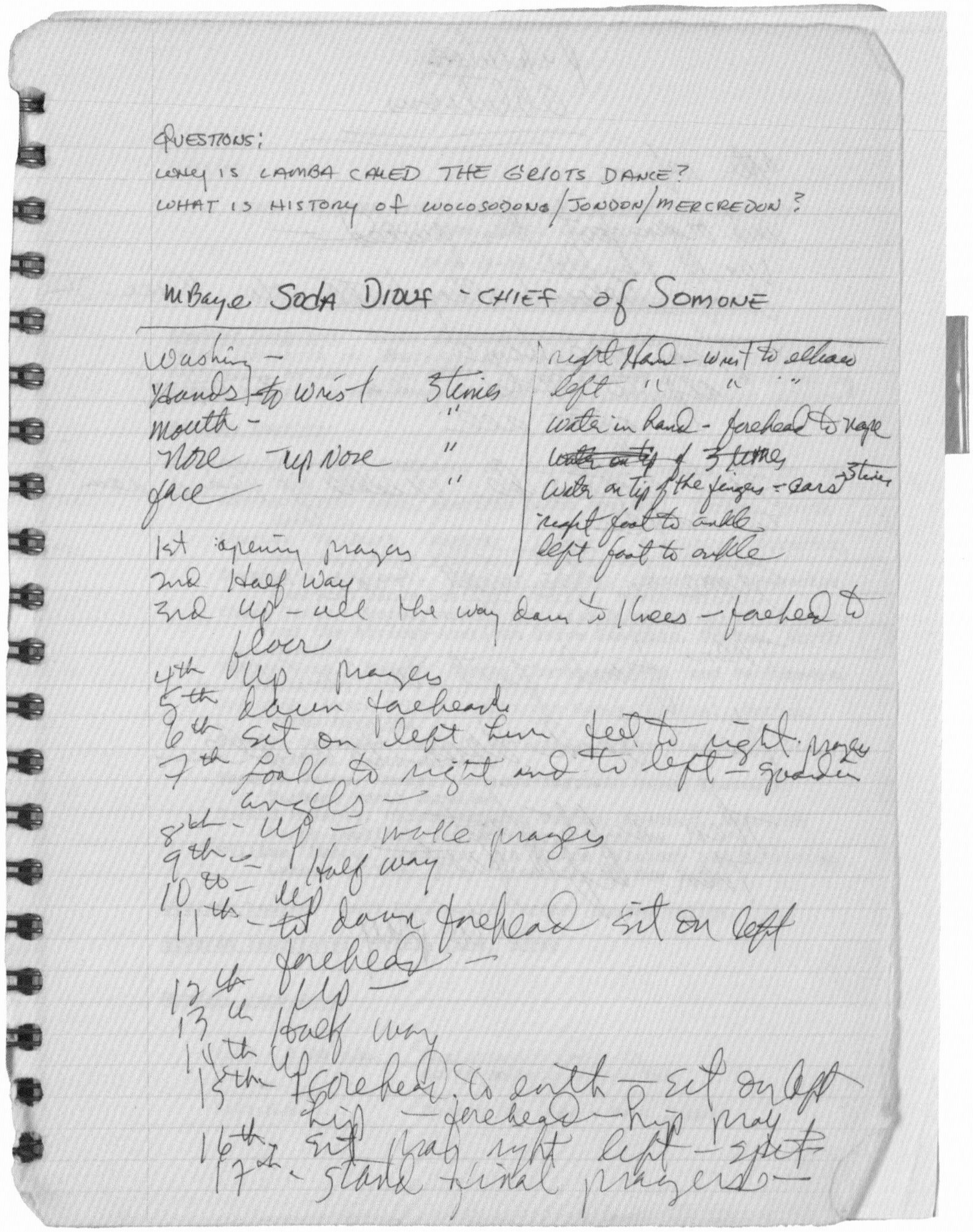

QUESTIONS:

WHY IS LAMBA CALLED THE GRIOTS DANCE?

WHAT IS HISTORY OF WOLOSODONG/JONDON/MERCREDUN?

mBaye Soda Diouf - CHIEF of Somone

Washing —	right Hand - wrist to elbow
Hands to wrist 3 times	left " " "
Mouth — "	water in hand - forehead to nape
Nose - up Nose "	water tip of 5 times
face "	water on tip of the fingers - ears 3 times
	right foot to ankle
1st opening prayers	left foot to ankle

2nd Half Way

3rd up — all the way down to knees — forehead to floor

4th Up prayers

5th down foreheads

6th Sit on left turn feet to right - prayer

7th foall to right and to left — guardian angels —

8th — up — make prayers

9th — Half way

10th — up

11th — to down forehead sit on left forehead —

12th Up

13th Half way

14th

15th Up forehead to earth — Sit on left hip — forehead — hip pray

16th Sit pray right left — spit

17th — stand final prayers —

change and drew his inspiration as an educator and choreographer from the dances of Africa and the African diaspora throughout his lifetime. He founded the Chuck Davis Dance Company in New York in 1968 and the African American Dance Ensemble in Durham, North Carolina, in 1983. He was also founder and artistic director of DanceAfrica, a festival held each Memorial Day weekend at the Brooklyn Academy of Music. Davis frequently traveled to Africa. This spiral notebook is just one of the many he used to record his daily observations and impressions during his trips to Africa, choreography ideas, instructions for certain rituals, notes, letters, itineraries, and expenses.

While dancers were pursuing their own artistic voice in the field of modern dance, others were trying to break down brick walls that stood between African American artists and classical European dance. Arthur Mitchell (1934-2018) parlayed his success with the New York City Ballet and partnered with Karel Shook to establish the community-based Dance Theater of Harlem (DTH) in 1971. Since the Company's founding, ballerinas with DTH have used customized mixtures of dyes, makeup, and paint to color pink tights and ballet shoes to match their skin tones. The dyed ballet shoes and tights from the 2013-14 season on display in the Museum's ongoing *Taking the Stage* exhibition, are not only a reflection of the history of DTH and its commitment to empowering young people in the community, but also a symbol of the way American ballet continues to struggle to accept African American ballet dancers as professionals in the field. The detail (above) of a photograph by Anthony Barboza captures members of the Company at rehearsal and confirms Arthur Mitchell's point that: "The myth was that because you were black... you could not do classical dance. I proved that to be wrong."[10] DRR

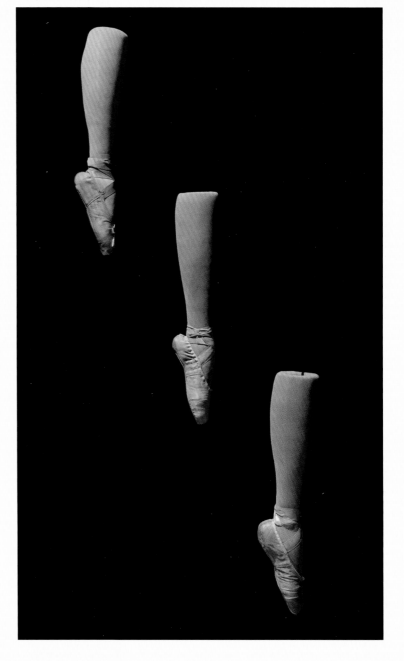

Innovations in Sound

African American music research has benefited tremendously from studying musical instruments. Examining the physical appearance of instruments and their use emphasizes the human stories behind these tools in ways that enrich musical discourse. Approaching instruments from a material culture lens contributes to understandings of how music intersects with technological, social, and cultural histories. This is apparent in a selection of instruments at the NMAAHC that reflect African American culture's creolization and significant innovations.

It is not easy to write anything definitive about this antebellum gourd banjo. Nowhere on the instrument is there a maker's mark, nor is there a written date of manufacture. Information such as this, which often accompanies an object when it is acquired by a museum, generally guides researchers in establishing basic documentation. Frets are missing from along the rough neck of the banjo, and no skin remains to stretch across the scored rim. Two broken strings curl as they extend from an asymmetrical tin tailpiece anchored to the dowel stick holding the neck and body together. A rounded headstock has four tuning pegs that jut out behind. Centrally placed on the headstock is a hole that perhaps held the banjo when it was hung safely on a wall while not in use. This use for the extra hole is consistent with a ca. 1840 Haitian four-string gourd banjo in the collections of Paris's Musée de la Musique and a contemporary illustration depicting an enslaved Jamaican family's dwelling.[11] The NMAAHC's banjo has a sense of mystery about it that begs for further research and underscores how musical instruments can offer more information beyond their capabilities to make sound.

As with many musical instruments associated with eighteenth- and nineteenth-century African American music, the unknown early history of this banjo echoes the invisibility and exploitation of African Americans during this time. Still, the combination of the gourd body, four strings, and twelve fret spaces hints at the banjo's development after enslaved Black musicians in the Caribbean first conceived the instrument and then carried it throughout the American colonies. This banjo moved between several collectors after it was purchased in 1985 from a family living in Savannah, Georgia. Though the provenance leaves much to be desired, the instrument's unique features become a vehicle for analyzing the hybridity of African American culture that was the product of different African ethnic groups blending and adapting influences from the European and Indigenous cultures they lived among.

Upon first glance, many would assume this tall drum was African. A stretched animal hide secured onto nine wooden pegs covers the mouth of the drum before it tapers down into a rounded foot. The two carved faces adhered to either side of the belly are reminiscent of many drums found in West Africa and demonstrate retentions of African traditions in the Gullah communities living in the coastal Sea Islands of the southeastern United States. When Black Codes prohibited drumming in the wake of the 1739 Stono Rebellion, drum traditions were thought to have largely disappeared. The Sea Islands drum's physical appearance and history provide an intriguing opportunity to examine how cultural practices persisted, even in the face of oppression.

The provenance of the drum traces its origins to the traditions of Black secret societies shortly after the time of emancipation. These societies first emerged in the United States during the eighteenth century. They became important spaces for organizing to support members and social justice efforts. They also preserved African-born cultural traditions that cultivated a sense of identity among enslaved populations. The drum's reported use in these ceremonies reveals the continuities of African culture that survived suppression and contributed

to secret societies' efforts to aid their members in finding community and confidence after the traumas of slavery.

Like their historical counterparts, modern musical instruments also lend themselves to examinations and document how African American musicians spur on innovation. Equipped with his Akai MPC and Moog synthesizer, James Yancey, a.k.a. J Dilla (1974–2006), exemplified the instrumental possibilities of hip-hop production. He wove songs together on this gear by chopping, looping, and manipulating samples drawn from across the broad spectrum of music he encountered while flipping through records and experimenting with live instrumentation. Wear on the MPC's gray drum keys are the residual marks caused by hours Dilla spent tapping beats. Studying the loss of paint and heavy use of some keys might provide further insight into the producer's preferences. Dilla's music projected his cerebral aesthetics and keen ear for crafting head-bopping beats that occasionally confounded rappers with their intricacies. Using electronic instruments to express his vision also created intergenerational musical experiences as he re-worked older music to articulate his imaginative grooves. HG

Diasporic Expressions

While promoting her album *Black Gold*, which was recorded in 1969, Nina Simone (1933–2003) supplied disc jockeys with a copy of the record and an accompanying necklace with a gold-plated pendant in the shape of the African continent. The pendant's surface lifts and sinks to depict Africa's majestic mountains and rivers in careful topographical detail. The necklace's distribution as part of the marketing around *Black Gold* suggests the political stance Simone asserts through the album. It indicates her desire for listeners to carry the profound, revolutionary message of her music with them into their lives. It is not only a gift but an invitation to join her activist crusade for global Black Freedom.

Simone's music took on increasingly political tones amidst the Black Arts Movement of the 1960s, and her performance wardrobe gradually shifted from the tailored gowns of a nightclub chanteuse to a uniform of bright African prints, large dangling earrings, and cascading necklaces. This adoption of African dress developed following her 1961 travels to Lagos, Nigeria, to perform in the Dinizulu Festival.[12] While meandering about the city, she began contemplating more earnestly her connections to the African continent and its far-flung diaspora of Black people. Donning African-inspired clothing facilitated Simone's presentation of a soul aesthetic that was bold in its political alignment with the oppressed. Subverting notions of respectability that often dictate how Black women should dress and behave, Simone's new tastes contributed to this mid-century reimagination of Blackness grounded in performative solidarity with the global populations comprising the African diaspora.

On the backs of Black people in the past and present, pan-African dress and adornment emphasize how marginalized groups use clothing and accessories to honor their ancestral heritage while visually commenting on their complex relationships with mainstream cultural practices. For example, in the Democratic Republic of the Congo, the Maison Dorcas Women's Singing Group (right) uses patterned textiles along with music therapy to aid its members, many of whom are recovering from experiences with sexual violence, in healing and regaining confidence. African American musicians and performers engage this type of fashionable negotiation throughout the United States in ways that highlight how artists understand and communicate their Blackness.

Hip-hop group X Clan used their music to meditate on Blackness and futurist ideas lyrically. These themes proliferated in the work of their

Brooklyn-based collective, the Blackwatch Movement. Decked out in "boots and beads, bags and braids, stick and scroll, rings and shades,"[13] X Clan's performance uniform made it abundantly clear, if their lyrics were not explicit enough, that they viewed themselves as carrying on the traditions of their politically minded predecessors. Around the time their debut album, *To*

the East, Blackwards, was released in 1990, X Clan's five emcees—Professor X the Overseer, Isis, Suga Shaft the Rhythm Provider, Brother J the Grand Verbalizer, and Paradise the Architect—stoically posed for photographer Ernie Paniccioli. In his photograph, they stand before two pan-African backdrops, complementing their matching black kufi caps

emblazoned with red or green ankhs. As it captures X Clan's fashionable challenge, the photograph recalls bell hooks's statement about photography being "a powerful location for the construction of an oppositional black aesthetic."[14] X Clan's clothing, accented by dangling hoop earrings and nose piercings, was a meaningful extension of their musical performance. The group's style fit into hip-hop's Africanist aesthetics. These aesthetics went beyond the bling and bravado to cultivate symbolic capital that unified different communities within the African American population by embracing diasporic cultural pride. Music and dress were critical components of this project. They supported artists' critiques of the harsh realities that Black people globally confronted.

Like their more famous counterparts, community performers similarly utilize costuming alongside music and dance as part of staged unifying spectacles of cultural expression. Since the 1990s, the Bahamas Junkanoo Revue has participated in Miami's Junkanoo parades celebrating Bahamian culture alongside other Junkanoo groups. A front-line dancer representing the Bahamas Junkanoo Revue dazzled spectators wearing this Wilshire Dames-created costume made from cardboard, aluminum rods with eye-catching feathers and bright yellow, red, and aqua colors, tissue, and other decorative materials. Adhering to the Middle Eastern theme for the 2015 Christmastime parade, the costume hints at mosaics with gleaming beads and prominent vegetal designs. Details like a two-headed viper curving out from the waist into lifted heads flashing long white fangs add to the arresting appearance this costume must have made, while its wearer danced to the rhythms of Goombay drums with accompanying cowbells and bright brasswind instruments. HG

Hall Johnson's Spiritual Quest

Hall Johnson was arguably the most visible and influential proponent of Negro spirituals in the first half of the twentieth century. However, as director of the Hall Johnson Choir, he also performed in more than thirty feature-length films, appeared on Broadway, and toured across the country and internationally for over thirty years. Johnson had a platform and profound influence in shaping public perceptions about African Americans and their musical traditions.

Dr. Eugene Thamon Simpson donated the Hall Johnson Archive to the NMAAHC in 2013. Dr. Simpson, who had met Johnson in 1959, became custodian of the Archive at the family's request after Johnson died of burns he received in a fire at his Harlem apartment in 1970. The Archive includes business papers, royalty statements, correspondence, photographs, music manuscripts, orchestral scores, personal diaries, programs, and a camera. The Archive is a record of Johnson's professional career and artistic output, and offers insight into his interests and hobbies.

Johnson took up photography when he was a young man, and was known to have a camera with him at all times. This Rolleiflex Automat Model 1 (or

Model RF 111A, according to the serial number) was manufactured between August 1937 and March 1939. Notes on the camera's condition after inspection by NMAAHC conservators reference extensive damage to the exterior by extreme heat or fire, "causing loss and shrinkage of leatherette and loss and cupping of the remaining paint." Given the circumstances of Johnson's death, the camera was most likely retrieved from his apartment after the fire.

Johnson's interest in spirituals was inspired by the songs that his grandmother, who lived in slavery for thirty years, sang to him. Early in his career, he realized the sounds of the spiritual as they were meant to be sung would eventually disappear, and so he committed himself to educating audiences about the way "the American Negro slaves…created, propagated and illuminated an art-form which was, and still is, unique in the world of music."[15]

In addition to composing and directing the Choir, Johnson was interested in the careers of other musicians. Programs in the Archive are not only a record of the performances he attended but also of the number of Black classical musicians and composers who were active at the time. As a vocal coach, Johnson was said to be quite meticulous. He insisted that

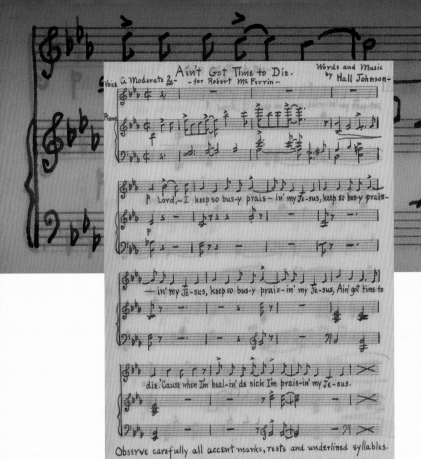

every marking and accent be observed as written. Johnson was baritone Robert McFerrin Sr.'s first vocal coach when he arrived in New York City in 1948.[16] This version of "Ain't Got Time to Die" is inscribed "for Robert McFerrin." Among several versions of the piece in the Archive, this is the only one written for a particular person. Its annotation of reminders for accents, rests, and underlined syllables is unique to this copy and hints at Johnson's detailed coaching.

Part of Johnson's advocacy for the spiritual required defending the performances of the Choir when it became a target of racialized scrutiny, caricature, objectification, or misinterpretation. Johnson's responses to these insults usually took the form of long, detailed letters. This letter addressed to "Mr. Kosson" refers to a separate seven-page typewritten letter that Johnson wrote in November 1937 but did not mail at the time. After a performance at the University of Washington the month before, Johnson read the University newspaper's articles to promote the event. In that typewritten letter, he refutes every statement falsely attributed to him, moving back and forth between righteous indignation and snarkiness. On page 4, he writes, "It should not be necessary to point out to any University student that the suffix 'ster' (appended to a noun) signifies occupation; as in gangster, trickster, teamster, etc.

When one wishes to speak contemptuously of Negroes, the correct term is 'darkies,' not 'darksters.'"

Johnson's effort to educate and present spirituals as an original work of art was always in tension with the inclination of some audiences to interpret the Choir's performance as a justification for their own biases and racist attitudes. Johnson closes this handwritten letter with a note of contrition and expression of his frustration with the challenges he faces in realizing his goals:

Though this whole affair was, to us, miserable, I am writing with no real ill-feeling toward you or the author of the articles. It is just another example of the failure to take Negroes seriously that is so common in this country. I am sure that such a thing could never have happened to a group of visiting artists of any other race. DRR

65

Concert Stage

On April 9, 1939, contralto Marian Anderson (1897-1993) stepped before nine radio microphones to deliver a recital on the steps of the Lincoln Memorial. She wore a lush fur coat over an eye-catching bright orange jacket, paired with a floor-length velvet black skirt. Gracefully standing before the imposing seated figure of Abraham Lincoln's statue near a grand piano played by her accompanist, Kosti Vehanen, Anderson sang a program that scholars describe as the first public triumph of the modern Civil Rights Movement. Looking up at her, 75,000 people listened transfixed while she performed a mixed repertoire of classical vocal music. The recital's seven songs included favorites such as Donizetti's aria "O Mio Fernando" and Franz Schubert's "Ave Maria," alongside spirituals such as her encore "Nobody Knows the Trouble I See." Anderson's carefully selected clothing was a visual complement to her aural challenge to the racism exhibited by the Daughters of the American Revolution (DAR) in their refusal to let Anderson perform at Constitution Hall. The DAR's response led First Lady Eleanor Roosevelt to resign from the organization and paved the way for Secretary of the Interior Harold Ickes and NAACP Secretary Walter White to organize the momentous event.

Over the years, Anderson's historic ensemble was lovingly maintained by her nephew James DePreist and his wife Ginette. In 1993, when the original orange velvet had aged beyond preservation, Ginette arranged for the jacket to be remade so that she could wear it to the Academy Ball in Philadelphia in honor of Anderson. She replaced the velvet with a shimmery Shantung silk of the exact same color, to which the original trim was attached so the jacket's story could continue. Her acts of care are a reminder of the fastidious attention that classical musicians like Anderson devoted to every minute detail of their performances. The clothes take the viewer back to Anderson in the moments she stirred the hearts of high society in the nation's capital, when she and her supporters protested segregation's broad impacts. This concert introduced Anderson to wider audiences in the United States as a rising concert vocalist. Her belongings join other material culture in the Museum's collection that assist in communicating the brilliant legacies of Black musicians, such as the detail above of a photograph of Leontyne Price performing at Carnegie Hall. They speak to the obstacles their owners surmounted while chipping away at racist assumptions. Using artifacts like clothing, a holiday card, and a photograph ignites a discussion of how African Americans in classical music have persistently worked stateside and abroad, despite minimal opportunities, in ways that inspire younger artists.

William Grant Still (1895-1978) was going on his third year living in Los Angeles when he signed this holiday card to Mr. Frank H. Bolner in 1937. When he had applied for the Guggenheim Fellowship that took him back to Los Angeles in 1934, he explicitly stated his intentions to move to the city, where he found "an atmosphere conducive to creative effort."[17] He sent the elegant card from his new home, signing below a

dark purple square announcing "Lenox Avenue and I / Wish You / A Happy New Year," accompanied with a start to a syncopated melody in E-flat major. Still discovered his preference for Los Angeles while working as an arranger for Paul Whiteman's radio show in 1929. His first year in the city kickstarted a period of productivity in his composing. When he returned to New York in 1930, he quickly premiered compositions including the ballet *Sahjdi* and the *Afro-American Symphony*.[18] The two cities that were central to his work are celebrated together on this card, as well as the popular versus classical music divide that his oeuvre straddled. The nod to his piece "Lenox Avenue" references the familiar street in Harlem where he worked during the 1920s, conducting and arranging for jazz orchestras. His present location in Los Angeles acknowledges where he found the inspiration for his neo-romantic style.

Still's success in the 1930s excited many young musicians who continued breaking down barriers in classical music. Conductor Dean Dixon (1915–1976) was one such up-and-coming classical star, who formed the Dean Dixon Symphony Orchestra in 1932 while still a student at DeWitt Clinton High School in New York City. When Arthur Leipzig took this photo of him conducting in the 1940s, Dixon was fresh from his recent studies at Juilliard and Columbia, where he specialized in violin and music pedagogy. The young phenomenon had already performed before illustrious persons, such as First Lady Eleanor Roosevelt, who had given him positive reviews. He also became the first African American to conduct the New York Philharmonic Orchestra, in 1941. Baton in hand, Dixon was the first Black person to conduct a major symphony orchestra and inspired a generation of young maestros who, following in his footsteps after seeing him in action, went on to take up positions with prestigious institutions such as the Chicago Symphony Orchestra and the San Francisco Ballet Orchestra. HG

The Saxophone in Black Music

On September 26, 1890, composer Will Marion Cook (1869-1944) featured the unfamiliar "saxaphone" in a Washington, DC concert.[19] The saxophone has occupied a special place in African American culture ever since. From its beginnings in Black ragtime and vaudeville bands, like those of the Six Musical Spillers, to its central place in jazz and its supporting role in later Black popular music styles, the saxophone has become associated with African American musical traditions to an extent unknown with other European instruments.

Saxophones failed to make inroads into European concert music prior to their adoption by ragtime and jazz musicians in the early twentieth century. Even in France, where the saxophone received positive attention after its inventor Adolphe Sax was granted a patent in 1846, composers had little interest in expanding the traditional orchestra to incorporate it. The saxophone's lack of an extensive literature or a place in the orchestra made it a blank slate which Black musicians could use to their own ends. Its expressive timbral flexibility—enabling a range of honks, growls, wails, and screams, along

with conventional pitches—fits comfortably within what musicologist Olly Wilson has called the "heterogeneous sound ideal" of Black music.[20]

The instrument's relative newness also made it a symbol of modernity at a time when a new generation of Black Americans were forging a path away from painful legacies of slavery and blackface minstrelsy in the nineteenth and early twentieth centuries. Charlie Parker (1920-1955), whose musical innovations blended experimentalism with a deep commitment to the blues and jazz traditions, exemplified that modernist spirit. In 1947, after Parker emerged as his generation's leading saxophonist, the H.N. White Company of Cleveland gave him an endorsement deal and produced this customized engraved King Super 20 saxophone for him.

The custom horn features an enlarged bore and a modified key action to support Parker's virtuosic technique. Parker used this horn on many of the recordings he made between 1948 and 1954. Its association with him has made it into a powerful symbol of Black genius and the birth of modern jazz. Indeed, because it was modified to Parker's specifications, his saxophone is a concrete manifestation of his musical aesthetic. His horn is part of the history of Black musicians altering their instruments, either physically or electronically, to achieve new sounds. Other examples include trumpet player James "Bubber" Miley (1903-1932), who used an array of mutes to create vocalized sounds, and blues harmonica player "Little" Walter Jacobs (ca. 1930-1968), who added a microphone and tube amplifier to his harmonica to create a new sound dubbed the "Mississippi saxophone."

In the 1950s and '60s, John Coltrane (1926-1967) extended Charlie Parker's innovations into new directions. Coltrane combined complex improvised

melodies with emotive shrieks, honks, and other unorthodox sounds that represented a distinctively African American approach to the saxophone. A manuscript part from Coltrane's first big band arrangement hints at his early musical development. "Nothing Beats A Trial But A Failure" was one of Coltrane's first compositions and one of his first attempts to arrange for a large jazz ensemble. Coltrane arranged this song for Jimmy Heath's big band while based in Philadelphia in the early 1950s. After the orchestra performed his arrangement once, Coltrane collected the parts and threw them into the gutter on his way home in frustration. This tenor saxophone part is likely the only surviving fragment of the arrangement. Coltrane's destruction of his music, which baffled his saxophonist friend Benny Golson (b. 1929) at the time, represented the perfectionism that elevated Coltrane's music to new heights by the late 1950s.

Material culture can point us to the work of underrecognized saxophonists, too. This photograph depicts saxophonist Willene Barton (1928–2005) performing at Jimbo's Bop City in San Francisco in the mid-1950s. Barton toured nationally in the 1950s in all-woman jazz combos, earning compliments from influential saxophonists Johnny Hodges and Charlie Parker. Her collaborators included vocalist Anna Mae Winburn—best known as leader of the International Sweethearts of Rhythm—and trombonist and arranger Melba Liston. Barton finally attracted the attention of jazz critics in the late 1970s as a member of a group called the Jazz Sisters and through prominent appearances at events including the Universal Jazz Coalition's "Salute to Women in Jazz." Her career reflects obstacles that continue to face Black women saxophonists. Although Black women have been performing as professional saxophone soloists since the early twentieth century, they have often been marginalized in favor of their male colleagues. Materials like this photograph help us to reconstruct these musicians' lives and contributions. SWL

Chapter 3

MUSIC IN THE COMMUNITY, MUSIC OF THE COMMUNITY

The importance of community is always central to discussions about African American music-making. A community is defined in this context by a shared cultural heritage and experience and a collective sense of purpose in the struggle for freedom. It is demonstrated in a variety of cultural practices and performance traditions, such as the circle in the ring shout, call and response, improvisation, and the equal value placed on individual performance and group participation. Community is also celebrated in the value of communal music-making and the power it has in putting movements into action and being the force of real social change.

However, the meaning of community also extends to the countless ways music lives in society and is activated by a broad network of smaller community formations that serve multiple purposes and goals. These formations can be defined by relationships (families of origin or by design); location (city, state, region, or neighborhood); shared values and beliefs (religion or education); identities (ethnicity, gender, sexual orientation, religion, or class); businesses and organizations (stores, entertainment venues, and professional associations); and common interests, activities, or goals (self-sufficiency, personal development, musical genres, or hobbies). None of

these formations are mutually exclusive and they frequently overlap.

As discussed in Chapter 1 (see p. 15), a material culture methodology is well suited to understanding the many pathways music leads to, and the networks it creates. Thinking of music as a social process, whether through creating, performing, identity formation, or community building, opens the door to a wealth of interpretive possibilities in understanding the centrality of music in our lived experiences. For example, a photograph of The Gap Band member Robert Wilson (1956–2010) with his guitar as he stands in front of an image of country music legend Hank Williams in Tulsa's historic Cain's Ballroom (see opposite) offers an opportunity to scratch the surface of Tulsa, Oklahoma's complicated history.

African American music-making, both by individuals and communities, has shaped and been shaped by a sense of place. Identified by cities such as New Orleans (jazz), rural (Mississippi Delta Blues) and urban (Chicago Blues) regions, West Coast and East Coast (hip-hop and rap), our musical and personal identities reflect and speak to the environments that influence us. Tulsa natives, Robert Wilson and his two older brothers, Charlie (b. 1953) and Ronnie (1948–2021) were the founding members of The Gap Band, one of the most popular funk/R&B groups of the 1970s and '80s. The Wilson brothers grew up in a religious family in Tulsa's Greenwood District, where they sang every Sunday during worship at the Pentecostal church where their father preached and

Robert Wilson of The Gap Band poses in front of a photograph of country singer Hank Williams inside Tulsa's historic Cain's Ballroom in 1973. Robert, along with his brothers, Ronnie and Charlie, founded The Gap Band in 1967 and would become one of the most popular R&B/funk groups in the 1970s and '80s.

their mother accompanied them on the piano. Their grandparents settled in Greenwood during a wave of Black migration to the western territories that started after the Civil War and led to the establishment of several Black towns and neighborhoods. While these towns were created out of necessity due to the same type of racial segregation practiced in the South, they also evolved into thriving communities where businesses, entertainment, churches, schools, and other services catered to the needs and interests of the community.

Greenwood was a popular destination. The neighborhood spanned thirty-five blocks and included Black-owned businesses and its own schools, libraries, hospitals, and public transportation. By 1919, Tulsa had risen to national prominence for being home to one of the most prosperous Black neighborhoods in the country. Nicknamed "Black Wall Street," Greenwood was a symbol of Black pride that exemplified a philosophy of racial solidarity, self-help, and economic advancement.

However, on May 31, 1921, a mob of Tulsa's white residents viciously attacked Greenwood's Black residents and decimated everything the community had built and represented. Residents were shot and killed, homes and businesses were looted and ransacked, and virtually every standing structure was set on fire and burned to the ground. Dynamite was even dropped by air to ensure that the entire neighborhood was wiped out. After two days, what is believed to be the largest incident of racial violence in American history left 300 people dead, 8,000 people homeless, and an entire neighborhood and community spirit devastated.

Many witnesses to what happened in 1921 were too traumatized and fearful to even verbalize what they had seen. Nevertheless, the story of the Massacre and the symbol of Black pride and accomplishment that existed before the tragedy was passed on from generation to generation. Charlie Wilson said he learned about the Massacre from his grandparents. When he and his brothers were deciding what to name their new group, they knew they wanted it to have some connection to the history of Greenwood, explaining, "The original name was the Greenwood Archer and Pine Street Band. We decided on that because we were all told what happened in Greenwood in 1921. I knew we were going to go all over the world and we were going to have to talk about all of that and where the name came from."[21]

When people think about the regional areas that had a pivotal role in Black music, South Central states like Oklahoma do not immediately come to mind. As African Americans began to settle in Oklahoma, however, they had the means and access to schools, music lessons, and instruments that helped aspiring musicians develop the skills to foster a climate for jazz and blues guitar. Tulsa's Black musicians are shaped by the history of Greenwood and, just as The Gap Band made that history part of their own identity, contemporary artists like Steph Simon (b. 1987), whose 2019 album *Born on Black Wall Street* commemorates the Greenwood neighborhood, are committed to making sure that the story of Tulsa's Black history and the reimagining of its futures continue to be told through the voices of its own community.

Education has always had an important role in the quest for freedom, allowing African Americans to further their efforts to acquire the same rights and privileges that were supposed to be granted to all citizens. Music education served a unique purpose. It not only provided basic musical training, but was also used to enhance students' awareness of the history, heritage, and accomplishments of African Americans, as well as to instill the value of discipline, practice, and working together toward common goals to inspire self-confidence and affirm the importance of perseverance and fortitude in negotiating the

Classical Music in the Community

Joseph Douglass (1871–1935) was the most celebrated Black violinist of the early twentieth century. A grandson of influential abolitionist Frederick Douglass (1818–1895) (pictured together in Boston in this 1894 photograph), the younger Douglass studied at the Boston Conservatory and rose to national prominence after performing at the 1893 Chicago World's Fair. He spent more than three decades crisscrossing the country on tours and working as a music educator at Howard University and New York City's Music School Settlement for the Colored. By the end of his career, Douglass had performed at every Black educational institution in the United States.

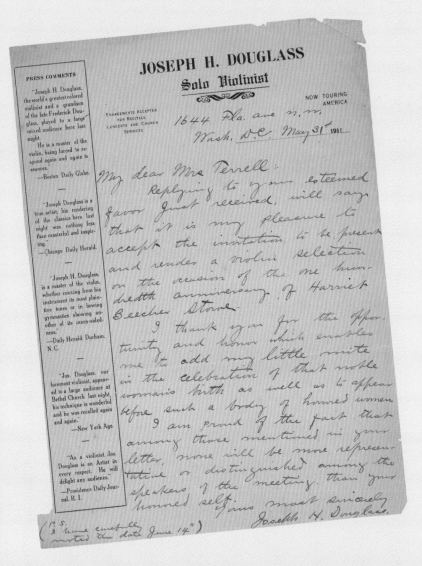

A 1911 letter from Joseph Douglass to activist Mary Church Terrell (1863–1954) illustrates the challenges faced by Black concert soloists of the era. Douglass's personalized stationery advertises his availability "for recitals[,] concerts[,] and church services." The mention of church services is important. Ignored by white audiences, Black artists often depended on Black community institutions like churches and colleges. Douglass writes to Terrell accepting her invitation to perform at a celebration of what would have been Harriet Beecher Stowe's hundredth birthday. Like other Black concert soloists of the period, Douglass would have relied heavily on friends and personal connections to find performance opportunities.

Douglass's correspondence with Terrell also underscores the important role that Black women's clubs and community organizations played in the musical lives of their communities in the early twentieth century. As a founder of the National Association of Colored Women, Terrell was a leading figure in the development of a national network of Black women's associations. In addition to their work to fight racial discrimination and to aid poor families in their communities, Black women's clubs often sponsored performances of classical music and music appreciation classes. SWL

challenges that come with being Black in the United States.

In 2004, the National Academy of Recording Arts & Sciences recognized folk singer and educator Ella Jenkins (b. 1924) with a Grammy Lifetime Achievement Award for her lifelong commitment to the music education of children. Over her sixty-year career, Jenkins made music for and alongside children, engaging them as participants in their discovery through learning and creative self-expression. Jenkins's unique gift was not just as a performer but in the way she created an environment for music education that also included skill development. She drew upon African American musical traditions of call and response, game songs, and ring chants that required group participation, allowing children to think independently, develop leadership skills, and learn to improvise, all while increasing their self-confidence.

Until 1954, when the Supreme Court ruled in *Brown v. Board of Education* that the segregation of public schools by race was illegal, the education experience for Black students was curtailed by limited resources but also strengthened by a community of teachers and educational institutions that had an unwavering commitment and investment in the personal development, education, and cultural enrichment of each student. While there were differences of opinion in the type of education that would best serve students and advance the quest for racial equality, the ultimate goal for educators of African American students was to prepare young people to have the best opportunity to be self-sufficient and lead purposeful lives.

From 1900 to 1935, manual training and industrial schools were the model for public education for Black students throughout the South. These schools were modeled on the Tuskegee Normal and Industrial Institute, in Tuskegee, Alabama—a school for Black students that was established in accordance with founding principal Booker T. Washington's educational philosophy that extolled the value of a practical education and focused on vocational and manual labor skills as the key to economic security and self-reliance.

The Bordentown School was founded in 1886 by Rev. Walter A. Rice, a formerly enslaved minister, in Bordentown, New Jersey. Although the school

Ella Jenkins is one of the most celebrated and influential folk musicians of her time. For over sixty years, she has instilled a love of music in children all over the world, which has passed on from one generation to the next. In 2004, Jenkins became the first professional children's musician to receive the Grammy Lifetime Achievement Award.

The Bordentown School was a symbol of excellence in providing a well-rounded education for Black students. Around 1935, sociologist and photographer Lewis Wickes Hine (1874–1940) made a series of photographs at the school, highlighting the various courses and opportunities available to students. Although girls were admitted to the school from its founding, this photograph depicts an all-male band in rehearsal.

was not originally founded as a manual training and industrial institution, the state of New Jersey took over its operation in 1894 and decided to model the curriculum on Washington's Tuskegee example. When William R. Valentine was appointed principal in 1915, he recognized the school's potential and knew Bordentown could offer Black students a practical and uplifting education. Valentine believed that, under the right conditions, industrial education could play a key role in progressive education, and he sought to blend vocational training with academic subjects.

Under Valentine, Bordentown expanded the curriculum to include literary clubs, choir, drama, sports, a glee club, and a school band. These additional activities promoted cultural enrichment and cultivated values of moral character, self-confidence, and cultural pride as additional tools that would ensure the student's chances in surviving life off-campus and maximizing their opportunities to achieve success. Valentine believed that fostering a strong work ethic and sense of personal responsibility was important to every student. Since Black students

were regularly excluded from extracurricular activities in most racially "mixed" Northern high schools, these were an important part of the school's attraction to Black families. By 1930, Bordentown School had a national reputation as a leading educational, athletic, and cultural institution for Black youth.

Bordentown closed after the *Brown v. Board of Education* case legally ended school segregation. While the climate for public education has changed, the value that music instruction brings to Black students has not. Particularly in schools where a large number of students are disenfranchised

Dr. Foster, FAMU, and the Marching "100"

This 1968 photograph depicts Dr. William P. Foster (1919–2010) standing proudly with five of his students from the Florida A&M University (FAMU) Marching "100." When Foster arrived as band director in 1946, he found the band struggling with a lack of resources. The group had only sixteen members and many instruments were damaged beyond repair. Foster set about making enormous improvements. He transformed the group by introducing complex routines and, beginning in the early 1960s, energetic choreography into their halftime shows. Soon the band was performing frequently on television, at national football championships, and at multiple presidential inaugurations. The performance style Foster introduced, combining traditional techniques with vibrant interpretations of Black popular music and dance, shaped the direction of college bands around the country. His innovative vision extended the work of earlier groups, like James Reese Europe's 369th Infantry band and the FAMU marching bands

of the 1910s and '20s, which had combined military precision with popular elements borrowed from traveling circus bands.

In addition to reinvigorating the college marching band tradition, Foster served for decades as Chairman of the FAMU Department of Music. He was also elected President of the American Bandmasters Association and was appointed by President Clinton to serve on the National Council on the Arts. Foster's influence stretched across generations of FAMU graduates, and his former students' reverence for him emphasizes Black band directors' roles as mentors to young musicians. Music educators like Foster, working at historically Black colleges and universities (HBCUs), teach music skills along with important life lessons, such as character, self-discipline, and etiquette, in an effort to cultivate the whole student.

This jacket and shako were worn by Ernest Brown, who played tenor saxophone in the Marching "100." Signs of extensive wear on the jacket's interior lining, along with a missing patch on its right wrist, point to its having been used by successive students over many years. This Marching "100" uniform illustrates the reality that, like other Black institutions, HBCUs have often had to make creative use of limited resources. After graduating from FAMU, Brown went on to serve as Director of Bands at Suncoast High School in Riviera Beach, Florida. Brown's experience shows how collegiate band programs like Foster's have trained generations of Black music educators, who in turn have taught music students around the country. SWL

by race, poverty, geographical location, or family circumstances, music is an important factor in self-expression and sense of belonging. Music education for Black students is not only about developing skills and increasing knowledge, but also instilling discipline, pride in one's heritage and culture, and self-esteem, in order to excel in music and to be able to negotiate the obstacles and challenges that come with being Black in American society.

Black photographers played a vital role in documenting music through the lens of the African American experience. From portraits of well-known artists, concert and club performances, and festivals to worship services, social protest gatherings, and musical experiences in the home and on the streets, Black photographers portrayed the breadth of African American music-making in an honest and respectable way. Photographer Lloyd W. Yearwood (1925–2011) was known for his work documenting the African American community in Harlem from the 1950s through the early 1990s. In addition to community scenes, Yearwood's portfolio includes portraits of musical artists such as Clara Ward, Miles Davis, Marian Anderson, and Sam Cooke, and the music traditions of churches and other religious organizations in and around Harlem.

African Americans follow a variety of religions, each with their own musical styles and worship traditions. In the early 1900s, African Americans formed a number of small religious organizations around religious identities that fell outside the Christian-based Black Church. The Commandment Keepers, a congregation of Black Hebrews founded by Rabbi Wentworth Arthur Matthew (1892–1973) in Harlem in 1919, was one of these organizations. Matthew was an immigrant from St. Kitts and his arrival in Harlem coincided with the emergence of new ideologies related to Black identity and a pan-African solidarity.

Inspired by a doctrine that recognized African Americans as descendants of Abraham, Isaac, and Jacob of the Old Testament, Matthew created The Commandment Keepers as a congregation that provided an ancestral identity and a symbol of human dignity to African American followers in Harlem. Matthew's work in Harlem became the inspiration for Black Jewish congregations in cities around the country, including Beth Shalom B'nai Zaken Ethiopian Hebrew Congregation in Chicago. Although music in Jewish religious services generally centers around oral recitation and chanting, the use of instruments is not uncommon. For example, an ancient instrument made from a ram's horn known as a *shofar* is traditionally blown during services on Rosh Hashanah to mark the beginning of the new year (see opposite).

Like Lloyd W. Yearwood on the East Coast, Steve Jackson Jr. (1923-1999) on the West Coast had intimate access to his community. After moving to San Francisco in 1951, Jackson met John "Jimbo" Edwards (1913–2000), the proprietor of the Bop City nightclub. The two soon entered into a special arrangement, whereby Edwards gave Jackson free access to photograph the club's musicians and customers, and also set up a dark room so he could develop the photographs right in the building. Jackson's photographs depict musicians both performing and sitting in the audience with other customers, wait staff, and musicians enjoying themselves.

As a jazz club in San Francisco's Fillmore District, Bop City was a popular destination for musicians and the local community from 1949 to 1965. The club initially started out as Jimbo's Waffle Shop. However,

This photograph by Lloyd W. Yearwood depicts Rabbi David Matthew Doré, the grandson of Rabbi Wentworth A. Matthew, blowing a *shofar* by the East River in Harlem on Rosh Hashanah in 1983.

This *shofar* belonged to Rabbi Abihu Reuben, who led Chicago's B'nai Zaken Ethiopian Hebrew Congregation from 1947 to 1991. It was later passed on to Rabbi Capers Funnye after he assumed leadership of the Congregation.

Customers enjoy themselves at Jimbo's Bop City, a jazz club in San Francisco's Fillmore District, also known as the "Harlem of the West." Bop City was a legendary hangout on the West Coast in the 1950s and '60s, where customers could hear the best Black musicians of the day.

when musicians started to drop by after an evening gig to play in the shop's backroom, Jimbo built a bandstand, got a piano and drum set, and re-opened as Bop City. It was an important training ground and West Coast venue for Black musicians who would drop in to perform or listen to others perform in legendary late-night jam sessions. The club was a showcase for bebop and attracted a steady stream of the most renowned artists of the day, such as Dexter Gordon, Chet Baker, Carmen McCrae, Johnny Mathis, Sarah Vaughan, Dizzy Gillespie, and John Coltrane.

Even though the musicians played to an integrated audience, Bop City was also a community space where African Americans felt welcomed in an era of Jim Crow segregation. The role Black nightclubs played as a communal space for music is evident in Steve Jackson Jr.'s photograph of three men in uniform and a waitress sitting in a booth at Bop City. Wearing a military uniform did not protect Black servicemen from harassment and racial discrimination. Off the base, or during a stop in another city, a club like Bop City would have been one of very few places where Black soldiers could relax and be appreciated for their military service.

During the mid-twentieth century, radio was the most popular form of entertainment and communication for African American communities. It played a critical role in building a broad audience for Black music, influencing musical tastes and styles, and creating a

Afro-Caribbean Voices

When Brandy Barretto donated percussionist and bandleader Ray Barretto's (1929–2006) archive to the NMAAHC, it resituated the music of a native New Yorker of Puerto Rican descent into the narrative of African American music. Barretto started out as a jazz musician but embraced a syncretic mix of music styles drawn from the Caribbean and the United States. He disliked being pigeon-holed and found creative autonomy in permeating the boundaries of genre, geography, nationality, ethnicity, and race. This drum is covered in multicolored scuffs and the metal surface of its handle is abraded, speaking to its heavy use and to Barretto's preference for the conga, his primary instrument. He often stood behind his drums lined out, or if he was seated, they were positioned between his legs. Staining and shallow scrapes on the surface of the drumhead secured by a screw-and-lug tension system help in recalling Barretto's hand techniques as he rapidly struck the instrument's surface with intention. The instrument preserves Barretto's performance of Caribbean-born rhythms and grooves, which he helped firmly integrate into the American soundscape.

Barretto was among a generation of Americans with Latin heritage who infused popular music with Afro-Latin musical styles and traditions from Cuba and Puerto Rico. Barretto's archive is not just a record of his own personal story; it also resonates with the stories of other people, places, and events that are included in the archive. This photograph of Barretto with the "Queen of Salsa", Celia Cruz, illustrates the high-energy nature of their music, which had global appeal. Their charisma and musical versatility influenced the American musical landscape but also challenged people's perceptions of race, ethnicity, and authenticity through a lens of cultural authority, ownership, and appropriation. Although these barriers are much more fluid today, the issues continue to hover around the perimeter and occasionally rise to the surface. **HG**

Black Radio

In 1948, Herman and Minnie Roundtree of Lyles Station, Indiana, sprang for a new top-of-the-line tabletop radio. The Philco model 48-482 was the brand's most deluxe tabletop radio in 1948. It could receive AM, FM, and short-wave broadcasts. Radio was an important source of entertainment for the family: Minnie, for example, used it to listen to her favorite baseball team, the St. Louis Cardinals, play. Especially with the growth of Black radio programming in the late 1940s, radios provided Black families with a wide range of programs that catered to Black community concerns. In many parts of the country, these programs were the only way to enjoy events without being denied access or negotiating demeaning race-based restrictions such as separate entrances and separate seating for Black patrons.

Radios, and other objects including record players and player pianos, point to the important place of popular media within twentieth-century Black domestic and community life. The development of new ways of distributing music gave Black communities access to musical genres and styles that were otherwise unavailable, while also inspiring community musicians with new sounds and techniques. In the decades before the introduction of television, radio broadcasts helped to bring families and even whole communities together. People without radios would often gather around those in their neighbors' homes, listening to live broadcasts of news, sports, and musical performances. This would have been even more important for Black communities in relatively isolated rural areas, like the Roundtrees' native Lyles Station, which was far from regional entertainment hubs like Indianapolis and Louisville.

The Roundtree family's radio also points to the central role that new mass media technologies played in the popularization of Black music in the twentieth century, beginning with sheet music and piano rolls, continuing through the development of recordings and radio, and persisting into the present in media such as podcasts and streaming services. American radio stations began broadcasting classical performances in 1910, and an increasing number of stations started regular broadcasts of jazz and blues during the 1920s.

Although Black radio personalities were active by the mid-1920s, the late 1940s and early 1950s saw the proliferation of Black-owned radio stations and Black DJs. In addition to their importance in promoting music, Black DJs strengthened community bonds by highlighting local and regional causes and organizations, providing an important venue for Black social and political commentary. By the time the Roundtree family purchased this radio in 1948, stations like WDIA in Memphis and WERD in Atlanta had become successful with all-African American on-air formats. SWL

Rev. Glenn T. Settle founded the Wings Over Jordan Choir when he was assigned as Cleveland's Gethsemane Baptist Church's new pastor in 1935. The Choir quickly became one of the city's most popular performing ensembles and would eventually have a national weekly radio program from 1937 to 1949 (first with WGAR, then with CBS, and finally with Mutual). This page from a 1948 Wings Over Jordan promotional pamphlet lists the names of eight scholarship winners for 1947–48.

larger sense of community for African Americans who lived in different regions throughout the country.

A national audience began hearing about the struggles of African Americans on the *Wings Over Jordan* radio program when it first aired nationally on CBS in January 1938. The half-hour broadcast included a performance by the Wings Over Jordan choir, brief commentary by the choir's founder and director, Rev. Glenn T. Settle (1894–1967), and a segment featuring prominent national leaders such as Langston Hughes, Adam Clayton Powell, and Mary McLeod Bethune. The program was a hybrid mix of activities that served as a platform to address the needs and interests of the larger Black community. It also introduced white audiences to issues that were of interest to African Americans. Wings Over Jordan operated as a nonprofit organization and was essentially the first Black-run radio production company. It earned income by touring across the US and worked with local sponsors to support community projects.

Even a solo venture is supported by a network of other communities. Nina Simone began playing the piano at a young age and was able to take formal piano lessons after a music teacher raised funds in the community for her education. She saved a card that promoted a recital she gave in Philadelphia when she was still known by her birth name, Eunice Waymon (see p. 84). The card could have been an advertisement or an actual ticket for admission.

While the allure of this particular object rests in the knowledge of its original owner and its connection to the earliest days of Simone's career, when she performed under a different name, it also carries another narrative about the network of communities and organizations that played a role in her musical training and formation.

The event sponsors included the Philadelphia branch of the National Association of Negro Musicians (NANM) and the Young People's Music Club. NANM was founded in 1919 to support the needs of professional musicians, particularly those who specialized and trained in classical traditions. It provided workshops, concerts, recitals, youth programs, and panel discussions about issues that were important to the membership, and served as a resource and support system for Black musicians who struggled to get the same opportunities and respect that white musicians received. This record of Nina

IN RECITAL . . .

EUNICE WAYMON, PIANIST

NEW CENTURY AUDITORIUM
One Twenty-four South Twelfth Street
Friday Evening, February 19th, 1954
at 8:30 o'clock

SUBSCRIPTION   (INCLUDING TAX) $1.30

SPONSORS
Philadelphia Branch N. A. N. M., Inc.
and Young People's Music Club

Eunice Kathleen Waymon, also known as Nina Simone, grew up in Tryon, North Carolina, and started playing piano at a very young age. After studying for a summer at Juilliard, she and her family moved to Philadelphia, where she started her professional career. This card, a personal keepsake, advertises a piano recital she gave just before her twenty-first birthday.

Simone's early years is just one of many examples of the varied ways that African Americans came together to support the aspirations of an individual, with the understanding that one person's success was an achievement that could be embraced as a sign of progress and validation for all.

Music organizations can also take a more activist approach. These alliances are agents of change. They are not created just because the members play the same instrument, work in the same profession, or are interested in a particular musical genre; they are created to challenge and dismantle the structures and practices that continue to uphold systemic racism. African American music has been front and center in conversations about race, in terms of authenticity, identity, ownership, appropriation, power, social change, the creative process, recognition, and economic reward.

Rock and roll's pioneers—Louis Jordan, Chuck Berry, Little Richard, Sister Rosetta Tharpe, and Willie Mae "Big Mama" Thornton, just to name a few—were Black. The exciting innovations in sounds, playing techniques, performance styles, and technology marked the beginning of a new revolution

that caught the attention of white listeners. The public erasure of the Black roots of the genre started in the 1950s, when Elvis Presley was marketed to audiences as the "King of Rock and Roll." By the 1960s the face of the genre had totally changed. Even though Black artists were still recording, the British invasion of musical groups such as the Beatles and the Rolling Stones—who were self-tutored on the records of Black artists in America—along with other primarily white bands, were promoted as the authentic purveyors of rock and roll. The music industry was so successful in promoting the genre through the lens of whiteness that even Jimi Hendrix, who was recording at the same time as many of these other acts, seemed more like an anomaly, as great as he was, to many audiences.

The Black Rock Coalition (BRC) was organized in 1985 in response to the obstacles a new generation of Black rock and roll musicians were facing with the music industry. Refusing to acknowledge that African Americans were the architects of the genre, many producers would not sign Black artists because audiences would not accept them as legitimate rock and roll musicians. The BRC's manifesto was not

Colored Performing Rights Society of America

Upon looking at this embosser's rather mundane outward appearance, some might wonder what about it could be musical. Its chunky metal visage seems like an unassuming piece of office equipment. When the curved lever is depressed on paper, it leaves an impression of a seal with two concentric circles separated by a dotted boundary. On the outer circle, a star appears at the bottom sandwiched between a line of text that stretches its way around, reading "COLORED PERFORMING RIGHTS SOCIETY OF AMERICA, LTD." The inner circle states "CORPORATE SEAL 1957 NEW YORK." And with that, the seal opens a window into evaluating the role of professional societies that gathered African American performers in community and aided them in navigating the business of publishing, performing, and working in a competitive music industry.

In the late 1950s, the embosser likely sat on a desk in the offices of the newly founded Colored Performing Rights Society of America (CPRSA), which was presided over by show-business veteran Perry Bradford (1893–1979). In 1957, Bradford was past his prime when he joined music publisher Barney Young in forming CPRSA. The pair sought to provide more exposure to music written by African Americans by working with composers to get their material licensed for use on radio and television.

Bradford, a songwriter and former vaudevillian from Montgomery, Alabama, was a natural choice for this position. His role in kickstarting the Race Records craze that began with Mamie Smith's 1920 recording of his composition "Crazy Blues" forever changed American music. Prior to the song's release, he had spent months appealing to record label executives and aides who doubted the commercial viability of such a venture. Advice he sought while crafting his sales pitch from older entertainers at the Colored Vaudeville Benevolent Association in Harlem critically aided him in reaching this historical achievement. HG

ASSOCIAZIONE CULTURALE
iZIMBRA

LA GAZZETTA DEL MEZZOGIORNO

MINISTERO DEL TURISMO E DELLO SPETTACOLO

COMUNE DI BARI
Assessorato allo Spettacolo

BLACK ROCK
FESTIVAL

tributo a Jimi Hendrix ~ da Hendrix alla Black Rock Coalition

RENOIR CLUB - BARI
VIA M. LOSACCO 8
~ ore 21.00 ~

24 GIUGNO
JJ JUMPERS
JEAN PAUL BOURELLY
KELVYNATOR X SLAM-FUNK POSSE

25 GIUGNO
P.B.R. STREET GANG
TASHAN
GANGSTARR

★ DOCTOR MUSIK ★
NICE PRICE

1988
DOCTOR MUSIK
~DISCHI~

26 GIUGNO
GOOD GUYS
D-XTREME
BLACK ROCK ORCHESTRA

~ PREVENDITE ~
DOCTOR MUSIK NICE PRICE
Via Putignani, 215 - BARI
Tel. 080/5246686
DOCTOR MUSIK
Via P. Amedeo, 154 - BARI
Tel. 080/5210856 5244686
CANTON BLUE
V.le Unità d'Italia, 63/8 - BARI
Tel. 080/ 5575532

27 GIUGNO
MICHAEL HILL'S BLUESLAND
BLACK ROCK ORCHESTRA
Featuring BERNIE WORRELL

RACCOMANDATO DA

radionorba

just limited to rock, but highlighted the larger issue that has dominated the music industry and the way audiences listen to and buy music—namely, that the conventions of genres are not random categorizations but a systemic method of codification and control that ensures that the boundaries are carefully policed and guarded.

The BRC serves the needs of its members by providing resources and giving maximum exposure to artists who defy convention. This poster for a Black Rock Festival tribute to Jimi Hendrix in Italy features a roster of musicians whose creative voices defy categorization. The poster design, with the colors red, yellow, green, and black, incorporates the symbols of a pan-African ideology where solidarity and collaboration among people of African descent form the path toward liberation for all.

The material culture of music methodology invites one to engage with African American music through multiple lenses that draw attention to the role people play in bringing the art form to life. This chapter explores people building alliances and communities through social identities, organizational structures, practices and values where music is the foundation or route to other community goals, and the impetus for communal gatherings or social change. The history of Motown Records, interpreted in light of the Detroit Riots of 1967, is a perfect illustration of the multiple ways music lives in communities, but also the differences of opinion as to what purpose the music is supposed to serve.

The Motown legend, from its earliest days as a community of people living in one city, brought young creative entrepreneurs together with aspirations to break through the barriers to achieve racial integration and social change through music. When Berry Gordy (b. 1929) borrowed $800 from the Gordy family savings co-op to start his own record company in 1959, he was following the family blueprint for success. His parents, Berry Sr. and Bertha Gordy, sold a track of land in Georgia for a sizeable profit and moved to Detroit in 1922. The Gordys became one of Detroit's prominent African American families, establishing numerous businesses to serve the community. Some of these ventures, like a record store, were connected to music.

The Gordys moved north for a variety of reasons. Detroit was a popular destination due to the employment prospects offered by the city's auto industry. Steady work provided the foundation for Detroit's African American middle class, which supported a robust music environment in the city. Another beneficiary of this prosperity was the Detroit public school system, which had gained national recognition for its strong music curriculum. Students learned to read music, learned about composition, and performed a variety of musical styles. This instruction extended to homes within the neighborhood, and demonstrates the network of formal and informal musical training and exposure that was common in many Black communities.

By 1967, Motown was one of the country's most visible Black-owned businesses. Berry Gordy had changed the music industry, the trajectory of American popular music, and the blueprint for African American success in the field of entertainment. The fact that African Americans reaped the economic rewards of this success is equally significant. Motown served a variety of markets with over a dozen imprints, including Tamla, Gordy, Mel-O-dy, Divinity, Soul, and Black Forum, as well as Jobete Publishing Company and International Talent Management Inc. For example, Gladys Knight and The Pips, who signed

The Black Rock Coalition (BRC) was founded in 1985 by Living Colour guitarist Vernon Reid (b. 1958), musician and cultural critic Greg Tate (1957–2021), and producer Konda Mason (b. 1955) to fight the "racist and reactionary forces in the American music industry" that deny Black musicians the same creative freedoms and economic rewards that are afforded to white musicians.

with Motown in 1966, had their first hit on Motown's Soul Records label, working with the company's team of songwriters and producers on "I Heard it through the Grapevine," which reached No. 1 and No. 2 on the Rhythm and Blues and Pop charts, respectively.

However, even though Motown was enjoying great success, internally things were changing. The heralded songwriting team of Holland-Dozier-Holland left the company due to royalty disputes, and Motown's success and marketing to appeal to the crossover market was increasingly viewed to be out of sync with the immediate concerns of the Black community. As in many urban cities across the country, a simmering anger was emerging as Black radicalism began spreading in Detroit. On the morning of July 23, 1967, about a half-mile from Motown's Hitsville studio on the city's West Side, a police raid at an unlicensed bar sparked four days of civil unrest. Widely known as the

Detroit Riots, what is now understood as a "rebellion" was an eruption fueled by the Black community's growing frustration with the City's unwillingness to address the racial disparities in housing, employment, social services, education, economic investment, and the judicial system.

The events and their aftermath received national attention. Photographers from the Detroit Free Press won a Pulitzer Prize for their coverage. Most of the images included looted stores; people throwing rocks and bottles; police in riot gear barricading city streets and businesses, and arresting residents; community leaders on bullhorns trying to restore the peace; and multiple images of community members and police warily observing each other from a distance. Amidst these images, a photograph of one man walking down the street with a lantern in his left hand and his right arm wrapped around a string bass stands out. The man is apparently responding to the moment and the call to evacuate the neighborhood, leaving with two possessions, one out of necessity to navigate the current environment and the other because it is something of value to him. This photograph is a poignant reminder of how central music has been to the history of Detroit and its African American community.

Photographers for the Detroit Free Press won a Pulitzer Prize for their coverage of the Detroit Riots in July 1967. While most of the photographs document the police in riot gear, the damaged and looted storefronts, and neighborhood residents being arrested or kept at bay, this photograph, taken by Ira Rosenberg, stands out by offering a different perspective on the city and its residents.

Resurrection City

In 1968, Dr. Martin Luther King Jr. and the Southern Christian Leadership Conference launched the Poor People's Campaign—a multiethnic, multicultural movement to demand equal access to economic opportunities and security for all people. Weeks after King's assassination on April 4, protesters traveled to Washington, DC, and built an encampment known as "Resurrection City" on the National Mall to honor King's vision and as an act of civil disobedience. For a period of five weeks—from May 21 to June 23, 1968—thousands of America's poor were joined by activists and artists, including Lou Rawls, Jimmy Collier, Dizzy Gillespie, and James Moody, to confront poverty as a national human rights issue.

Among the artists who joined the protest was musician and civil rights activist Rev. Fredrick Douglass Kirkpatrick (1933–1986), who throughout his life used music to teach about African American history and the Civil Rights Movement. A photograph of Kirkpatrick playing the guitar is among the Museum's collection of over three hundred photographs from Resurrection City taken by Baltimore-based photographer Robert Houston (1935–2021). In this photograph, Kirkpatrick plays the guitar, while participants holding lyric sheets join him in song.

Musical performances and impromptu singing took place all around Resurrection City—from outside the Department of Agriculture and on the steps of the Lincoln Memorial to the encampment's Many Races Soul Center. This Center was a major venue for

concerts, meetings, education, and activism—where Resurrection City's many music and multicultural programs took place. The Center was built with plywood walls, one of which was transformed by demonstrators into a twelve-panel mural known as "Hunger's Wall." From the multilingual slogans, symbols, and art on the walls of the building to the freedom songs that were sung inside, the Many Races Soul Center was a place where protestors could come together and create a sense of unity and hope for the movement. DTR

Music and Family Life

Gathering in familiar spaces to share stories and songs is a valued tradition for many Black households. For families of different configurations around the country, including these children gathered around a piano at an orphanage in California (above), such moments of coming together happen in the home, around an instrument. Those who grew up with a piano in the living room may remember the dread of practicing scales, excitement when it was time to put on a show for the family, or nerves after the last run-through before a recital. All stories about music in the home are different, but many are connected to a shared instrument like the piano.

In 1911, Henry L. Long (1882–1935) purchased a ca. 1898 E.P. Carpenter & Company parlor-style pump organ for his family in Seneca, South Carolina. Long worked as a Pullman Porter and his wife, Ida, worked as a washerwoman. They added regular payments on the instrument to their household budget until it was paid off. Documenting their middle-class home was so important to them that, decades later, a leather folder with the paperwork and receipts for the organ and other household items was still hidden away inside the instrument. After all, during the late nineteenth

and early twentieth centuries, no parlor was complete without a piano or pump organ.

While the Long family did not play music outside of the home, the children were encouraged to explore their musical interests and talents. They used the organ for informal gatherings and large celebrations alike. The organ stayed with family members as they moved from Seneca to Atlanta, Georgia, then to Fort Washington, Maryland. It was there that, in 2011, Frankie Long, Henry's daughter-in-law, shared the organ with the Museum and donated it as a gift of the family of Henry L. Long.

Like the Longs, the Freeman children in Cleveland, Ohio, grew up exploring music in their family's home. Four-year-old Ernie Freeman is pictured sitting on a bench in front of his family's piano, holding a small

violin. His feet barely reach halfway to the ground, but his hand confidently grips the violin bow. Born into a musical family, Ernest "Ernie" Freeman's (1922–1981) musical journey started at a young age. He played violin with his family's classical ensemble, picked up the saxophone and joined his sister's swing band, and even performed in local nightclubs, all before graduating from high school. After joining the Navy and graduating from the Cleveland Institute of Music, Freeman moved to Los Angeles and obtained a master's degree in music composition from the University of Southern California while honing his skills as a sideman and arranger. His career flourished during the 1950s and '60s through his work in jazz, R&B, popular music, and television and films (see pp. 130 and 158).

Taking piano lessons often includes performing during recitals for family and friends, even for a member of the world's most famous musical family. Janet Jackson (see also p. 30) wore this pale blue chiffon dress for her first piano recital when she was eight years old. The tenth and youngest of a talented family, Jackson had already performed on stage in Las Vegas a year before she wore this dress.

The Jackson family's journey from Gary, Indiana, to Los Angeles, California, was centered around the career trajectory of Janet's brothers in the Jackson 5. Everyone in the family went through rigorous rehearsals at home and was expected to present polished appearances in public, whether performing on a major stage for thousands or in a living room for a small group. Jackson not only developed her remarkable stage presence at a young age, but through her lessons, she also learned fundamental elements of music theory. This training served her well when she began writing music and forging her path as a solo artist. TAB

The Black Church

Beginning within the dark period of American slavery, the Black church has been the central anchor institution in Black communities across the United States. In addition to their priestly and prophetic roles in leading communities in protest and praise, in seasons of suffering and hope, Black churches have long offered everyday Black Americans opportunities for human dignity, social interaction, and leadership training—intangibles long denied Black people within the broader American society. Moreover, the Black church has also played a pivotal role in broadening America's (and the world's) cultural soundscape. Through the application of an African-derived musical aesthetic and experimentation with new forms of instrumentation, the Black church has produced a sound and musical culture that has influenced the world, while fostering a distinctive African American musical identity. At various points in history, the music of the Black church has also given voice to the church's position as a base for civic engagement and social activism.

As music director of Chicago's Pilgrim Baptist Church for more than thirty years, beginning in the early 1930s, the "father of gospel music" Thomas A. Dorsey (1899-1993) used this piano for rehearsals with choirs and soloists, including Albertina Walker, Mahalia Jackson, and Aretha Franklin. The piano, a Conover "Fairy Grand," was the smallest of the five grand piano models manufactured by the Conover Cable Company of Chicago. Conover's instruments were well-regarded at the time—the renowned Chicago Symphony owned one of their larger Model 100 pianos—and the quality of the piano's construction points to Pilgrim's status as one of Chicago's most prominent and prosperous Black churches by the mid-1920s.

Dorsey's piano also hints at Chicago's centrality to the Great Migration. The Black churches of the North and Midwest were sites where southern Black folk culture developed into new traditions. Dorsey, a former bluesman who had migrated to Chicago from Georgia in the early 1920s and was steeped in the Southern traditions of the blues and Black folk music, used Pilgrim's rehearsal piano to work out the foundation of gospel music. His ideas were an important influence on choirs like the one shown in the above photograph of the Ebenezer AME Church in Fort Washington, Maryland. Dorsey's piano acquired another, more tragic, significance in 2006, when a fire gutted the historic church and destroyed Dorsey's manuscripts and other priceless artifacts. As the only surviving object from the church's early years, the instrument highlights the vulnerability and irreplaceability of cultural heritage.

In addition to nurturing musical innovation, Black churches embraced music's role in building political consciousness. A 1932 hymnal insert of James Weldon Johnson (1871-1938) and John Rosamond Johnson's (1873-1954) "Lift Every Voice and Sing" reflects the important role that Black churches have played in fostering a sense of pride and an activist spirit in Black communities. Inserts like this were often added to hymnals to supplement the standard repertoire of worship music. Black congregations adopted the song shortly after its introduction in 1900. In 1919, the NAACP designated the hymn the "Negro National Anthem," as reflected in the title of this insert. By the 1920s, it was commonly performed in Black churches around the country. Inserts of "Lift Every Voice and Sing" fell out of use beginning in the late 1970s, as hymnals incorporated the song. For example, the 1984 edition of the African Methodist Episcopal Church's

official hymnal included the song for the first time. Its existence as an insert, decades prior to its formal incorporation, illustrates just how receptive Black churches were—and still are—to the song's message of hope and activism grounded in religious faith.

Finally, a trumpet played by Elder Roosevelt T. Hunter of the Church of God in Christ further illustrates the diversity and creativity of twentieth-century Black worship traditions. It was donated to the NMAAHC by his son Ralph Hunter, a longtime resident of Atlantic City, and founder and president of the African American Heritage Museum of Southern New Jersey. Elder Hunter (1903-1980), a street preacher and native of Memphis, Tennessee, played this trumpet during his sermons on Beale Street in the 1930s and '40s. His instrument demonstrates the significance of alternative forms of instrumentation in the music of churches within and influenced by Black Holiness and Pentecostal movements. Beginning in the early twentieth century, as Southern Black migrants carried their sacred traditions North and West, urban congregations began to incorporate musical instruments that were frowned upon in mainline Methodist and Baptist churches for their association with secular music forms like jazz and blues. This innovative approach and openness to experimentation with sound was a key influence on gospel artists like Rosetta Tharpe, Arizona Dranes, Edwin Hawkins, and Andraé Crouch. ELW

Dirr Street Methodist Episcopal Church

S. P. JENKINS, *Minister*

Negro National Anthem––Johnson

Lift every voice and sing, Till earth and heaven ring,
Ring with the harmonies of Liberty;
Let our rejoicing rise, High as the list'ning skies,
Let it resound loud as the rolling sea.
Sing a song full of the faith that the dark past has taught us
Sing a song full of the hope that the present has brought us;
Facing the rising sun of our new day begun,
Let us march on 'till victory is won.

Stoney the road we trod, Bitter the chast'ning rod,
Felt in the days when hope unborn had died;
Yet with a steady beat have not our weary feet
Come to the place for which our fathers sighed?
We have come over a way that with tears has been watered
We have come, treading our path thro' the blood of the slaughtered,
Out of the gloomy past, Till now we stand at last
Where the white gleam of our bright star is cast.

God of our weary years, God of our silent tears,
Thou who has brought us thus far on the way;
Thou who hast by thy might, Led us into the light,
Keep us forever in the path, we pray
Lest our feet stray from the places, our God, where we met Thee
Lest our hearts, drunk with the wine of the world, we forget Thee;
Shadowed beneath Thy hand, May we forever stand,
True to our God, True to our Native land.

Musical Life at Historically Black Colleges and Universities

In this October 1937 photograph, composer William Levi Dawson (1899–1990) stands proudly in front of the Tuskegee Choir. Dawson inscribed the image to fellow Black composer Hall Johnson, who kept it among his personal papers for the rest of his life in a sign of respect for his colleague. Dawson attended Tuskegee before studying at the Horner Institute of Fine Arts in Kansas City, Missouri, and the American Conservatory of Music in Chicago. He joined the Tuskegee faculty in 1931, after a stint playing first trombone in the Chicago Civic Symphony Orchestra. One of Dawson's most important roles was as director of the Tuskegee Choir, a position he occupied from 1931 through his retirement in 1956. Under his leadership, the choir rose to national prominence, embarking on nationwide tours and giving an acclaimed series of performances in New York City at the opening of the Radio City Music Hall in 1932. Dawson's Tuskegee Choir was part of a lineage of choral ensembles at historically Black colleges and universities (HBCUs), which, beginning with the triumph of the Fisk Jubilee Singers in the 1870s, had done the crucial work of fundraising for their institutions, preserving the African American spiritual repertoire, and embodying Black musical excellence for global audiences.

Decades later, Dawson's famous student Ralph Ellison remembered Tuskegee as "one of the major musical centers of the South."[22] Ellison's comment illustrates how dedicated educators and performers made HBCUs into hubs of musical life in Southern communities. During the Jim Crow era, when many concert venues were off-limits for Black people, HBCUs welcomed Black audiences to musical performances that would have been inaccessible otherwise. They were also an essential training ground for generations of Black classical musicians. Some of these artists, such as vocalist and Fisk student Roland Hayes (1887–1977), went on to become world-famous. Many others would occupy important roles in their communities, serving as music educators and providing music for church services and community functions.

Marching bands represent an especially distinctive facet of the HBCU musical tradition, one that provides the public "face" of HBCU music departments in communities around the country and the world. This left-handed baritone horn made by the German

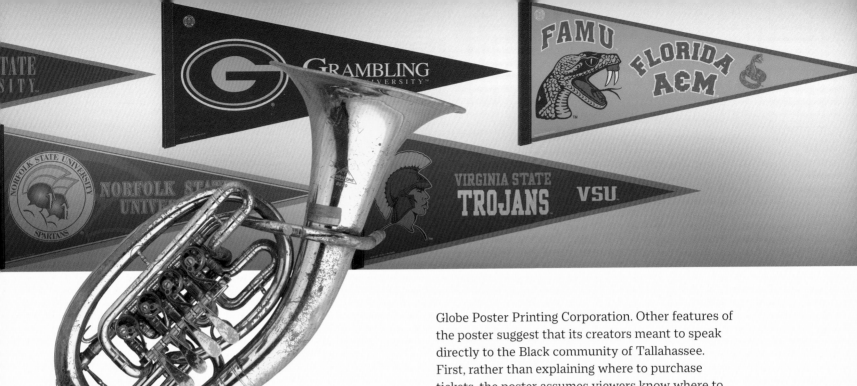

Mirafone company was used by members of the Florida A&M University (FAMU) Marching "100" from the mid-to-late twentieth century. Its lacquer has considerable wear, indicating that the instrument had heavy use. Baritones with rotary valves were much less common in American marching bands than those with piston valves. The instrument's nonstandard design hints at the financial constraints that faced the Marching "100" and many other HBCU marching bands (see also p. 76). This horn was likely one of the many that director William P. Foster and his students found in local pawn shops and used to fill in gaps in the marching band's instrumentation. Despite the financial challenges Foster faced when he accepted the position of band director at FAMU in 1946, he soon transformed the marching band into a world-renowned ensemble by incorporating elements of contemporary popular music and dance into their halftime routines. In 1970, Foster outlined his techniques in his manual *Band Pageantry: A Guide for the Marching Band*.

Just as HBCUs have been important venues for classical music in Black communities, they have also been key sites for popular music performance. This 1969 poster for a James Brown concert at FAMU, with its large print and bright colors, bears the usual characteristics of posters from the Baltimore-based Globe Poster Printing Corporation. Other features of the poster suggest that its creators meant to speak directly to the Black community of Tallahassee. First, rather than explaining where to purchase tickets, the poster assumes viewers know where to look, simply instructing them to find tickets in the "usual places." Second, the advertisement promises "a show for the entire family," inviting residents from all over the city, not just FAMU students, to attend. These elements highlight HBCUs' role in connecting southern Black neighborhoods to the wider world of Black entertainment and culture. For much of the twentieth century, Black colleges and their surrounding communities attracted outstanding Black musicians on tour, along with visiting Black intellectuals and political leaders. In this way, HBCUs continue to inject contemporary popular culture and current events into small southern communities—such as Tallahassee, Florida; Hampton, Virginia; and Tuskegee, Alabama—that might otherwise be passed over by high-profile figures. SWL

FLA. A & M UNIV.-Tallahassee
SAT. MAR. 1 8:30 P. M. CONCERT
Advance Admission $4.00 - At Door $5.00 - Students $3.00
TICKETS ON SALE AT USUAL PLACES

A SHOW FOR THE ENTIRE FAMILY

MR. DYNAMITE

James BROWN

18 PIECE BAND
and his REVUE

We Are Americans Too

The long history of Black service in the military reflects the paradoxical position that Black people have long held in American society. In every American war, from the Revolutionary War to contemporary military conflicts, Black men and women have fought bravely to protect their communities and their country. They have done so despite America's longtime refusal to grant Black Americans full citizenship rights. Indeed, military service has played an important role in the struggle for Black equality. Black veterans throughout American history have pointed to the remarkable Black military legacy to demand an end to racial discrimination. Military music has played a key role in this struggle. The outstanding performances of Black military musicians, whose role required their participation in various aspects of military life, helped open doors for Black entry into various other aspects of military service.

Objects from the NMAAHC collection add to the extensive documentation of Black musicians in the military. Beginning with the French and Indian War and continuing through the Revolutionary War, the

War of 1812, and the Mexican American War, Black musicians served as fifers, drummers, and buglers. With the formation of African American regiments in the Union Army during the Civil War, Black musicians were recruited to play in all-Black regimental brass bands under the command of white officers. This Black brass band tradition continued after the end of the war, and several of the Black regiments stationed in the Western states, including the 25th Infantry, featured bands famous for their musicianship.

Regimental bandsmen in the 25th Infantry used drums like this one from around 1930 while stationed at Fort Huachuca in Arizona. The 25th Infantry was one of several regiments of Black men that were organized in the years immediately after the Civil War. Known as "Buffalo Soldiers," these regiments

served in a variety of capacities in the Great Plains and Southwestern states, fighting the Indian Wars as well as patrolling communities to discourage illegal activities like cattle rustling. Bands like the 25th Infantry regimental band had a wide repertoire of classical and dance music and would have performed for civilian engagements as well as traditional military functions, playing an important part in public outreach. During World War I, James Reese Europe's 369th Infantry band, shown in the image above, would earn acclaim from French audiences for its exciting performances of blues and ragtime.

A five-page booklet containing Alton Adams's Continuous Service Records documents the career of an especially distinguished Black military musician who was active at around the same time. The booklet, bound by metal fasteners and backed with cardboard covered in green fabric, includes information about bandmaster Adams's duty stations and ratings of his leadership abilities and technical skills. Alton A. Adams Sr. (1889–1987) was born in St. Thomas, Virgin Islands, and earned a bachelor's degree in music, going on to found the St. Thomas Juvenile Band in 1910. After the Virgin Islands became a territory of the United States in 1917, Adams's band was inducted into the Navy, making Adams the first Black bandmaster in the US Navy. He served until his retirement in 1934, but returned to the Navy at the start of World War II and remained until the end of the war in 1945. One of the bands he led during the war, at Guantanamo Bay, Cuba, in 1942, was the first racially integrated band in the history of the US armed forces. Adams also worked as a composer, a public-school music educator, and a music journalist. His personal papers became available in the early twenty-first century, leading to a 2008 scholarly edition of his memoirs and to his family

commemorating his legacy by donating materials from his career to the NMAAHC.

Black military musicians like Adams had long seen military service as a gateway to full civil rights. During World War II, the *Pittsburgh Courier* spearheaded the "Double V" campaign, a push to defeat fascism in Europe and racism at home. The sheet music for "We Are Americans Too," a song written in 1941 by Andy Razaf, Eubie Blake, and Charles L. Cooke, is of a piece with the outspoken advocacy of Black activists and soldiers during this period. The sheet music cover features images of Black men in uniforms associated with American wars, including World War I, the Civil War, and the Revolutionary War. It was published by the Handy Brothers Music Co. Inc., the publishing company founded by William Christopher Handy, known as "father of the blues." The songwriters and publishers of "We Are Americans Too" amplified Black soldiers' call for equality as recognition for their patriotic service.

The experiences of Black military musicians point back to fundamental questions of Black American identity. What motivated Black bandsmen to maintain such high standards of musicianship? How did Black musicians recruited to regimental bands obtain their early musical training? Ultimately the paradox of exemplary Black performance despite white supremacy points to a core element of the Black experience in America. SWL

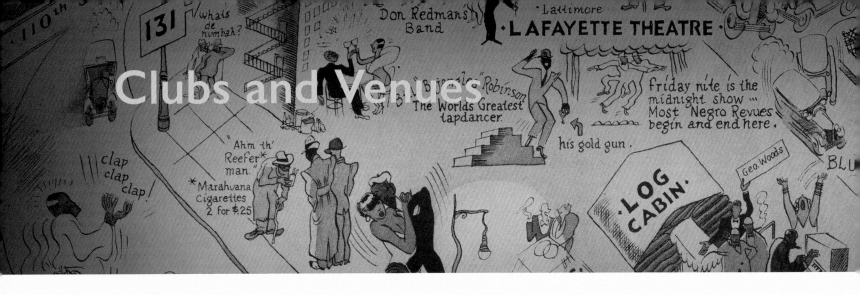

Clubs and Venues

As demonstrated by Elmer Simms Campbell's "Night-club Map of Harlem," shown in the image above (see full image on pp. 170–71), nightclubs and similar venues in Black neighborhoods around the country have long been essential showcases for Black music. For example, this clear glass ash tray is associated with Club Harlem, a nightclub that operated in Atlantic City, New Jersey, from 1935 through its closure in 1986. Club Harlem was founded by Leroy "Pop" Williams, who converted a former dance hall into a large club with two cocktail lounges and a main showroom with seats for nine hundred patrons. Located at 32 North Kentucky Avenue, in the African American Northside neighborhood, the club was an icon of Atlantic City's famous entertainment scene.

During its heyday, the Club Harlem's floor show approached the polish of the best Broadway shows, featuring elaborately costumed dancers and an excellent house orchestra led by drummer "Crazy" Chris Columbo. The club hosted an integrated audience and consistently attracted outstanding Black entertainers, including musicians like Billie Holiday, Lou Rawls, Aretha Franklin, and Dinah Washington; comedians Dick Gregory and "Moms" Mabley; and dancers Sammy Davis Jr. and Clayton "Peg Leg" Bates. The cocktail lounges, which offered drinks and preshow entertainment, often featured jazz organist "Wild Bill" Davis. Another well-known feature of Club Harlem was its 6:00 am Breakfast Show. After the featured Saturday evening performances had ended, headlining acts from venues around the city would come to Club Harlem and give unscheduled performances.

When Club Harlem closed and was set to be demolished in the 1980s, Atlantic City residents who had been the club's former patrons gathered mementos of its storied past, including chairs, booths, photographs, and other objects. This ash tray was one such piece of memorabilia, and its preservation by Atlantic City native Vicki Gold Levi speaks to the important place Club Harlem still holds in the history of the city. Despite the discrimination that Black people faced in Atlantic City as elsewhere, Club Harlem, with its integrated audience, extravagant interiors, and celebration of Black artistry, pointed toward a future that most of America had yet to reach in the mid-twentieth century.

A photograph from a more modestly sized club on the opposite coast highlights the importance of clubs and other venues as places where Black artists were able to hone their craft. Jimbo's Bop City was a San Francisco jazz club owned and operated by John "Jimbo" Edwards from 1949 through 1965 (see also pp. 69 and 78). Bop City was an important part of the jazz scene in the Fillmore District and attracted many of the leading jazz musicians of the 1950s and early 1960s. It became well-known for its competitive jam sessions, which usually extended into the early morning. Because of its late-night hours, the club served as an important social hub where local musicians and visiting artists could meet after their regular gigs elsewhere in the city. Clubs like Bop City, where young musicians joined more experienced players on the bandstand, were informal "schools" where jazz artists could develop their skills.

Steve Jackson Jr., an aspiring photographer, befriended Edwards and became a regular at Bop City. Over the course of Jackson and Edwards's thirty-year friendship, Jackson's photography skills grew, and he left behind a priceless archive of jazz in San Francisco. Jackson's photography helped make Bop City a center of Black creativity that extended beyond its exciting musical offerings.

In fact, a variety of spaces within Black communities have embraced and encouraged developing musicians. Harry Allen's photograph of James Todd Smith (b. 1968)—known professionally as LL Cool J—during his first performance at New York City's Benjamin Franklin High School in 1984 is the third in a series of four photos of LL Cool J's debut. The photograph in the NMAAHC collection came from the archives of Bill Adler's Eyejammie Fine Arts Gallery (see also p. 134). As he raps, LL Cool J holds a copy of "I Need a Beat," his first release, which had been issued as a 12-inch single by Def Jam Recordings that year. LL Cool J was one of the fledgling Def Jam's first few recording artists, and he maintained a longstanding association with the label for much of his career.

Allen's photograph of LL Cool J challenges us to expand our definition of "music venue" beyond clubs, dance halls, and theaters to include various gathering places in Black communities that played host to talented artists. As participants in a grassroots cultural movement, hip-hop artists in the music's early years often performed at venues like house parties, community centers, and high schools, which were readily accessible to their young peers and fans. SWL

Neighborhood Record Store

A glossy Cleveland Clinic medical campus now sprawls along Carnegie and Euclid Avenues in Cleveland's Cedar-Central neighborhood, where the city's thriving African American business district once stood. Only a few landmarks from that period, like East Mount Zion Baptist Church, have survived the tumultuous decades of racial strife, economic instability, and encroaching new development. However, a small collection of materials from storyteller W. Allen Taylor documents the optimism and sense of community that his father, Bill Hawkins (1909-1975), cultivated as Cleveland's first Black disc jockey. Photographs of Hawkins at the mic with stars like Mary Lou Williams (below) or with crowds of teenagers in auditoriums capture the relationship between Hawkins and Cleveland's Cedar-Central African American community.

Hawkins's activities as a leading radio personality in the city played an essential role in creating a space for locals to gather around music and meet their favorite entertainers.

As with so many Cleveland residents in the mid-twentieth century, Bill Hawkins's journey began in the South, specifically in Alabama. He was born to a religious family who resided in Birmingham before relocating to Indiana. As a young man, Hawkins studied at Chicago's Radio School of Technology and sang with the Riff Brothers quartet, who later re-branded themselves as the Ink Spots. Hawkins ultimately settled down in Cleveland, Ohio, with his wife Blanche in 1936 as the city's population continued to swell with Southern migrants. Based in Cleveland, Hawkins worked with the New York Central Railroad Company as a Pullman Porter on the Mercury Line in the mid-1930s, traveling between Midwestern cities. On this route, Hawkins encountered many people, allowing him to keep in touch with cultural movements. He also tapped into Southern oral traditions while a Porter to develop his smooth-speaking rhyming style that characterized his radio programs.

Hawkins leaned further into his entrepreneurial ambitions after reading a December 1947 *Ebony* article proclaiming that out of 3,000 DJs working for over 1,300 radio stations nationwide, only 16 were African American. He moved forward first by studying the model of Chicago-based DJ Jack Cooper, a former vaudevillian and comic. Cooper had established a successful radio operation in the 1930s with gospel, jazz, and R&B programs by partnering with local Black businesses. Modeling that relationship, Hawkins began his first radio program at Cleveland's WJW in 1948 with local barbecue restaurant Hot Sauce Williams as his sponsor. After his show quickly gained

a sizable audience, Hawkins debuted his show "Ridin' 'n Jivin' and Talkin' with Bill Hawkins" on Cleveland's WHK. On air, he played popular songs and games with listeners who could call in with answers to win cash on his program.

As he built his listening empire in Cleveland, Hawkins appealed to teens and their parents alike with programs that ranged from live gospel broadcasts held at local churches to dances hosted at the Pla-Mor Roller Rink for teens. Hawkins also embraced unconventional ideas like broadcasting live from the Warrensville Workhouse in 1955 to fundraise for improved recreational equipment for inmates. Most of his decisions were driven by a desire to uplift the African American community in Cleveland and he situated his programs as essential ways of connecting businesses to potential customers.

The pinnacle of Hawkins's connection to Cleveland's African American community came through his shop at Carnegie and 105th Streets. Here, he sold records, recorded up-and-coming musicians on

the Hawk Record imprint, and hosted broadcasts from the shop's window where crowds gathered to watch his live interviews. The shop was a favorite of local children growing up in the nearby Outhwaite Homes Estates, who eagerly looked forward to the allowance provided by their families to spend on new records. Likewise, teens and adults made the trek to Hawkins's store to see their favorite artists who visited to meet with their fans. The store served as Hawkins's home base through the 1950s until he stepped away in 1958 after a car accident caused a jaw injury that made it difficult for him to speak.

As the years went by and Cleveland's bustling Cedar-Central area struggled in the aftermath of the 1966 Hough Riots, the city's landscape gradually changed, and Bill Hawkins's legacy faded from memory. In recent years, though, Hawkins's son, W. Allen Taylor, has resurfaced his father's career and his quest to know him in the play *In Search of My Father... Walkin' Talkin' Bill Hawkins*. Taylor, who grew up unaware that Hawkins, whom he knew as a family friend, was his father, centers the play around the curiosity of learning about a parent you never got to know deeply. The result celebrates Hawkins's path to becoming Cleveland's first Black DJ and the reverberating impacts of his work influencing Cleveland's community from the window of his shop. HG

Music in the Black Mecca

Atlanta, Georgia, has been called a "Black Mecca" since the early 1970s. Beginning with the election of Maynard Jackson as its first Black mayor in 1973, the city has amplified its longstanding association with Black activism, education, and wealth to establish itself as a center for Black culture. Music, first R&B and eventually hip-hop, played a central role in cultivating Atlanta's image, as the city's profile rose from the late 1970s through the early twenty-first century.

The Atlanta-based funk group The S.O.S. Band released its third album, *S.O.S. III*, in 1981 while they were still riding high on the commercial success of their 1980 single "Take Your Time (Do It Right)." *S.O.S. III* was recorded during the band's close association with Burnella (or "Bunnie") Jackson-Ransom, the ex-wife of mayor Maynard Jackson, who discovered the group and handled their public relations needs during the early 1980s. Through her leadership of public relations agency First Class, Inc., Jackson-Ransom—along with First Class co-founders Linda Gulley, Anne Allison, and Billye Aaron—played a central role in turning Atlanta into a cultural

powerhouse, boosting the careers of Atlanta groups such as The S.O.S. Band, Brick, Cameo, and Kris Kross.

This 12-inch LP appeared during the early years of the Atlanta Bureau of Cultural Affairs, an office of the city government established by Mayor Jackson in 1974 and dedicated to the support of artists and arts organizations. Through city-funded grants, Atlanta built a vibrant community of musicians in genres ranging from jazz and classical to R&B and funk, beginning in the 1970s. Materials like *S.O.S. III* complicate the well-established narrative that Atlanta's musical prominence started with the popularity of Southern hip-hop, demonstrating that the groundwork for the city's musical influence was laid at least a decade earlier through the work of The S.O.S. Band and fellow Atlanta-based funk groups like Cameo.

Undoubtedly, however, one of Atlanta's most important contributions to popular music started in the 1990s with the rise of Southern hip-hop. This fitted baseball cap and colorful costume trace the story of OutKast, the Atlanta-based hip-hop duo of Big Boi and André 3000, whose commercial and critical success in the late 1990s and early 2000s established Atlanta as a new hub of hip-hop culture. In 2013, the New Era Cap Company created a limited-release Atlanta Braves hat to coincide with the release of Antwan "Big Boi" Patton's (b. 1975) album *Vicious Lies and Dangerous Rumors*. The cap features the Major League Baseball Atlanta Braves logo, with the iconic "A" in rainbow colors to match the front cover of Big Boi's new album. It was distributed to fans who attended a CD signing at the New Era store in Atlanta in June 2013. Big Boi often wears Atlanta sports apparel and made it part of his stage persona while still a member of OutKast—for example, the cover art of OutKast's 1996 album *ATLiens* features

Big Boi in an Atlanta Braves cap like the one shown here. As Southern hip-hop scholar Regina Bradley has observed, while OutKast was not the first prominent Atlanta hip-hop act of the early 1990s (two earlier examples include Arrested Development and Kris Kross), they were the first to make Atlanta central to their image.[23] Big Boi's caps and jerseys were an important way to highlight the group's association with the city.

André "André 3000" Benjamin (b. 1975) wore this multicolored cape while performing "B.O.B.," the lead single from OutKast's 2000 album *Stankonia,* on the Chris Rock Show. The costume creates a rainbow effect using multiple feather boas in different colors attached to a set of oversized black shoulder pads. The flamboyant aesthetic of the object reflects changes to OutKast's look after the commercial and critical success of their 1994 debut album *Southernplayalisticadillacmuzik.* Within the broader cultural landscape of the early twenty-first century, André 3000's feather boa cape represents a challenge to narrow concepts of masculinity imposed upon hip-hop culture. After their record label, LaFace Records, granted the group increased control of their image, OutKast adopted a style reflecting the Afrofuturist aesthetic of artists like George Clinton and Sly Stone. With its influences drawn from 1970s funk artists, André 3000's costume resonates with hip-hop's roots as an outgrowth of funk and disco, while also recalling the futuristic style of first-generation hip-hop artists like Afrika Bambaataa and Grandmaster Flash.

The histories of Big Boi's fitted cap and André 3000's costume are part of the much larger story of Atlanta's development into one of the early twenty-first century's most prominent centers of Black American culture. As the booming "Black Mecca" attracts Black talent from around the country, the work of Atlanta hip-hop artists complicates simplistic narratives of Atlanta as a center of Black prosperity and progress by highlighting the persistence of problems like poverty, violence, and gentrification in the city's working-class Black community. SWL

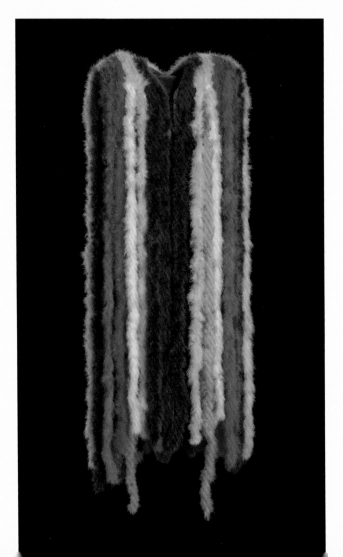

Ain't That a Shame

The red leather on the curves of the Spanish-made loafers is cracked. Some areas are lifting, revealing discolored patches caused by the waters that devastated most of the Ninth Ward in the days after Hurricane Katrina passed over New Orleans in August 2005. Residents who remained found themselves trapped by the levees that broke and submerged their beloved city as they waited for help that was slow to come. Such was the case for rock pioneer Antoine "Fats" Domino (1928–2017), the owner of these loafers.

The loafers, made by the French company Pierre Cardin, have elegant lines, and likely looked sharp paired with a suit. They recall the polished style Domino developed at the height of his career when he brought the rollicking R&B of New Orleans's honky-tonks to mainstream audiences during the 1950s. Suits, dress shoes, and flashy jewelry became his uniform as his fanbase grew beyond his working-class neighbors. Domino came to prominence in an age of impeccably dressed young rock-and-roll musicians challenging tradition and segregation through the appeal of their music. Like other children of New Orleans before and after him, Fats injected sounds from the vibrant musical ecosystem of the city into American popular music to great success. His music is littered with references to the city, food, and culture he longed to go home to during the grind of grueling, star-studded packaged revue tours across the nation.

By 1960, Domino and his growing family were settled into their home on the corner of Caffin Avenue and Marais Street. Domino purchased the lot next door and converted the existing shotgun house into an office where he could record and conduct his business. The bright yellow portico of Fats's offices, emblazoned with his initials and black stars, proclaimed to the world that his music represented the Ninth Ward community. Ultimately, home was where Fats and his wife, Rosemary, weathered Katrina, since she had not been healthy enough to evacuate.

Days after they were stranded in the upper reaches of their flooded home, Coast Guard officials rescued the Domino family. Using orange and black spray paints they marked the Dominos' home to indicate that the area had been searched. In a news interview with local CBS-affiliate WWL-TV weeks later, Domino walked with reporter Eric Paulsen through the ruined rooms of his home and business. He mentions, as they look upon his office, that he saw it while watching the television coverage of the storm. He did not raise the media's false reporting of his death, though, which took hold after someone spray-painted "R.I.P. Fats You will be missed" on the front of his home. This was just one of many unsubstantiated reports that made their way into the chaotic coverage of the aftermath in New Orleans.

Inside, Domino points out his white Steinway grand piano, which had been tipped over in the

flooding and now rested against a wall with the lid strewn open, caked in dark gray grime. Local artist Charles Gillam (b. 1945) chose to paint Domino playing that piano on a piece of wood from a dresser salvaged after the storm. He named the piece after Domino's 1955 hit, "Ain't That a Shame." Gillam presents Domino standing in a powder-blue suit in the painting, defiantly playing his piano on the roof of his studio as the floodwaters carry away his records and memorabilia, along with the pink Cadillac he once drove around town.

Art made from salvaged materials from the hurricane included paintings like Gillam's and instruments like Don Moser's Voodoo guitar. The pieces demonstrate New Orleanians' creative resilience and their cultural commentary on what they endured. Gillam's work reminds viewers of the cultural loss New Orleans suffered in addition to the physical devastation. Moser built guitars from debris he found after the storm as part of a larger project to help put instruments back in the hands

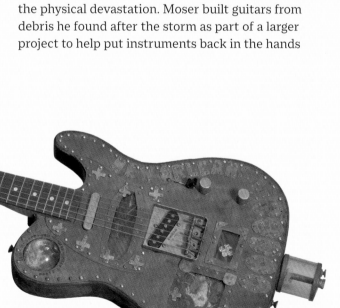

of musicians. He salvaged parts he came across and produced decorative instruments that paid homage to New Orleans and its resilience. The artist was fond of this guitar, which he called "Marie." In describing the guitar, he likened its sound to "the devil moving furniture." Moser filled the guitar with cultural symbolism associated with the Ol' Big Easy, like a fleur de lis and a voodoo doll, which drew in different elements of Southern African American folk culture beyond music. In the traumatized post-Katrina context, music and art came to symbolize the city's loss and frustrations with the botched responses that endangered residents and ultimately forced many to leave their homes behind for good. HG

Singing for Justice

The Civil Rights Movement of the 1950s and '60s is indelibly associated with "freedom songs" like "We Shall Overcome" and "This Little Light of Mine" in the popular imagination. These songs, many of which were adapted from traditional spirituals, epitomized the righteous fervor of the demonstrators, and symbolically connected them to the long struggle for freedom expressed in the songs of the enslaved. Despite the central position they quickly took within the image of the Movement, songs did not become a major part of civil rights demonstrations until the early 1960s. The popularity of freedom songs can be traced back to the work of the Freedom Singers, formed in 1962 by Student Nonviolent Coordinating Committee (SNCC) field secretary Cordell Reagon.

We Shall Overcome was the Freedom Singers' first and only album. They recorded it for Mercury Records in October 1963 before disbanding at the end of the year. Pictured on the cover from left to right are: Cordell Reagon (1943-1996), Rutha Mae Harris (b. 1942), Bertha Gober, Bernice Johnson (b. 1942), and Charles Neblett (b. 1941). The album's title comes from the freedom song "We Shall Overcome," which was adapted from Charles Tindley's 1900 hymn "I'll Overcome Some Day." *We Shall Overcome*, along with other high-profile performances by the Freedom Singers in 1962 and 1963, popularized freedom songs as emblems of the Civil Rights Movement. Reunion concerts over the subsequent decades brought songs from the Freedom Singers' repertoire, such as "Oh, Freedom" and "Ain't Gonna Let Nobody Turn Me Around," to new generations. Commercial recordings like the *We Shall Overcome* LP also invite us to consider the complex relationship between the music of protest and struggle and the business of music, and how the entertainment industry can amplify, co-opt, or even stifle political messages.

Freedom Singer Bernice Johnson, who became Bernice Johnson Reagon after her marriage to Cordell Reagon, went on to a distinguished career as an activist, musician, and music historian. After the breakup of the Freedom Singers, Reagon started a cappella groups of her own. The first, the Harambee Singers, began in 1966 and was connected to the 1960s struggle against South African apartheid. Reagon founded her second and best-known group, Sweet Honey in the Rock, in 1973, while she was a graduate student at Howard University. After completing her PhD in American History, Reagon spent twenty years as a cultural historian and curator at the Smithsonian Institution. In the 1980s, she received a MacArthur "Genius" Grant and went on to serve as a music consultant on multiple award-winning film projects, while also teaching at American University.

TO AID SOUTHERN STATES SIT-IN MOVEMENT
MARTIN LUTHER KING DEFENSE

AN EVENING OF
MUSIC AND DRAMA
FOR FREEDOM NOW
★ ★ STARRING IN PERSON ★ ★

HARRY **BELAFONTE**

MAHALIA **JACKSON**

SIDNEY **POITIER**

SHELLEY **WINTERS**
(1960 ACADEMY AWARD WINNER)

DIAHANN **CARROLL**

PRODUCTION SUPERVISED by
OSSIE DAVIS and RUBY DEE
FREEDOM DRAMA WRITTEN by
LORRAINE HANSBURY • JOHN KILLENS • GEORGE TABORI
Author of 'Raisin In The Sun'

FULL STEREOPHONIC
SOUND SYSTEM

TUES.
MAY 17
8 P. M. to 11 P. M.

Mail Orders For Tickets To
Committee To Defend
Martin Luther King, Jr.
And The Struggle For
Freedom In The South
312 W. 125th St., N. Y. 26, N. Y.
UN 6-1700

369th
ARMORY
142nd St. & 5th Ave., NYC

All Balcony Seats $2.00 — Orchestra Seats $2.00 & $3.00 — Small Reserved Section $5.00

—— TICKETS ON SALE ——

MANHATTAN
Committee
312 West 125th St. — UN 6-1700
Friendship Baptist Church
HOUSE OF FRIENDSHIP
170 West 130th St. — FO 8-6623
District 65 (AFL-CIO)
13 Astor Place — OR 3-1520
Frederick Douglass Book Store
141 West 125th Street

BROOKLYN
Antioch Baptist Church
828 Greene Ave. — GL 5-8990
President Pharmacy
1265 Bedford Ave. — MA 2-0526
Mason & Williams Realty Co.
275 Reid Ave. — PR 3-4745

NEWARK, N. J.
Afro-American
190 Clinton Ave.
Bigelow 8-3636

S. A. WARNER POSTER CORP., 458 11th AVE., N. Y.

Celebrities played important roles in the Civil Rights Movement, complementing and supporting the work of activist groups. A 1960 poster for "An Evening of Music and Drama for Freedom Now" announces an all-star performance in New York City to raise funds for the sit-in movement and Martin Luther King Jr.'s legal defense (see previous page). Produced by Ossie Davis and Ruby Dee, it starred Harry Belafonte, Mahalia Jackson, Sidney Poitier, Shelley Winters, and Diahann Carroll. The evening also featured a "freedom drama" written by Lorraine Hansberry (misspelled on the poster), John Killens, and George Tabori. Beyond its significance as an example of celebrities' involvement with the Civil Rights Movement, this poster points to the fact that the movement was nationwide rather than simply Southern. Black people in Northeastern cities contributed their funds and their time to support the activists on the front lines in Southern states.

Prominent musicians in recent years have continued to use their platforms to contribute to contemporary civil rights struggles. Before he was killed in March 2019, hip-hop artist and entrepreneur Nipsey Hussle (1985–2019), born Ermias Asghedom, became famous for investing his wealth in Los Angeles's Crenshaw District and for his outspoken political statements. One of his best-known recordings is "FDT," a collaboration with fellow artist Keenon Dequan Ray Jackson, better known as YG (b. 1990). The track, which articulated a blistering critique of Republican presidential candidate Donald Trump, found Nipsey and YG applying the spirit of N.W.A.'s classic "Fuck Tha Police" to the volatile political climate of the 2016 presidential election.[24] Nipsey has remained a symbol of musical activism in the years after his death.

This photograph, taken by Tommy Oliver during the 2020 protests following George Floyd's murder by Minneapolis police, demonstrates Nipsey's continuing relevance to contemporary activist struggles. The image depicts YG at a Los Angeles Black Lives Matter protest that he organized. In his left hand, he holds a large color photograph of his deceased collaborator, Nipsey Hussle. People in the crowd around him hold signs expressing their anger at police and their embrace of the Black Lives Matter movement. The prominence of Nipsey's image in this photograph emphasizes his significance as a symbol of Black political and economic empowerment, his importance to the Black residents of Los Angeles in particular, and, more broadly, the influential role of hip-hop in contemporary activism. SWL

Baltimore, Prince, and the Rally 4 Peace

Emblazoned with a bold graphic of Prince's oh-so serious, yet cool visage framed by a haloed-Afro and wearing dark shades to match against a background of purple and gray over the word 'Baltimore' in yellow lettering, this T-shirt was designed for the *Rally 4 Peace* concert held in Baltimore on Mother's Day, May 19, 2015. In the wake of the massive Black Lives Matter protests which erupted for weeks after the death of Freddie Gray (1989-2015)—who suffered a broken neck and almost severed spinal cord while in police custody on April 12, 2015—Prince arrived to anoint and heal with his sonic medicine. A statement released by the streaming service, Tidal, said that the concert was meant to "be a catalyst for pause and reflection." The city of Baltimore was ablaze in righteous fury and fire, which culminated in the declaration of a State of Emergency and the presence of the National Guard. Prince composed a song for the occasion, "Baltimore," and used his voice to express solidarity for the movement and to raise funds for Baltimore-based youth charities.

This T-shirt reminds us that, like many others before him, Prince was never just a brilliant musician. He created his unique brand of multi-genre funk within the context of the beautiful, yet troubled world around him, and his sounds reflected all of it and more. The T-shirt, and the accompanying concert, sing a narrative of the role that musical artists like Prince have played and continue to play in the realm of social activism—as beacons of light, town criers, and prophets. It hearkens back to such concerts as the James Brown performance in 1968 in Boston after the assassination of Dr. Martin Luther King Jr. and the recently discovered footage of the *Summer of Soul* concert series held in Harlem in 1969, which featured artists known for their activism, such as Nina Simone and Mahalia Jackson. Those concerts bookmarked

that tumultuous era, and this one underscores our own. It also tells the story of the commodification of social activism in the form of swag like T-shirts, buttons, and even coffee mugs. What does it mean to purchase and wear a statement T-shirt? Beyond the politics of the wearer, it also raises questions of who manufactured the item, who designed it, and where is the money going?

Prince died before the Black Lives Matter movement reached a crescendo after the murder of George Floyd during the summer of 2020, but this T-shirt reminds us of his prescience and that he was more than just a multifaceted musical genius; he was also a very thoughtful and engaged human being who understood the power of his creative voice.

During this same time of upheaval, in the days after Freddie Gray's murder, local photographer

Devin Allen (b. 1989) took this black and white photo of a young Black child at a rally holding a sign with the handwritten text, "Community Band / Funding / We come in peace / #BmoreUnityBand." In the background, several other children stand nearby, holding up signs that are mostly illegible and out of frame. The sign's text references the long tradition of community bands in Baltimore that can be traced as far back as 1870, when members of the city's newly freed Black community held one of the largest parades in the country to celebrate the 15th Amendment, which gave Black men the right to vote. These bands continue to thrive, despite a constant need to raise funds. Together, the Prince T-shirt and the Allen photograph illuminate the intersection of music and social activism as a central element of African American cultural expression. One can almost imagine Prince leading a community band and parading through the streets, followed by these children, in a funky demonstration that Black Lives do truly Matter. KEN

115

Chapter 4

I WISH I KNEW HOW IT WOULD FEEL TO BE FREE

After the 13th Amendment to the US Constitution abolished slavery in 1865, the African American struggle for freedom took another direction.[25] Even though newly freed African Americans were legally afforded the same rights as all citizens, the social and political climate of the country did not drastically change their circumstances. As new towns and territories were established in the West, communities followed the same discriminatory practices and unwritten laws that enforced racial segregation and second-class status. These attitudes were shaped and reinforced by a new form of theatrical entertainment that had swept the American stage, blackface minstrelsy.

The first minstrel shows were produced in New York theaters around 1829. The cast included a roster of recurring characters that presented exaggeratedly caricatured racial and gendered stereotypes as authentic portrayals, including the dim-witted Jim Crow; the maternal Mammy; a hypersexualized temptress or tragic Jezebel; the arrogant, slick, and shifty dandy, Zip Coon; and the lazy, childlike Sambo. The caricatures took shape through makeup that escalated over time—faces covered in burnt cork, black curly wigs, big red lips, and popping eyes—as well as costume, gestures, and speech. Performances were constructed for laughs, and characterizations could often go beyond simple ridicule to brutal dehumanizing caricatures.

The characters in these shows appealed to the sensibilities of white audiences who easily accepted the humor and derision, along with the lack of humanity, because it was not a threat to their own sense of racial superiority. By the 1850s the minstrel show had become the most popular form of American entertainment. As much as it entertained, blackface minstrelsy also promoted stereotypical representations of African Americans that introduced and reinforced beliefs of white supremacy.

Music, the entertainment industry, and mass media are arguably the most powerful forces in perpetuating the values of white supremacy and anti-Black racism. However, in these arenas African Americans can also contest the racial stereotypes and categorizations that are used to uphold and justify the values of white supremacy and obfuscate the existence or adverse impact of systemic racism. The transformative power of dismantling the impact of racist ideologies in arts and entertainment lies in acts of resistance involving self-definition. Personal liberation comes by transcending the mindset of imposed limitations on artistic expression and musical innovation,

To entertain the guests that they boarded in their home, the Sugg McDonalds, an African American family living in California during the turn of the twentieth century, purchased sheet music of popular songs for the boarders to use while playing the family's organ. Music from the family's home, like "He's Up Against the Real Thing Now," composed by Black minstrel performer Bert A. Williams, illustrates the far-reaching impact minstrelsy had offstage in music-making practices within domestic spaces.

The Poet II

Standin' on the road side,
Waitin' for the ball an' chain.
Say, if I was not all shackled down
I'd ketch that wes' boun' train

—Excerpt from "Chain Gang Blues"[26]

Claude Clark Sr. (1915–2001) was a prolific artist and educator who was known for his paintings that addressed racial and economic injustice and illuminated Black rural life. He decided early in his career to use his art to alleviate the sufferings of humanity. He stated, "Today, [the Black artist] has reached the phase of Political Realism where his art becomes even more functional. He not only presents the condition but names the enemy and directs us toward a plan of action in search of our own roots and eventual liberation."[27]

The Poet II pays homage to the thousands of African American men imprisoned under the forced labor system called the "chain gang." Sanctioned by the state, the chain gang was used throughout the South for building projects such as roads and railroads. These men faced brutal treatment, often resulting in death. The system flourished during the 1920s and '30s and was notorious for its inhumane work conditions and harsh corporal punishments. As evidenced in the painting, many chain gang convicts were required to wear striped uniforms and ankle shackles to prevent escape. Members of the gang would often sing in rhythmic call-and-response verse to alleviate the monotony of the labor, to help them work in tandem with one another, and as a creative outlet to express the pain and injustice they endured through the poetry of song. Individuals were often chosen to lead these work songs, particularly if they had a clear loud voice and the ability to play an instrument. *The Poet II* recognizes the humanity and value of these men, who were treated by the legal system as disposable commodities. **TF**

and through civic engagement, social activism, professional opportunities, and autonomy over creative control and one's own identity.

Visual and performative caricatures of blackface minstrelsy were easily absorbed into all segments of American life. Racial caricatures appeared on sheet music (see p. 116), instruments, artwork, magazines, newspapers, toys, games, household items such as salt and pepper shakes and cookie jars, and other ephemera. The popularity and widespread use of this material culture illustrated how easy it was for audiences, as consumers, to be complicit in both the ridicule of an entire culture and the structures, policies, and practices which ensured that perceived Black inferiority continued to restrict the actual freedoms of African Americans despite their legal rights. Ironically, it was the minstrel show that opened the doors to a host of employment opportunities to African Americans. The caricatures were so embedded into American entertainment that any route African Americans pursued to establish a career in music, or any other related field or industry, was always within the context of the social attitudes of Black inferiority.

The popularity of blackface minstrelsy extended far and wide, and its legacy has continued to inform and support racist beliefs, practices, and structures throughout society. In addition to feeding fears of "otherness" and reducing human beings to mere archetypes, blackface minstrelsy stereotypes have led people to rationalize or dismiss the impact of the

emotional, spiritual, and psychic harm that African Americans are subjected to on a daily basis.

In her book, *Art on My Mind: Visual Politics*, cultural theorist bell hooks argues that Black liberation is as much about dismantling racial stereotypes as it is about equal access and opportunity.[28] No place is this more evident than in the fields of music and entertainment, where the dialogue about the impact of negative versus positive representations of African Americans underscores their power in shaping public opinion.

Even as blackface minstrelsy's popularity waned on the professional stage, many elements were incorporated into new theatrical formats such as vaudeville, cabaret, and musical theater. Minstrelsy's popularity in the field of amateur entertainment continued well into the twentieth century as schools, fraternal lodges, and other organizations produced minstrel shows in local communities. For example, this painted drum with a large blackface caricature

Blackface minstrelsy was a theatrical format that enjoyed tremendous popularity in the mid-nineteenth century. Minstrelsy's visual and performative conventions had a pervasive influence in shaping and reinforcing negative stereotypes about African Americans to justify white supremacy, which continued to proliferate in amateur and professional entertainment.

caricature with yellow eyes and a broad smile with thick red lips, surrounded by nine musical notes with smaller blackface caricatures, was created around 1925 (see p. 119). Given the estimated date of manufacture, this drum was most likely used in a local minstrel show as a musical instrument or a stage prop. The drum, with smiling caricatures and musical notes, emphasizes the connection between blackface, humor, music, fun, and entertainment.

The impact of blackface minstrelsy carried over into mass media, as recording, radio, film, and television developed into important outlets for musical performance. For African Americans, the field of entertainment was a double-edged sword. While the country's growing entertainment industry offered an array of new professional opportunities for African Americans, the legacy of blackface minstrelsy worked inside the industry to objectify, constrain, and diminish the presence and contributions of African Americans in multiple ways. African Americans strategically navigated a complicated path in maintaining a sense of dignity and creative autonomy as they struggled for opportunity and the right to control their own narratives.

Eleanora Fagan, more commonly known as Billie Holiday (1915–1959), one of the most celebrated vocalists of the twentieth century, was once made to wear "special dark grease paint"[29] makeup while performing with the Count Basie Orchestra in Detroit in 1937. She publicly struggled with the constraints of racism and sexism throughout her career, and the manner in which she retained a sense of autonomy in her life, musically and socially, is part of her allure.

One way that Holiday broke through these stereotypes was through her fashion. She was always up to date with the current styles of the day and would accessorize in ways that were equally stylish and recognizable, such as wearing a white gardenia in her hair. By the time she died in 1959, Holiday retained very few personal belongings, so examining unique objects that are directly tied to her is particularly useful. Her tailored curve-hugging dresses of the 1930s were replaced in later decades with ankle-length gowns, like the one pictured here.[30]

Audiences were equally as fixated on Holiday's voice as they were on her fashion sense. When Holiday released her first recording in 1933, she followed in the tradition of the classic blues singers of the 1920s, who boldly set in motion a cultural revolution that foregrounded the voices of Black women. These blues predecessors claimed their sexual liberation and personal agency despite the social dictates of the day and cultivated a new sound and attitude for popular song. Holiday's vocal style took the blues and jazz in new directions, as her sound resonated with her own musical influences and keen understanding of the realities she and her audiences faced every day. With a creative sense of rhythm and phrasing, Holiday had the ability to convey the tumultuous feelings of joy, heartbreak, resignation, and longing, capturing the breadth of human emotion. From her evocative description of the horrors of lynching in "Strange Fruit" (1939), to the moody lover's goodbye in "I'll Be Seeing You" (1944), Holiday's personal and professional story illustrates how she resisted, maintaining her own sense of humanity and artistic agency despite the external forces that fought to control her.

As a self-described "hip kitty," Billie Holiday was attentive to fashion and used clothing as an extension of her creative and political expression. During the height of her career, she performed in custom-made clothing. However, by the early 1950s, she was earning much less money and had to find clothing off the rack, like this Chantilly lace ankle-length dress made by Andora.

Diahann Carroll won the 1962 Tony Award for Best Leading Actress in a Musical for her performance in *No Strings*. The medallion features the masks for tragedy and comedy on one side and the winner's name and year on the reverse.

Like Holiday and the many other African American women who worked to retain a sense of autonomy and self-respect in the face of the racism and misogyny they experienced, Diahann Carroll, born Carol Diann Johnson (1935–2019), asserted her independence and rightful sense of entitlement to be treated fairly, and challenged attempts to diminish and erase her power and individuality as a Black woman.

By 1962, Diahann Carroll was already a well-seasoned veteran with several accolades on her resume. She had modeled for *Ebony* magazine; won the top prize three times in a row on the television program *Chance of a Lifetime*; had roles in the films *Carmen Jones* (1954), *Porgy and Bess* (1959), and *Paris Blues* (1961), where she co-starred with Sidney Poitier, Paul Newman, and Joanne Woodward; and received a Tony nomination for her 1954 performance as Ottilie in the Broadway musical *House of Flowers*.

However, while she sat in the audience during the 1962 Tony Awards ceremony, she was astounded when she heard her name announced as that year's winner for Best Performance by a Leading Actress in a Musical—the first African American to win in that category—for her performance as Barbara Woodruff in the musical *No Strings*.[31] According to Carroll's daughter, Suzanne Kay,[32] winning the Tony Award was the moment her mother started to see her accomplishments and the course of her career in a new light.[33]

As one of the many trailblazers who opened doors for other Black artists to enter, Carroll had a public persona which radiated with a sense of glamour and self-assuredness that spoke to her pride as a Black woman. She led her life and career in the belief that she had the right to expect and seek the best opportunities, and to be seen and treated fairly and

Ebony Magazine

In 1945, Johnson Publishing Company launched *Ebony* magazine. Modeled after *Life* magazine, *Ebony* chronicled all areas of Black life, including politics, civil rights activism, entrepreneurship, religious life, sports, music, and entertainment. The publishers also devoted space to in-depth reporting on issues and current debates that spoke to concerns of the community. In a Publisher's statement, founder John H. Johnson wrote, "*Ebony* was founded...to project all dimensions of the black personality in a world saturated with stereotypes."[34]

This October 1967 issue of *Ebony* features the original members of The Fifth Dimension. From left to right, Ron Townsend (1933–2001), Florence LaRue (b. 1944), Billy Davis Jr. (b. 1938), Marilyn McCoo (b. 1943), and Lamonte McLemore (b. 1939) are pictured

beaming, clapping, and dancing on the cover in patriotic red, white, and blue ensembles. Positioned among other headlines on the front cover, delving into topics including the 1967 riots, Black leadership in the West Indies, and Chicago Cubs home run hitter Ernie Banks, is a six-word subtitle over the photo that reads: "White sound in a black group." This headline indicates how *Ebony*'s staff contextualized the contested idea of "Black sound" for their readership within other cultural happenings.

Inside the magazine, the cover story describes The Fifth Dimension as "one of the hottest and vocally most unusual acts in show business," while noting they had "no brown sound" in most of their work released to date. Questioning the authenticity of some Black musicians was common in publications such as *Ebony*, especially when musicians subverted essentialist notions of how they should sound and presented their own identity through their music. *Ebony*'s statements bring the publication's perspective into the broader conversations of Black music and sound. The magazine, in turn, is a valuable resource in tracing how The Fifth Dimension was characterized in press coverage and how their reception by the Black community evolved over time. VLM

as an individual. Carroll's sense of herself as a Black woman and as an artist rested in the self-confidence she fearlessly displayed as someone who knew her worth and the value of her own authentic voice. As a singer and actress on stage, television, and film, she challenged essentialist constructions and constraints defined by race and gender to free herself and others from systems of oppression.

Racism permeated all areas of the music and entertainment industry, not just on the stage and screen. However, African Americans found opportunities and persevered against other forces within the business to pursue their own careers and create opportunities for others to follow. Because of this, African Americans could share in the profits, allowing them to negotiate more favorable deals, work autonomously, establish their own record labels, publishing houses, or management companies, and move up the corporate ladder within large recording companies.

Black songwriters were largely excluded from the early music publishing business and unable to benefit from copyright protection. Only a handful of Black musicians were included among the charter members of the American Society of Composers, Authors and Publishers.[35] The situation improved somewhat in 1939 with the founding of Broadcast Music, Inc. (BMI), which published the songs of early R&B artists like Fats Domino and Etta James.[36] In 1960, Ray Charles (see also p. 21) made history as one of the first artists to own his master recordings, meaning that he would reap the financial benefits of any use of these recordings. His groundbreaking deal with ABC Records came as other Black artists sought to exercise increased control over their intellectual property.

In 1965, Otis Redding (1941–1967) and Steve Cropper (b. 1941) signed an agreement with Stax Records co-owner Jim Stewart (b. 1931) that established payment distribution for royalties for the song "Mr. Pitiful" (see opposite). Stax guitarist Steve Cropper was one of Redding's frequent collaborators and it was he who suggested they write a song around the "Mr. Pitiful" nickname that A.C. "Moohah" Williams, a DJ on Memphis's WDIA radio station, gave him. Redding was dubbed "Mr. Pitiful" because he was never too proud to beg in any song. Released as a B-side, "Mr. Pitiful" peaked on Billboard at No. 10 and at No. 2 on the Cashbox chart.[37] A slight departure from the standard ballads Redding had sung up until this time, the song met with commercial success that did a great deal to broaden his audience.

Recording artists who wrote their own songs could write something that was suited to their own voices and personalities. They also had the benefit of earning more money, with the additional royalties a songwriting credit brought. Redding, who was the label's premier artist, renewed his recording contract with Stax the same year this agreement was executed. His new deal included an increase in his percentage in royalties and a one-third interest in the publisher's share of his songs, which made him co-owner of the copyrights to his original songs. Secure with a profitable new contract, Redding started several new business ventures, including a publishing company, Redwal Music; co-ownership in Jotis, a new boutique record label; and Big O Productions, inspired by Sam Cooke's management firm, to produce new artists.

Establishing a recording studio was another lucrative venture for African American artists, enabling them to save thousands of dollars that would have been spent renting studio time for jams and official recording dates. On August 26, 1970, Jimi Hendrix (1942–1970) hosted the grand opening of Electric Lady Studios in Greenwich Village, New York City. Electric Lady was designed to inspire and support Hendrix's expansive sensibilities in pushing boundaries in the direction towards a universal musical language. This quarter-inch magnetic tape recording, housed in a vintage Electric Lady Studios

AGREEMENT made this 19th day of May 19 65 between

East Publications Inc. hereinafter designated as PUBLISHER and

Otis Redding .... of 3226 Commodore, Macon Ga. ....

Steve Cropper .... of 2582 Capewood, Memphis, Tenn. ....

.... of ....

jointly and/or severally designated as WRITER.

WITNESSETH:

(1) The Writer hereby sells, assigns, transfers and delivers to the Publisher, its successors and assigns, all of his rights, title and interest in and to a certain heretofore unpublished original work, as annexed hereto, written and/or composed by the Writer, now entitled,

"MR. PITIFUL"

including the title, words and/or music thereof, as well as the entire exclusive right to publicly perform and televise, together with the right to secure copyrights and renewals therein throughout the world, as proprietor in its own name, or otherwise, and to have and to hold the said work, copyrights and renewals thereof and all rights of whatsoever nature thereunder existing.

(2) The Writer hereby warrants that the said work is his sole, exclusive and original work, that he has full right and power to make the within agreement, and that there exists no adverse claim to or in the said work, which is free from all liens and encumbrances whatsoever.

(3) In consideration of this Agreement, the Publisher agrees to pay the Writer, jointly, only the following royalties:

(a) .05 ¢ per copy, in respect of regular piano copies and/or orchestrations, sold in the United States and for which the Publisher received payment.

(b) .50 % of the net amount received by the Publisher, in respect of regular piano copies and/or orchestrations sold and paid for in any foreign country.

(c) .50 % of the net amount received by the Publisher, in respect of any licenses issued authorizing the manufacture of parts of instruments serving to mechanically reproduce said work, electrical transcriptions, or to use said work in synchronization with sound motion pictures.

(d) .50 % of the net amount of performing fees received by the Publisher in the United States, only provided said fees include both Writer and Publisher shares and are payable on a fixed and determinable basis.

(4) The Publisher agrees to render to the Writer on or about February 15th, and August 15th. of each year, so long as it shall continue publishing or licensing said work, covering the six months ending December 31st, and June 30th, of each year respectively, royalty statements accompanied by remittance of the amount due.

(5) All sums hereunder payable jointly to the Writer shall be divided and paid in the following manner:

50 % to Otis Redding .... of ....

50 % to Steve Cropper .... of ....

...... % to .... of ....

(6) The Publisher shall have the right to alter, change, edit or translate the work or any part thereof. in any way it may be necessary. In the event it be necessary for the Publisher to cause lyrics to be written in other languages for and as part of the work, the publisher shall in such event have the right to deduct from the heretofore agreed royalties payable to the Writer, the cost or obligation thereof, but in no event more than a sum equal to one-half.

(7) The Writer hereby grants and conveys an irrevocable power of attorney authorizing and empowering the Publisher, its nominees, successors and assigns, to administer any and all rights in and to the said work, and collect and receive any and all the fees therefrom; also to file application and renew the copyrights in the name of the Writer, and upon such renewals, to execute proper and formal assignments thereof so as to secure to the Publisher, its successors and assigns, the renewal terms of, in and to said copyrights and/or works.

(8) The Writer hereby agrees to indemnify and save harmless the Publisher against any loss, expense or damage by reason of any adverse claims made by others with respect to the work, and agrees that all expenses incurred in defense of any such claims, including counsel fees, as well as any and all sums paid by the Publisher, pursuant to a judgment, arbitration or any settlement or adjustment which may be made in the discretion of the Publisher, or otherwise, shall at all times be borne by the Writer, and may be deducted by the Publisher from any money accruing to the Writer under this agreement or otherwise.

(9) The Writer agrees that he will not assign this Agreement nor any sums that may become due hereunder, without the written consent of the Publisher first endorsed hereon.

(10) Except as otherwise herein provided, this Agreement is binding upon the parties hereto and their respective successors in interest.

WITNESS: .... *Steve Cropper*
Writer

.... *Otis Redding jr.*
Writer

....
Writer

WITNESS:

By .... *Jim Stewart*

East Publications Incorporated was the publishing arm of Memphis-based Stax Records and its sister label Volt Records. This contract—signed by co-writers, recording artist Otis Redding and guitarist Steve Cropper, and Stax co-owner Jim Stewart in May 1965—establishes the payment distribution terms for "Mr. Pitiful." The song was Redding's first top ten single.

Mississippi *@!!?*@!

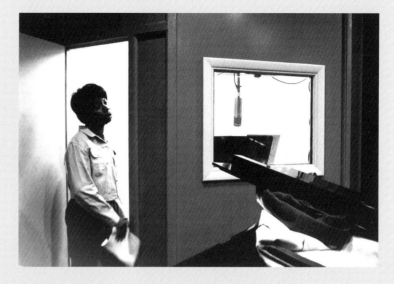

When Nina Simone introduced her song "Mississippi Goddam" at a Carnegie Hall performance, she told her audience that the song was a show tune for a "show that hasn't been written yet."[38] A promotional copy of the 45 RPM single from Simone's personal collection has a disc sleeve with the song's title censored. The text below indicates the single has been "specially edited for air play, featuring the 'BEEP-BEEP'" instead of Simone's pointed exclamation, "Goddam," hinting at her daring bravery and creative expression.

During a September 1964 appearance on *The Steve Allen Show*, Simone recalled the moments that led her to compose the stinging commentary. "First you get depressed," she shared while reflecting on her emotional reaction to violent current events instigated by white nationalists, "and then you get mad." Over a jaunty chordal accompaniment more reminiscent of Broadway choruses, Simone boldly lists her grievances, presenting listeners with insights into how Black women like herself participated in and supported the Civil Rights Movement. The song embodies acts of Black female empowerment and agency modeled by women like Simone that frequently get overshadowed by men's actions.

The disc's presence in the NMAAHC collection gains deeper meaning as Simone's song is put into context with material culture associated with the very events that drove her to write "Mississippi Goddam." Her comment about the "children getting bombed" becomes more visceral when the record is considered alongside ten shards of glass from the 16th Street Baptist Church. The pieces fell to the streets of Birmingham, Alabama, on September 15, 1963, after a bomb placed underneath the church's stairs exploded as the congregation began their Sunday services. Joan Trumpauer Mulholland (b. 1941), a white civil rights activist, later picked them off the ground and carried them home. The shards and the 45 record offer two different perspectives that contribute to understanding the 16th Street Baptist Church Bombing's impact on American society. HG

electric lady studios
52 west 8 street new york city n y 10011 212 777-0150

"Hey Baby (New Rising Sun)"   6:00
"Earth Blues"
✗ " Room Full of mirrors "   4:10
"Look Over Yonder "   3:20
"Bleeding Heart"   2:25
✗ "Dolly Dagger "   3:06
                                   4:40

Jimi Hendrix

COPY ☒
MASTER ☒   1/4 TE.

This master tape contains several tracks from Jimi Hendrix's 1971 album *Rainbow Bridge*. The soundtrack, compiled posthumously, draws upon music that Hendrix was working on at his Electric Lady Studios before his death in 1970. Songs like "Earth Blues," featuring the Ronettes, captured the new musical directions Hendrix pursued while weaving tapestries of sound in his studio work.

tape box, includes some of the material Hendrix was working on for his fourth studio album. Unfortunately, that album was never completed, as Hendrix died a month after the studio opened. The recorded tracks handwritten on the box, except for "Bleeding Heart," appeared on his second posthumous album, *Rainbow Bridge* (1971).

When Hendrix and his manager, Michael Jeffrey, took over an old nightclub in Greenwich Village, the plan was for Hendrix to open his own private club. However, he was eventually convinced to build a professional recording studio instead. John Storyk (b. 1946), a young architect who had studied at Princeton and Columbia, was hired to design the space. In discussing the vision for the building, Storyk recalls

Hendrix saying, "I just want things to be soft and curvy. I want things to be white, and then I want the light to be able to change."[39] Electric Lady Studios was as much of an artist's room as it was a studio space. In an interview on Recording Studio Rockstars, Storyk explained that the magic of Studio A at the venue was the ceiling: "It was a kind of a flat curved propeller shape that was made of...very lightweight plaster, which I specified because I didn't want to have a flutter echo between [the ceiling] and the wood floor. But, inadvertently, what I ended up making...was a membrane absorber, and that's what's holding in the low frequency; that's what makes that tight sound in that rock and roll music room."[40]

It was because of that tight sound, and the opportunity to record in a space that was designed by an artist for artists, that musicians of all genres flocked to Electric Lady to cement Hendrix and the studio's legendary status. Albums such as Stevie Wonder's *Talking Book* (1972), Patti Smith's *Horses* (1975), David Bowie's *Young Americans* (1975), The Roots' *Things Fall Apart* (1999), and D'Angelo's *Voodoo* (2000) were all recorded at Electric Lady.

As an African American rock musician steeped in the traditions of R&B, performing in a genre that was largely misunderstood as being the domain of white performers and audiences, Hendrix was the quintessential symbol of freedom and independence for his willingness to defy conventions in his musical sound and performance, resistance to essentialist notions about race and music, and ability to let his creativity and imagination inspire him toward new dimensions of being.

In the same way that recording studios owned by African Americans created opportunities for

Black artists, so did Black-owned record labels. In the late 1960s, one of the most powerful figures in the entertainment industry was Clarence Avant (b. 1931), founder and owner of Sussex Records. Avant learned the ins and outs of the music business under the tutelage of Joe Glaser, owner of Associated Booking Corporation (ABC) and manager of Louis Armstrong and Billie Holiday, whom he met early in his career when he was managing a nightclub in Newark, New Jersey. Under Glaser's mentorship, Avant learned where the wealth and power resided in the music business and became one of the toughest negotiators in the industry.

Working behind the scenes, Avant often took on the role of mentor, advisor, dealmaker, and business executive. In 1970, he signed 32-year-old Bill Withers (1938–2020) to Sussex when no other label would give him a chance. Withers released his first album, *Just as I Am*, in 1971 and followed soon after with a second album, *Still Bill*, in 1972. At first glance, the album cover for *Still Bill* expresses a story about Bill Withers. However, looking at the inside cover brings forward possibilities for additional stories about the individuals—musicians, producers, and record label owners—who make producing an album possible. Withers's collaborators on this album included a group of musicians known as the Watts 103rd Street Rhythm Band, as well as producer Booker T. Jones of Booker T. & the MG's. Arguably, though, the most important collaborator on the album was Avant himself, who launched Withers's career, which spanned more than five decades.

In addition to founding Sussex Records and signing Bill Withers, some of Avant's more well-known accomplishments include brokering the sale of Stax Records at the request of Stax executive Al Bell Jr.,

"KISSING MY LOVE"
(There is young, reckless, energetic love:)
When I'm kissing my love, I can hear a thump
thumping in my head
When I'm kissing my love I close my eyes and
see a pretty city with a million flower beds
I can hear the angels sing, songs that only angels
sing and I can feel my heart just a-thumping and
a-skipping, when I'm kissing my love
when I'm kissing my love I feel the blood
pump-pumping in my veins — Bless her name —
when I'm kissing my love she's such a tender sender
with a sweet young frame.
She's so good at what she does, all she wants
to do is kiss and hug, she's got me in love
and I can feel my heart just a-thumping and
a skipping when I'm kissing my love
Used by Permission © 1972 Interior Music (BMI)

"I DON'T KNOW"
(There is mature, soft, secure love:)
I get a warm summer feeling walking through the snow
Even chilly darkness has the brightest glow
And I just love you so, sometimes I just don't know
Time just seems to help this wonderous feeling grow
maybe I might wake up early one morning
and find it isn't so
I just love you so sometimes I just don't know
feeling like a rich man haven't got a dime
feeling like a young man but I'm old as father
time and I just love you so sometimes I just don't
know, I just don't know
Used by Permission © 1972 Interior Music (BMI)

"ANOTHER DAY TO RUN"
(Lonely people are often confused by things around them and they withdraw and
go to "shrinks" But:)
If you don't look into your mind and find out
what you're running from
tomorrow might be just another day to run
If you just sit and waste your time you'll be
going where you're coming from (think about that)
tomorrow might be just another day to run
Someone must control your mind
you're the one
dark confusion's what you find when you run.
I don't want to waste your time but I'm talking
to you like a son
Tomorrow might be just another day to run
Walking down the road of life looking for direction sometimes
my mind gets so mixed up I can't tell lust from affection
Gonna stop in to a roadside church and get my mind a rest
and Lord Jesus, help me get my soul together in the process
Pretty ladies stand in line waiting for inspection
ragged old men drinking wine trying to drown rejection
I've been wasting too much time, I'm going to lose my
mind unless, Lord Jesus
You help me get my soul together in the process
I see Tony Jr. fill up his arm with dope and dream
about a valley but he lives in an alley
filled with papers thrown away — Lord tell me
Tony tell me why do you want to get high enough to die
He's long on dreams and short on hope and sometimes
he goes to rallies and stops by to see Sally just
to pass the time away
Lord tell me Tony tell me why do you want to get high
enough to die.
Used by Permission © 1972 Interior Music (BMI)

"I DON'T WANT YOU ON MY MIND"
(There are people trying to get out of relationships:)
I don't want you on my mind all the time
I believe that it shows a sign of weakness
I don't want no lonely nights to catch me crying
I found out I don't get no where with weakness
If I dream about you, I just wake up knowing that
I got to do without you. Don't want you all the
time doing up my mind. I don't want you on my
mind all the time
Used by Permission © 1972 Interior Music (BMI)

"TAKE IT ALL IN AND CHECK IT ALL OUT"
(So in the last analysis I guess we have to find each of our own loves, our own
causes, set up our own values and do the best we can. Information will probably
turn out to be our best friend so we just have to take it all in and check it all out
and make our decisions and hope for the best.)
You can fill up a room with idle conversation you can stir
up a whole darn nation with your mouth
but before you start to show your indignation
about a situation you ought to take it all in and
check it all out
You can create a boom with catchy information
you shake up a lot of people if you shout
but before you begin to grin about the
success of your creation, you ought to take it
all in and check it all out.
You can make out a plan with aimless
dedication you can hang up a million slogans
in your house
But before you put it into operation before
you man your station, you ought to take
it all in and check it all out, and find out
what it's all about.
Used by Permission © 1972 Interior Music (BMI)

Packaging: Milton Sincoff / Art Direction: Michael Mendel, Maurer Productions / Photography: Hal Wilson.
Also on Ampex 8-Track and Cassette Stereo Tapes / © 1972 Sussex Records, Inc. /
Distributed by Buddah Buddah Records, Inc. — A Subsidiary of Viewlex, Inc. /
℗ 1972 Sussex Records, Inc. — All Rights Reserved / ® TM Reg. U.S. Pat. — Member RIAA /
Sussex Records, Inc., 6430 Sunset Blvd., Hollywood, Calif. 90028

The interior album jacket of *Still Bill*, Bill Withers's second album for Sussex Records, includes the lyrics to the album's tracks along with the names of the studio musicians who appear on the recording. The prominent inclusion of Withers's lyrics highlights his contributions as a songwriter, while the names of the musicians connect *Still Bill* to recordings in a variety of genres.

Ernie Freeman

Ernie Freeman's long and successful career in Hollywood exemplifies the essential work that Black musicians performed behind the scenes as arrangers, composers, and accompanists.

In the 1950s and '60s, Freeman (see also p. 158) collaborated with Frank Sinatra, Sammy Davis Jr., Dean Martin, Ernie Fields, the Mills Brothers, Dorothy Dandridge, Sarah Vaughan, and the Platters among many others. He played on a number of recordings issued on the Specialty, Aladdin, and Modern record labels, helping to craft the sound of early rock and R&B. He also recorded several singles and albums as a band leader, including the 1957 hit "Raunchy."

Freeman was only one of many Black musicians whose supporting work for the stars helped define the sound of American pop music. Although relatively unknown to the listening public, his outstanding arrangements earned him 60 gold albums and 150 gold singles, along with a steady flow of high-profile jobs. He won his first Grammy Award, along with the gold record shown here, for his arrangements on Frank Sinatra's 1966 album *Strangers in the Night*. He won another Grammy in 1970 for his arrangements on Simon and Garfunkel's last studio album, *Bridge Over Troubled Water*. More than just symbols of record sales, awards like Freeman's gold record for *Strangers in the Night* reflect a lifetime of effort and the hard-won respect of his peers in the industry. Professional studio musicians like Freeman represent a crucial, if often untold, part of the story of Black musical achievement. SWL

serving as Chairman of the Board at Motown Records, becoming the first African American to be appointed to the board of Polygram Records, owning three record labels, and managing Michael Jackson's 1987 Bad Tour, his first without his brothers. Avant also intervened in 1973 when Dick Clark announced his plan to create a new program, *Soul Unlimited*, as a competitor to Don Cornelius's *Soul Train*. The latter was a symbol of pride in the Black community and many civil rights leaders were disturbed that Clark would try to undermine its success. After Avant met with the chairman and president of ABC, plans for *Soul Unlimited* stopped in their tracks, while *Soul Train* continued to entertain and uplift the Black community for the next thirty-five years. The power and respect Avant has earned go beyond music and can be felt in film, sports, and politics. When asked about how he is able to do what he does, he once said, "My job is to move us forward. Period."[41]

As opportunities for Black artists to create, record, and produce their own music continued to grow into the late twentieth century, so too did the opportunities for artists to expand their work to television, film, and music videos.

Music plays a prominent role in the body of work produced by filmmaker Spike Lee, born Shelton Jackson Lee (b. 1957). His third film, *Do the Right Thing* (1989), is no exception, with hip-hop, in the form of Radio Raheem's boombox, serving as an omen and catalyst in the film's climax. Raheem's boombox is a 'metaphorical' prop because it and the music it plays comprise his alter ego. It is the source of energy that fuels Raheem's existence and the message of resistance and collective action that he wants to share with everyone. Like a material culture artifact, a prop can acquire additional meaning when it is used to express a character's feelings, demonstrate a special talent or ability, initiate a series of actions or plot development, or focus attention on a primary theme. Props can serve a basic function and be used in films or on the stage as the audience would expect them to be used, or they can serve a metaphorical function as a symbol of a particular message or theme.

Do the Right Thing follows the activities of the residents in Brooklyn's Bedford-Stuyvesant

Actor Bill Nunn (1953–2016) carried this Promax Super Jumbo boombox, one of multiple used in the film, in his role as Radio Raheem in Spike Lee's 1989 film, *Do the Right Thing*. On the lower back of the boombox is a handwritten inscription in gold ink that reads: [BROOKLYN, N.Y. /3/17/90 / To Gene / RADIO RAHEEM LIVES / LOVE, Spike Lee / "FIGHT THE POWER"]. Spike Lee gave the boombox to film critic Gene Siskel in appreciation for his support of the film.

neighborhood over the course of the hottest day of the summer. Radio Raheem walks around the streets with his jumbo boombox blaring Public Enemy's "Fight the Power," which was written by Chuck D, born Carlton Douglas Ridenhour (b. 1960), specifically for the film. While Spike Lee's father, Bill Lee, wrote the score, Lee wanted Public Enemy to write "an anthem that could express what young Black America was feeling at the time."[42]

"Fight the Power" carries the DNA of such artists as James Brown and Sly Stone. It was a call to action for those who were held hostage by the politics of the 1980s and channeled the frustrations and the brewing anger-teetering-toward-rage around racism, poverty, the politics of disenfranchisement, policing, and the justice system. In a nod to the song's creators, one side of the boombox features a sticker with Public Enemy's name and crosshairs logo (see also below). As Chuck D stated: "The United States Constitution once considered black people to be three-fifths of a human being. If this is a public document, obviously we must be the enemy, so that's where the name Public Enemy came from."[43]

In the film, Radio Raheem appears to impose his music everywhere he goes, except inside Sal's Pizzeria. When Sal (Danny Aiello) prohibits Raheem from turning on his music, Raheem accompanies Buggin' Out (Giancarlo Esposito) and Smiley (Roger Guenveur Smith) on another trip to the pizzeria to threaten Sal with a boycott until he changes his rules. This time Raheem turns on his music full volume, but Sal's simmering frustration turns to anger as he grabs his baseball bat and proceeds to turn off the music by pummeling Raheem's prized boombox to pieces.[44] The characters in the film and the movie audience are frozen into silence as they grasp the significance of what has just happened. This destruction of Raheem's prized possession not only silences the music, but also the lifeline that is the symbol and power of his whole identity.[45] Chaos follows as Raheem attacks Sal in retaliation, the fight spills on to the streets, and Raheem is tragically killed when New York City police administer a chokehold around his neck. "Fight the Power" plays one more time as the camera pans over what remains of the pizzeria. Radio Raheem's boombox lies amongst the debris, silenced, like its owner, forever.

Do the Right Thing demonstrates a facet of hip-hop's transcendence into film, and the boombox pairs well with other materials in the NMAAHC collection that spotlight how the music was documented behind the camera by filmmakers and photographers. Photography is an especially powerful medium in conveying the growth, energetic vibrance,

Public Enemy front man, rapper Chuck D, says the group's name comes from the definition of a Black man that once appeared in the US Constitution. According to Chuck D in *Rolling Stone* magazine, "The crosshairs logo symbolized the black man in America.... The B-Boy stance and the silhouette was more like the black man on the target."

The Mothership Connection

The Mothership, a spaceship-styled stage prop, was the theatrical centerpiece of Parliament-Funkadelic's staged "funk opera" in the mid- to late 1970s. The awesome spectacle of its ritual descent during the climax of their stage shows became the ultimate symbol of an Afrofuturist vision manifested in popular music and catapulted the band to stardom. George Clinton (b. 1941) envisioned the large, flamboyant Mothership as part of his ongoing musical space odyssey and the vessel that would figuratively transport audiences away from the racist realities and the societal confines of Earth to the symbolic, liberated realm of the cosmos. This smaller replica was used to promote the 1996 album *T.A.P.O.A.F.O.M.*, an acronym for "The Awesome Power of a Fully Operational Machine." Devised by bandleader George Clinton and co-designed by Jules Fisher (b. 1937) and Peter Larkin (1926–2019), the concept and design of the Mothership was inspired by Clinton's fascination with sci-fi stories, the space program, and comic-book characters.

Reflecting on the experience of seeing Clinton emerge from the Mothership on stage, band promoter Darryll Brooks stated, "Here's a guy coming out of a Mothership with a mink coat and platform shoes.... Black folks been down so long.... It was jubilation."[46] Brooks's descriptions provide valuable insight into Clinton's larger goals to produce visual and sonic art that would work in tandem to transcend musical and social boundaries. Through the visual of the Mothership and the music of funk, Parliament-Funkadelic created a musical universe of their own, with sci-fi-inspired characters, stories, and a general philosophy that emphasized the unifying power of the "one" and the greater project to "free the minds" of the audience from musical, societal, racial, and gendered rules and "constrictions." With the Mothership stage prop, outlandish costumes, and cosmic-inspired funk, Parliament-Funkadelic were the progenitors of an Afrofuturist sound and vision in popular music. KMS

and cultural positioning of hip-hop music. In 2015, the NMAAHC acquired over four hundred photographs from Bill Adler's Eyejammie Hip-Hop Photography Collection. Adler, an author, documentarian, archivist, and former music journalist and publicist at Rush Productions and Def Jam Recordings, exhibited his collection in his Eyejammie Fine Arts Gallery from 2003 to 2008. His feelings that the music was overshadowing the visual art of hip-hop motivated him to open the gallery. As he explained, "I founded Eyejammie to do what I could to correct that imbalance."[47]

The Eyejammie collection features photographs documenting a wide swath of the world of hip-hop, including portraits, performances, backstage moments, parties, and sets of music videos. One such photo features Queen Latifah (b. 1970) on the set of the music video for "Fly Girl" (see opposite). Queen Latifah is photographed in an outfit typical of the way she presented herself early in her career—wearing African-inspired clothing and crown-like headpieces. In a 1989 episode of *Yo! MTV Raps*, she told Fab 5 Freddy, "By wearing African clothes, African accessories, not only am I supporting my African brothers and sisters who have these businesses, but it brings me closer to my ancestors."[48]

Many hip-hop pioneers adopted the same symbols of Black pride, Black Nationalism, and Afrocentrism that proliferated during the late 1960s and 1970s. Queen Latifah started her career with a public persona rooted in a strong sense of self-worth. Born Dana Owens, she renamed herself "Latifah" when she was a child, and lived into that identity. When she came on the scene, she projected the wisdom and strength of an elder, and infused hip-hop with a Black feminist message which ensured that her inheritance as an African American always received the respect it was due. Her rhymes were unapologetic and blunt, but could also celebrate femininity. Since her early days in hip-hop, Queen Latifah has gone on to appear in

over thirty films, host a talk show, star in a successful sitcom, receive an Oscar nomination for Best Supporting Actress, and found her own management and production company, Flavor Unit Entertainment.

For the African American performer, realizing true equality and freedom is a personal endeavor of self and of collective liberation. Approached from different perspectives, values, and beliefs, Queen Latifah's career and image marked a generational shift in traversing the barriers that limited opportunities to Black artists. Her pursuit of a career on her own terms is a product of self-confidence, pride, and perseverance, but also of the struggles, disappointments, and triumphs of the people who went before her in negotiating their way through the oppressive practices of racism, bigotry, misogyny, sexism, homophobia, classism, and other belief and value systems that marginalized and disenfranchised whole segments of society. From generation to generation, music continues to be the center of activity in the existential quest of learning how it feels to be free.

Hip-hop and sports photographer Al Pereira took this photograph of Queen Latifah while she was filming the music video for "Fly Girl," the lead single off her second album for Tommy Boy Records, *Nature of a Sista'*. The 1991 album, on which she also served as co-executive producer, features a range of musical styles and includes songs about gender politics and relationships.

Luther's Ballad

From afar, this sheet of paper torn from a spiral notebook does not immediately leap out as something historically significant. Nevertheless, the handwritten lyrics on the page in blocks below the underlined title "Dance with My Father" preserve the songwriting process of Luther Vandross's 2003 hit. Vandross (1951–2005) memorialized cherished memories with his mother and late father through the words written on the page. His close friend Fonzi Thornton preserved the lyrics for years before donating them to the NMAAHC. The song joined Vandross's body of "Quiet Storm" repertoire that dominated late-night urban radio and wedding playlists. His narration of the prominent position of fathers in family relationships employed a presentation of sentimental masculinity that he had actively crafted for two decades in the recording studio and onstage.

The throwback elegance and charm that suffused Luther Vandross's music extended from his vocal dexterity to the lush arrangements he concocted to accompany his romantic serenades. His music appealed to Black middle-class values, while quietly informing queer culture. In performances during the 1980s, glittering jackets and gowns adorning Vandross and his back-up singers—Ava Cherry, Kevin Owens, and Lisa Fischer—enhanced the drama of his songs. These heavily beaded Tony Chase-designed red, black, and white costumes accentuated the vocalists' simple movements. Cherry, Owens, and Fischer strutted across the stage, and side-stepped at their microphones in formation behind Vandross, in their flamboyant ensembles. The campy spectacle pulled on different threads of Vandross's personal history. A former background singer himself, Vandross developed his glamorous stage aesthetic in the 1970s, while collaborating with Broadway musicians and singing for major acts like David Bowie. Performing onstage in matching uniforms with his fellow vocalists helped ease the pressure on the introverted Vandross as he established his solo career following the great success of his 1981 debut album, *Never Too Much*. HG

The Legacy of Blackface

Retired blackface minstrel Bobby Newcomb's jokebook and instruction manual, *Tambo: His Jokes and Funny Sayings*, was published in 1882. At the time of its release, blackface minstrelsy had dominated American popular culture for more than forty years. Beginning in the 1830s, with star performers like George Washington Dixon and Thomas "Daddy" Rice, minstrels combined derogatory stereotypes of Black culture with imitations of Black folk dance and music.

In 1843, the Virginia Minstrels introduced the minstrel show's standard format, along with its standard instrumentation of fiddle, banjo, tambourine, and bones.[49] Minstrels usually sat onstage in a semicircle, with the tambourine player ("Mr. Tambo") and the bones player ("Mr. Bones") on either end, trading jokes between musical performances. Minstrel troupes proliferated in the 1840s and '50s, and

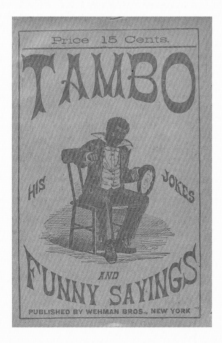

amateurs began staging their own shows, leading to a cottage industry of instruction manuals and jokebooks like Newcomb's. The first part of *Tambo* includes advice on topics such as "Banjo Playing," "Burnt Cork," and "Stump Speeches." The second part is a collection of jokes and lines to be delivered onstage. *Tambo*'s comparatively late date points to minstrelsy's enduring popularity at the community level, even as vaudeville began to eclipse minstrel shows in the 1880s.

After the Civil War, Black performers formed their own minstrel troupes, softening the racist humor and incorporating new material like Black religious songs. Among this new generation of Black performers was Charles P. Stinson (1854–1911), who co-designed this banjo with J.H. Buckbee (1832–1897) of New York in the late nineteenth century. Stinson worked as a professional banjoist in vaudeville and minstrelsy in the 1870s and '80s, touring the United States and Europe, and winning multiple playing competitions. In one 1888 competition in Kansas City, Stinson defeated eleven white players, becoming the first Black musician to win a banjo competition in a southern state. After the 1880s, Stinson returned to his native Pittsburgh and taught private lessons, profiting from the late-nineteenth-century banjo craze. Stinson and Buckbee likely designed this banjo as a beginner-level instrument for Stinson to distribute to his students. In a mark of respect unusual for a Black musician of the time, Stinson's name and hometown are engraved on the banjo's dowel stick.

Stinson achieved his greatest success in the 1880s and '90s, as the banjo was fading from African American popular culture. The banjo is the

quintessential African American instrument, and its history in America parallels the development of a distinctive African American culture in the eighteenth and nineteenth centuries. Enslaved Africans in the Caribbean developed the first banjos from West African lutes, beginning in the late 1600s. The instrument had arrived in North America by the first decades of the eighteenth century and spread throughout the English colonies. It became a distinctive feature of Black musical ensembles throughout the antebellum and Reconstruction periods.

In the late nineteenth century, the banjo's place in Black music was gradually superseded by that of the guitar, an instrument whose longer sustain and lower pitch made it better suited to the blues, a new musical form emerging in southern Black communities. The banjo diminished in Black culture but remained important in rural white communities, where white musicians had adopted it from Black musicians over a century earlier. In the twentieth century, the banjo's prominence in white-dominated genres like country and bluegrass obscured its African origins. Despite the changing image of his instrument, Stinson's story demonstrates how Black musicians negotiated the constraints of blackface minstrelsy to make successful careers in the entertainment industry.

The traditional minstrel show had largely disappeared by the turn of the twentieth century.

But the stereotypes of Black people popularized in minstrel shows continued to cast a long shadow over Black representation in twentieth-century media. Louis Armstrong (1901–1971), shown here on the set of the 1938 film *Going Places*, exemplified Black entertainers' efforts to negotiate and subvert the minstrel stereotypes foisted on them by the entertainment industry. In his many film and television appearances, Armstrong often embodied a grinning, eye-rolling persona redolent of blackface minstrelsy. This aspect of his work alienated many young and politically conscious Black listeners and viewers in Armstrong's later years. And yet, even as his onstage mugging conformed to stereotypes, the brilliance of his trumpet playing communicated a powerful rebuke to ideas of Black inferiority. This important dichotomy in Armstrong's work emphasizes the need to interpret even the most revolutionary Black artists in their historical and cultural contexts. Armstrong, like many other Black artists of his generation, made strategic concessions to Hollywood's racism while using his artistry to challenge audiences' assumptions. SWL

Black Music Takes Center Stage

Sandwiched between text on the front cover of sheet music for the song "Love Will Find a Way" are signatures from musical theater pioneers Adelaide Hall (1901–1993), Noble Sissle (1889–1975), and Eubie Blake (see also p. 33). From the "New York musical novelty success" *Shuffle Along*, the song by Sissle and Blake was nestled into this exciting new work penned by Black blackface comedians Flournoy Miller (1885–1971) and Aubrey Lyle (1884–1932). The duet with romantic lyrics—one of Blake's favorite pieces in the score—does not smack of anything immediately apparent as controversial. However, in 1921 when the song was first performed during the premiere, the show's creators feared their portrayal of Black love onstage during the delivery of this song might be their downfall.

Shuffle Along's comedic appeal, coupled with its ragtime score and dazzling dancers, attracted thousands of eager audience members every evening. The show's format and exciting music transformed Broadway by bringing jazz music and styles to the Great White Way. One of the most visible impacts of the show was the demand and work it established for Black entertainers that ushered in the Harlem Renaissance. Nearly a century after it first opened, producer George C. Wolfe (b. 1954) revisited the show to weave a 2016 revival that staged a narrative of how the musical's creators exerted artistic control over their story to present audiences with new perspectives of Blackness. The sheet music's signatures provide a jumping-off point to explore how *Shuffle Along* connects to other moments in theater where African Americans participated in reimagining Blackness onstage or reframed constricting scripts that perpetuated racial mimicry.

Fifty years after *Shuffle Along* premiered, the racial and class tensions it foregrounded continued to shape African American involvement with musical theater. The 1970s was an exciting period in Broadway history, with numerous African American productions successfully staged, including *Purlie* (1971), *A Raisin in the Sun* (1975), and *Ain't Misbehavin'* (1978) (see images from the 1978 Broadway cast album above). Amidst this growth in Black musical theater productions in the 1970s, *The Wiz* premiered.

Like *Shuffle Along*, *The Wiz* tapped into popular music and successfully brought contemporary trends into musical theater and created opportunities for Black creatives both on and off the stage. A tight cream-colored jumpsuit with flared bell-bottoms and decorative rhinestones placed along the perimeter of a flap,

paired with a similarly decorated pilot's helmet, preserves the Afrofuturistic elements in *The Wiz*'s re-telling of L. Frank Baum's *The Wonderful Wizard of Oz*. When Tony Award winner and Broadway veteran André De Shields (b. 1946) wore the costume during the musical's original production in 1975, he premiered the slinky movements and delivery of the Wizard of Oz. The show had hit songs drawing on popular music conventions. Songs like "Ease on Down the Road" even crossed over to Billboard's Soul charts and contributed to the show's lingering intergenerational appeal. Costumes including the glamorous jumpsuit worn by De Shields garnered critical acclaim. Along with others in the show, this ensemble earned the polymath director, choreographer, actor, and costume designer Geoffrey Holder (1930–2014) a Tony Award for costume design. Holder, a Trinidadian-American dancer, joined the production initially as a consultant and costume designer. Over the course of *The Wiz*'s production, however, he gradually took on additional roles as the musical's choreographer and director.

Costume design is one of many behind-the-scenes roles African Americans play in staging musical theater. Judy Dearing (1940–1995) was a multitalented artist whose career as a costume designer brought her international acclaim. She once described her style to *Essence* magazine as "something old, something new, and something African."[50] Born and raised in New York by her tailor father and crafty mother, Dearing began her adventures in show business as a child appearing in musicals and later studying dance with legends including Martha Graham. Her background and childhood making her own clothing informed her tremendously successful career as a designer working with performers. Dearing drew this costume design in the months before her death

for the 60th-anniversary revival touring production of *Porgy and Bess*. A stamp in the bottom left corner, with her signature inserted, documents her involvement in the United Scenic Artists association based in New York City. Intended for an unidentified character, the gathered folds at the waist and sharp appearance of the sketched woman hint at the ways Black artists interacted with the troublesome aspects of *Porgy and Bess*'s portrayal of Black southern life. In the article "'A Woman Is a Sometime Thing,'" scholar Dr. Daphne Brooks explores how Black women subverted archetypal representations permeating George Gershwin's so-called folk opera through their interpretive performances.[51] Perusing Dearing's costume design extends this conversation of Black women's cultural efforts beyond performance to other areas where women actively helped re-shape how Black performers appear onstage. HG

141

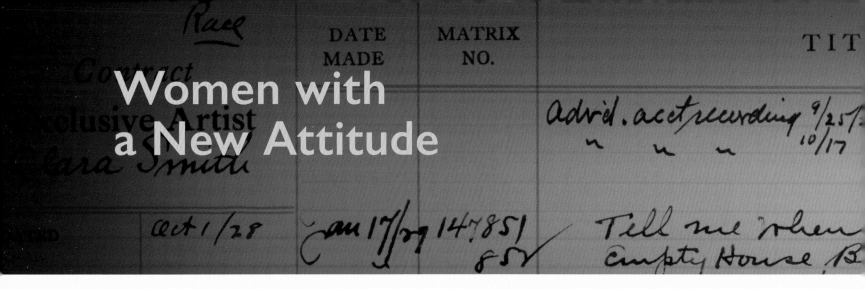

Women with a New Attitude

Reviewing a binder of century-old ledger pages listing contracted recordings for Columbia Records, it is clear that Black women had an indelible mark on the developing twentieth-century American music industry. Prepared by staff within Columbia's Race Records Division in black, blue, and red inks, the detailed administrative documents track session dates, payments, and song titles for popular blues singers such as Bessie Smith, Ethel Waters, and Clara Smith. In business fashion, Columbia's staff chronicled these women's significant achievements as they modeled their self-agency and spoke to women's issues in ways that presaged the feminist movement. In the wake of Mamie Smith's watershed release "Crazy Blues," Columbia and their competitors actively sought so-called "Southern coon shouters" for their Race Records rosters, where they transformed into legendary Blues Queens.[52]

Clara Smith (1894–1935) began her six-year journey with Columbia in 1923, and the company continually renewed her contracts through 1929. Under the auspices of Columbia's executives, she made history by recording the first devil-themed blues, "Done Sold My Soul to the Devil," in September of 1924. Years later, she closed out the decade with breakup anthems such as "Where is My Man" and "Papa I Don't Need You Now" that captured the pain, and relief, of separations familiar to her working-class audiences migrating around the nation in search of better opportunities.

Clara Smith was just one of many Black female singers who dominated the commercial blues market during the 1920s. These women delivered musical tales of female protagonists relishing in sexual entanglements with men and women, brandishing weapons to defend themselves, taking to the road to start anew after devastation, and subverting the patriarchal ideologies that governed American society. Crafting what Angela Davis in *Blues Legacies and Black Feminism* (1998) called "fearless, unadorned realism,"[53] Clara Smith and her many contemporaries, who crisscrossed the country performing in tent shows and the Black vaudeville circuit, created opportunities for generations of women who followed them. Treading the paths laid by their Blues foremothers, Black women in music continue to transform the music industry.

In the mid-twentieth century, Black women across the country expressed their visions of

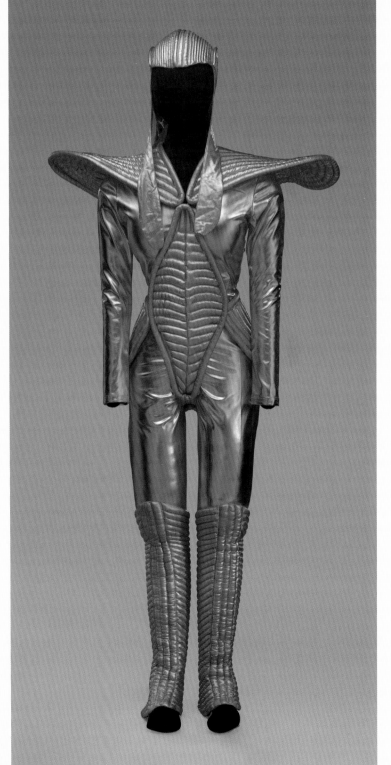

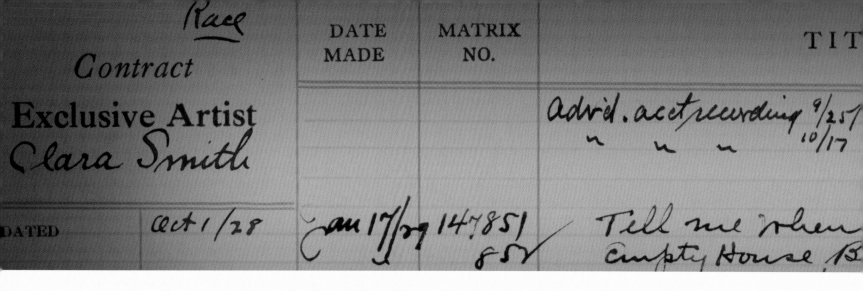

Race

Contract

Exclusive Artist
Clara Smith

DATE MADE

MATRIX NO.

TIT

advid. acct recording 9/25/
"   "   "   10/17

DATED   Oct 1/28   Jan 17/29 147851 /   Tell me when
                              85 /   empty House, B

womanhood through song, adding to the dialogue of female agency started by the Blues Queens. Nona Hendryx (b. 1944), for example, was a marvel to behold in April 1975, grooving across the stage of *The Midnight Special* in this gleaming silver Larry LeGaspi-designed costume. Its sculpted shoulders and contoured bodysuit accentuated her hip movements, perfectly synced with the percussionist keeping time on a cowbell. Alongside her Labelle bandmates Patti Labelle and Sarah Dash, Hendryx cultivated a unique brand of funky sci-fi-rock which staged futures that embrace Black women's joy, independence, and beauty. Promoting their 1974 album *Nightbirds*, Labelle partnered with LeGaspi to create costumes that channeled the energies of the Space Race and the Black Power Movement. Their transformation from ladylike doo-woppers to queering rock stars distinguished them from their contemporaries and clearly situated them in the lineage of the Blues Queens. Labelle's repertoire of the 1970s, characterized by Nona Hendryx's songwriting, saw the group stirring the imaginations of audiences young and old. Their empowering music and out-of-this-world costumes fabricated a limitless future for Black women by taking the familiar blues topics of overcoming oppression, heartbreak, desire, and hope to space.

The far-reaching influence of the Blues Queens is also felt in more contemporary historical artifacts, such as a sign carried by protesters in the 2017 Women's March in Washington, DC. In preparation for participating in the march, the maker of this sign used a black marker to write: "WHEN YOU HURT ME, YOU HURT / YOURSELF. WHEN YOU LOVE ME, / YOU LOVE YOURSELF..... / LOVE GOD HERSELF." The sign's inscription—lyrics drawn from Beyoncé's duet with Jack White, "Don't Hurt Yourself"— exemplifies how contemporary feminist movements absorb Beyoncé Knowles-Carter's (b. 1981) work into their public engagements. "Don't Hurt Yourself," from Beyoncé's culture-shifting sixth studio album *Lemonade*, ominously warned wayward lovers and governing bodies alike of the damaging consequences that come with violating the women in one's life. The album and its accompanying film were the latest installments of Beyoncé's feminist oeuvre. However, they critically introduced many mainstream audiences to her political stance and belief in woman's power. Traveling the streets of the nation's capital, this sign proclaims women as dragons breathing fire and extends Queen Bey's feminism to the contentious national dialogue following the 2016 presidential election. It is also a reminder of the strength she and Queens before her have instilled in audiences for over a century through their music. HG

E		PUB.	DATE O.K.'D	DATE PAID	AM'T PAID	MONTH LISTED
Auth 5476 - RD 26912 $25.00						
" 5508 RD 27117 25.00						
wls			Jan 24/29	Jan 26/29	100	may/29
			" 24 "	" " "	100	may/29

WHEN YOU HURT ME, YOU HURT YOURSELF. WHEN YOU LOVE ME, YOU LOVE YOURSELF....., LOVE GOD HERSELF

During and immediately after World War II, young Black musicians in New York City pioneered a new and challenging musical language. They were veterans of the dance bands of the swing era, and they sought to elevate their work to new heights of virtuosity and artistry. The music, soon to be called "bebop," paralleled the wartime Double V campaign for freedom from fascism abroad and from racism at home, in that it reflected the assertiveness and ambition of the rising generation of Black Americans. Although bebop developed within an impoverished community of bohemian artists, in the succeeding decades it found a relatively secure home within prestigious cultural institutions.

Charles "Teenie" Harris's (1908–1998) photograph of the New York-based Billy Eckstine Orchestra illustrates bebop's roots in big band and swing and its connections to urban Black communities around the country. Harris photographed Eckstine (1914–1993) conducting his band onstage at Pittsburgh, Pennsylvania's Aragon Ballroom in August 1944. The band shown in this photo features several of the young musicians who were about to reinvent jazz, including saxophonist Charlie Parker, bassist Tommy Potter, drummer Art Blakey, vocalist Sarah Vaughan, and trumpeters Dizzy Gillespie and Howard McGhee. Harris's photograph is one of many images of Black life in Pittsburgh that he took during his forty-year career in the mid-twentieth century as a freelance photographer for the *Pittsburgh Courier*, while also maintaining a personal photography studio. His photographs focused on Pittsburgh's working-class Black community in neighborhoods like the Hill District.

Although the Eckstine Orchestra was already popular with Black audiences when Harris photographed them, this photo only became more significant as many of Eckstine's sidemen went on to become jazz legends. Harris's photo, when viewed in the broader context of his body of work in Pittsburgh, contests the common image of bebop musicians as holding themselves aloof from developments in 1940s popular music. Instead, bebop was inseparable from the mosaic of Black life and pop culture during the war and immediate postwar years. Artists ranging from the crowd-pleasing proto-R&B of Louis Jordan to the more experimental orchestral jazz of Eckstine shared stages in Black neighborhoods around the country during the 1940s and '50s.

Materials including the neon Minton's Playhouse sign above and Thelonious Monk's Baldwin grand piano trace bebop's path into the cultural establishment in the second half of the twentieth century. This sign is a reconstruction of the sign that hung outside Minton's Playhouse in Harlem during the 1940s and until the club's closure in 1974. It was built and installed from around 1984, when the building was submitted to the New York State Historic Preservation Office, until the venue was remodeled in 2012. The original Minton's was opened by saxophonist Henry Minton in 1938, with a new music room opening after it came under the management of Teddy Hill in 1940, as shown in the invitation for the room's gala opening night (see p. 148). It became a regular after-hours meeting place for professional musicians, especially during its Monday-night jam sessions. In the early 1940s, musicians including Charlie Christian, Dizzy Gillespie, Charlie Parker, and Kenny Clarke laid the foundations for bebop during these informal performances.

This sign is interesting in part because it is not the sign that hung over Minton's during its glory days in the early 1940s. Instead, it was part of the effort to have the site recognized for its historic status.

Minton's shift from after-hours club in the 1940s to official historic landmark in the 1980s reflects jazz's institutionalization during the second half of the twentieth century. By the 1980s, when the Minton's sign was reconstructed, jazz was recognized by institutions like the Smithsonian as America's "classical music," enjoying a level of official recognition and support that would have been unimaginable earlier in its history.[54]

Thelonious Monk's piano likewise tells the story of jazz's path from the nightclub to the academy. This Baldwin grand piano is the only piano that Monk (1917–1982) ever owned. He purchased it in 1962, using his first advance payment from Columbia Records, and used it to write many of his later compositions, including "Green Chimneys," "Stuffy Turkey," and "Ugly Beauty." It also appears in his February 28, 1964, *Time* cover story. The piano's significance has grown as Monk's status as a major American composer has solidified. It has served as an important symbol of Monk as a jazz icon, especially from 1996 to 2018, when it sat in a classroom at the Thelonious Monk Institute of Jazz at UCLA. The instrument's early history illustrates the conditions of poverty that pioneer Black artists often faced. Despite his stature in the New York City jazz community, Monk could not afford to own his own piano until 1962, twenty years into his career. And yet, while Monk's Baldwin started as the personal piano of a struggling composer, it came to be housed in a university institute named for its owner three decades later, and finally in the Smithsonian. SWL

Announcing the

Gala Opening

of our new

MUSIC ROOM

❖

Minton's Playhouse

208 West 118th Street

Thursday, August 29th

10 P. M.

Morris Kilgore, Host

Morris Minton & Teddy Hill, Props.

UN. 4-9228   -   Reservations   -   UN. 4-9255

Richard Penniman's Freedom Blues

This tattered King James Bible belonged to rock and roll pioneer Richard Wayne Penniman (1932–2020), better known by his stage name Little Richard. The Bible, published by William Collins, Sons in 1959, is full of red ink, and the extensive notetaking and markings indicate that he likely used it for preaching and study. The wear and tear on its pages and binding indicates that Richard probably referred to it frequently over a long period—indeed, it was nearly falling apart when it arrived at the NMAAHC. Its fragile condition exemplifies the challenges of artifact care in a museum setting. The Bible was in urgent need of conservation by museum staff, but its physical condition, with markings and dog-eared pages, represented what it meant to its owner. In situations like this, museums walk a fine line between maintaining objects and preserving their distinctive character and history.

Little Richard's Bible points to his complicated relationship with his own sexuality and his long struggle for freedom in his personal and musical identities. Richard, who had started his career as drag performer "Princess Lavonne" and once described himself as "omnisexual," became famous for a flamboyant stage persona that reflected the gay subculture of Black show business. After experiencing visions and narrowly avoiding a plane crash in 1957, Richard abandoned secular music and enrolled at Oakwood University, a historically Black college affiliated with the Seventh-Day Adventist Church. He became ordained as a Seventh-Day Adventist minister and spent the late 1950s and early 1960s preaching, eventually recording a gospel album.

Even after returning to rock and roll in 1964, Richard continued to vacillate between sacred and secular expressions for the rest of his life. He made similar moves in and out of the closet.

In 1985, he publicly announced that he had "rejected homosexuality," but then said that he had "been gay all my life" in a 1995 interview. In 2017, several years after proclaiming himself "omnisexual," Richard implied that homosexuality was "unnatural."[55] Richard's bracketing of Revelation 14:4, with its reference to "they which were not defiled with women," suggests his efforts to reconcile his sexual orientation and his love of performance with his deep religious faith.

A photograph of four young men in front of Jack's Barber Shop points to similar themes in Little

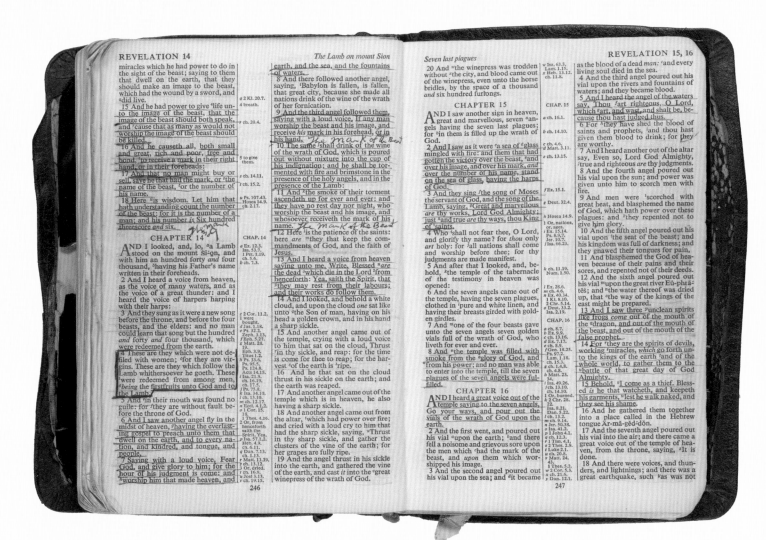

Richard's career. Richard stands at the far left. He and the man at the far right are holding books, possibly Bibles. This photograph was likely taken in the late 1950s, after Richard had embraced the Seventh-Day Adventist faith. It shows the distance between his colorful stage persona and the more conservative style he adopted after joining the church. Instead of the pompadour and flashy clothing that he sported in the mid-1950s (see photographs above), Richard appears with short hair and a more mundane outfit. Like Richard's Bible, this image of him after his conversion experience reflects conflicts in his life and music that he never fully resolved.

If Little Richard's move back and forth from the secular to the sacred mirrored his personal struggles with his sexuality, it also reflects the inseparability of secular and sacred African American music, as shown in Richard's own work. Some of his earliest musical experiences had been in the Pentecostal church that he attended with his family as a child in Macon, Georgia. The ecstatic Pentecostal style of worship became a key influence on Richard's famously energetic performances, both in rock and roll and gospel music. His sartorial style changed markedly as he moved between the sacred and secular spheres, but his singing remained notably consistent.

Richard's conversion experience did not stop him from returning to his roots in rock and roll, as demonstrated by this two-piece floral brocade costume. Melvin James likely made this costume for Little Richard in the late 1960s, and Richard wore it in publicity photographs of the period and on the covers of two of his albums, *Well Alright!* and *Freedom Blues*. It was one of several different costumes that James designed for Richard. Like Richard's other clothing from this period, it illustrates his transition from the ministry back to the world of secular music. The extravagant aesthetic reflects Richard's return to the flamboyant persona he had embodied in his early career, even as he continued to alternately celebrate and condemn his sexuality.

Importantly, Little Richard's return to secular music in the 1960s allowed him to reassert his place as one of the founding musicians of rock and roll. By the 1960s, with the popularity of British bands like the Beatles and the Rolling Stones, the African American roots of the music were diminished in favor of a narrative that advanced the music of white artists as the key architects and innovators of rock and roll. With his comeback, Richard claimed his rightful position as an inventor of music that had become a global phenomenon. SWL

The Black Press

Beginning in the late nineteenth and early twentieth centuries with publications like *Musical Messenger* and *Negro Music Journal*, and with regular music columns in prominent Black newspapers like *The Chicago Defender*, the Black press has paid special attention to music and to accomplished Black musicians. There are three important reasons for this: first, Black journalists were eager to give Black musicians the sympathetic hearing that they rarely received in white periodicals. Second, highlighting Black artistic accomplishment was (and continues to be) seen as a powerful way to subvert racist stereotypes. Finally, coverage of music and musicians proved enduringly popular with readers. Black music journalism was an important contributor to Black artistic freedom, articulating Black perspectives on the arts for a national readership and supporting and promoting Black musicians. Black periodicals have generated a rich material culture of objects that trace this history.

The staff of *The Chicago Defender* used this zinc plate around 1950 to print a photograph of Marian Anderson in a story about the renowned classical singer (see also p. 66). The *Defender* regularly featured coverage of classical music and Black classical artists, beginning as early as 1917 with the hire of Nora Douglas Holt, its first full-time music editor. This object, a seemingly candid image of a relaxed and elegant Anderson, points to the important role that Black classical musicians played in the Black press of the early to mid-twentieth century. In the context of Jim Crow America, these artists were held up by Black journalists as refutations of stereotypes and examples of education and cultivation for readers to emulate. By the mid-twentieth century, however, classical music was losing its central place as a representation of Black excellence. This image of Marian Anderson

would have appeared in the *Defender* as the Black music press was beginning to shift its attention away from classical music and towards more popular genres.

A February 1979 issue of *Black Stars* magazine demonstrates how much coverage of music in the Black press changed over the following decades. The cover features an image of Tina Turner (b. 1939), born Anna Mae Bullock, with other headlines referencing stories about Inez Andrews, Grace Jones, Chaka Khan, Lenny Williams, and Richard Roundtree. Published by Johnson Publishing Company, America's largest Black-owned publishing company of the twentieth century, *Black Stars* was a monthly entertainment magazine that ran from 1971 to 1981.[56] It featured coverage of living Black entertainers and often printed articles written by Black media figures. With its mixture of contemporary popular musicians, gospel legend Inez Andrews, and movie stars like Richard Roundtree, it exemplifies the populist direction that Black music

journalism took after World War II. Despite this shift in emphasis, *Black Stars* shared its mission with earlier publications, like the *Defender*, to popularize positive images of Black musicians.

The Black music press continues its focus on Black popular genres into the twenty-first century. This 2006 issue of *Vibe* (a hip-hop and R&B magazine founded by Quincy Jones) features a cover story on Atlanta hip-hop duo OutKast. The story focuses on the group's longevity, their place in hip-hop history, their new album *Idlewild*, and the upcoming release of their film of the same name. If this glossy magazine demonstrates hip-hop's prominence in American media, it also reflects the changes that had taken place on the hip-hop scene in the decades prior. By 2006, artists like OutKast had taken Southern cities like Atlanta from the periphery to the center of hip-hop music and culture, representing a significant shift from the 1980s and '90s, when the music was dominated by musicians from cities like New York and Los Angeles (see p. 106).

In retrospect, the magazine is situated within Black music journalism's transitional state in the first years of the new millennium, as digital formats began to outpace traditional print media. *Vibe* and many similar magazines moved to digital formats in the 2010s as sales of print media declined. Meanwhile, the development of social media platforms like Twitter and websites like YouTube changed the landscape of music criticism and journalism dramatically. These and other platforms allowed increasing numbers of opinionated music fans to add their voices to conversations around Black music and culture. The democratization of music commentary that has come from these developments raises questions about the future of traditional Black music journalism. The place of the Black press remains in flux in an era when musicians can advocate for their own work and when positive images of Black people are easier than ever to find. SWL

Getting the Music Heard

Black-owned record labels are among the most iconic examples of Black entrepreneurship. In the more than a century since the founding of the first Black record company, these organizations have attained a historical significance that goes beyond their financial success as Black business. Black record labels represent Black people's efforts to thwart patterns of cultural appropriation by maintaining ownership of Black culture and by reaping the economic benefits of Black music's popularity. The stories of image-conscious labels like Black Swan and Motown are important episodes in the long struggle to shift popular perceptions of Black people and Black culture in a positive direction. The material culture connected to this history—in the form of recordings, business documents, and other artifacts—provides valuable insight into the changing tastes, interests, and concerns of Black entrepreneurs and the Black listening public.

Ethel Waters's early recordings, such as her 1923 version of "Long Lost Mama," document the brief but influential existence of one of the first Black-owned record labels. Waters (1896–1977) was the star recording artist at Black Swan Records, which was founded in 1921 by Harry Pace (1884–1943) as part of his Pace Phonograph Company. Pace intended for his record label to produce outstanding recordings of Black musicians in styles ranging from jazz and blues to opera and classical music. He believed that by showcasing the excellence of Black Swan artists, he and his company would aid in the larger project of Black uplift. The iconic Black Swan logo on records was meant to evoke Black concert vocalist Elizabeth Taylor Greenfield (d. 1876), known as the "Black Swan" in the nineteenth-century press. This allusion to classical music illustrated the image of musical excellence and respectability that Pace sought to cultivate.

Although Black Swan Records declared bankruptcy in 1923—months after the release of Waters's recording of "Long Lost Mama"—it continued to hold major historic and symbolic importance. Pace's effort to leverage Black art in the service of Black advancement epitomized the spirit of what became known as the Harlem Renaissance. As the first prominent, ambitious, and politically engaged Black-owned record label, Black Swan presaged the more commercially successful efforts of Black music entrepreneurs during the next three-quarters of the twentieth century. Equally important, Black Swan launched the extremely influential careers of musicians including Ethel Waters, William Grant Still, and Fletcher Henderson.

The number of independent Black labels increased dramatically during World War II and remained large for decades. The 1942–44 strike by the American Federation of Musicians halted recording at the major labels and created an opening for small boutique record companies to meet public demand for music. Materials from the NMAAHC collection document the impact of the Black independent labels that proliferated during these years. Independent Black record labels remained an important force in popular

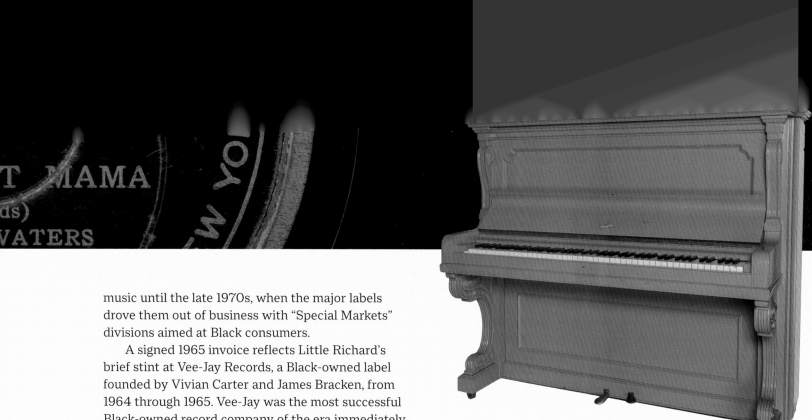

music until the late 1970s, when the major labels drove them out of business with "Special Markets" divisions aimed at Black consumers.

A signed 1965 invoice reflects Little Richard's brief stint at Vee-Jay Records, a Black-owned label founded by Vivian Carter and James Bracken, from 1964 through 1965. Vee-Jay was the most successful Black-owned record company of the era immediately preceding the appearance of Motown. The label recorded jazz, gospel, and R&B albums by major artists including Wayne Shorter, Wynton Kelly, The Staple Singers, The Five Blind Boys, and Jerry Butler. Notably, they also released music by white artists—the Four Seasons and the Beatles became the label's two biggest sellers. Despite Vee-Jay's commercial success,

its financial situation began to deteriorate in 1963 and worsened by the time of Richard's departure in 1965. Vee-Jay declared bankruptcy in 1966, ceasing operations later that year.

Even though Vee-Jay no longer exists, this invoice is a record of the company's historic significance as the first commercially successful Black-owned record label of the post-World War II period. Vee-Jay paved the way for Berry Gordy's work at Motown (see p. 87) in its ability to reach a crossover audience of white listeners. Where Motown did this through their carefully crafted aesthetic, Vee-Jay broadened their reach during their most successful period by recording and distributing hit recordings by white artists.

After the 1960s successes of Motown and Vee-Jay, Black music entrepreneurs would continue to set trends over the course of the next decade. This turquoise-blue Steinway upright piano sat in songwriter, arranger, and producer Thom Bell's office at the headquarters of Philadelphia International Records (PIR), one of the most prominent labels of the 1970s. Bell and PIR founders Kenny Gamble and Leon Huff, known as "The Mighty Three," were the architects of PIR's distinctive sound, which featured funk rhythms, jazz-influenced melodic structures, and lush orchestrations that included sweeping strings and blaring horns. SWL

Black Music and Hollywood

Black musicians had a complicated relationship with the Hollywood film industry for much of the twentieth century. Films provided talented Black artists with unparalleled visibility, but film studios often confined them to demeaning stereotypical roles. At the same time, the industry provided professional Black musicians with opportunities to build stable and distinguished careers. Materials from the NMAAHC collection document Black musicians' efforts to negotiate their sometimes-fraught positions in Hollywood.

Lena Horne (see also p. 24) wore this dress while appearing as Selina Rogers in the 1943 film *Stormy Weather*. 1943 proved to be an especially significant year in Horne's career, as she appeared in two all-Black Hollywood musicals—*Cabin in the Sky* (seen in the detail of a lobby card above) and *Stormy Weather*. Horne, who began her career as a Cotton Club dancer and vocalist with Charlie Barnet's orchestra before going to Hollywood, was a trailblazer for Black representation in films. Although she was not the first Black woman to sign a contract with a major Hollywood studio (Nina Mae McKinney, for example, signed with MGM in 1929), she was the first who was consistently able to avoid the domestic servant roles to which Black actresses were often confined. This breakthrough was due to both Horne's talent and to the pervasive colorism in Hollywood, which led studios to favor the light-skinned Horne over her darker-skinned peers.

Despite this historic step, many of Horne's film appearances in the 1940s were musical sequences in films focused on white actors, which could easily be edited out before being screened in southern theaters. The all-Black Hollywood musicals *Cabin in the Sky* and *Stormy Weather* were, in Horne's recollection, "the only movies in which I played a character who

was involved in the plot."[57] Horne's dress from *Stormy Weather* represents the rare opportunity these Black productions gave her to play an integral part in a Hollywood film early in her career. At the same time, her glamorous dress reflects the extent to which Horne broke away from the anti-Black stereotypes of 1940s Hollywood.

Black entertainers and musicians made important contributions to the American film industry behind the scenes as well, as demonstrated by Ernie Freeman's long career in Hollywood. After earning a master's degree in music composition from the University of Southern California, Freeman established himself as a studio musician and built a career as an arranger and composer in Hollywood. He

became an in-demand sideman and arranger, working with artists including Sarah Vaughan, Sammy Davis Jr., Frank Sinatra, and Dorothy Dandridge. He won Grammy Awards for his arrangements on Sinatra's 1966 album *Strangers in the Night* and Simon and Garfunkel's 1970 album *Bridge Over Troubled Water* (see p. 130). Among his many projects in Hollywood was the production score for the pilot episode of the 1967 television program *It Takes a Thief*. His work on *It Takes a Thief* provides a snapshot of a high point in Freeman's career, shortly after he received his first Grammy and only a few years before he received his second. A consummate professional, Freeman was able to carve out a distinguished place for himself in a demanding industry.

A few years after *It Takes a Thief*, Curtis Mayfield (1942-1999) demonstrated film soundtracks' potential for social commentary. He was given this plaque after the enormous commercial success of his 1972 soundtrack album *Super Fly*. It was the first Gold Tape Award ever given by Ampex. Mayfield established a brilliant career in the late 1950s and 1960s as a singer-songwriter and guitarist with the soul group the Impressions. During this early period of his career, his songs explored topics of freedom that corresponded closely with the progress of the Civil Rights Movement.

Mayfield left the Impressions in 1970, and *Super Fly* marked his first foray into film soundtracks. He joined Black artists such as Duke Ellington, Quincy Jones, and Isaac Hayes, who successfully explored film scoring after earning acclaim in popular music. The film, which tells the story of a Black cocaine dealer struggling to leave the drug trade in 1970s Harlem, was one of the most iconic films in the burgeoning Blaxploitation genre. Mayfield's soundtrack earned universal praise for its anti-drug message and its frank depictions of poverty, crime, and suffering in inner-city Black communities. His work on *Super Fly* pointed ahead to hip-hop performances exploring similar themes in the following decades, including most notably "The Message" by Grandmaster Flash and the Furious Five.

Mayfield's social commentary in his soundtrack for *Super Fly* exemplifies the ways that Black artists have used their work in Hollywood to call attention to injustices in American society. Although Mayfield did not appear in the film, his hit soundtrack brought new attention to the misery of America's neglected Black inner-city communities. SWL

APPLAUSE

At the turn of the twentieth century, African American musicians began to reach larger audiences performing in vaudeville, local theaters, clubs, and concert halls, launching recording careers, and appearing on radio broadcasts, film, and eventually television, which brought their music to homes across the country. Singer, songwriter, and pianist Una Mae Carlisle (1915–1956) had a career that straddled stage, radio, and screen. This photograph captures her on set at CBS studios in 1944. Sitting at an upright piano and surrounded by Roy Sneed Jr. and the members of the Southern Sons Quartet, Carlisle is only visible from her shoulders up. She is looking to her right and, assumedly, is playing the piano and singing. By 1944 the child prodigy had performed in Europe and the United States and had become the first Black woman to be credited as the composer of a song on Billboard's Harlem Hit Parade charts with her 1941 hit "Walkin' by the River." After years of success on stage and over the airwaves, Carlisle appeared on small screens in living rooms

across the New York City metropolitan area as the host of the *Una Mae Carlisle Show*.

As a pianist, arranger, composer, and vocalist active from the 1930s through the 1950s, Carlisle produced music that is often put into a jazz category, but her sounds were also an early blueprint for pop. Her successful navigation of the unique sonic spaces she created ran parallel with the colorism, racism, and misogyny she encountered in the music business. Carlisle is at the center of this photograph but still obstructed by the instrument she so beautifully commanded. Similarly, her presence as a Black and Indigenous woman making popular music that paved the way for so many others is crucial yet still somewhat hidden.

Black representation on television increased along with the role of mass media in popular culture during the 1970s and '80s. In 1971, Don Cornelius (1936–2012) premiered his long-running syndicated program *Soul Train* in Chicago. The musical variety show was the first of its kind and transcended social boundaries, disseminating positive images of Black youth to millions of viewers. Over time, *Soul Train* expanded its cultural influence by recording up-and-coming artists and hosting an annual award show. Vocalists Dionne Warwick and Luther Vandross hosted the inaugural Soul Train Music Awards on March 23, 1987, for a live broadcast audience. Thirteen years later, in 2000, Whitney Houston received this Female Artist of the Decade Soul Train Music Award.

The award features a metal statuette affixed to a cube-shaped green marble base with a gold plaque. It was one of several Soul Train Awards that Houston won over the years and marked the evolution of her relationship with *Soul Train*'s Black audiences. At more than one ceremony, audiences booed Houston when she won awards. Some booed her to voice

their skepticism of her authenticity, believing her musical talents and successful image were "too pop" or "too white" and not aligned within the canon of "Black" music that the Soul Train Awards celebrated. Houston's career was plagued with conversations about her not being "Black enough" for Black audiences and "too Black" for white audiences, and television programs like *Soul Train* were important spaces where this debate took place.

In the wake of Don Cornelius's entrepreneurship, Ralph McDaniels (b. 1962) started hosting a new kind of program centered around music videos and hip-hop in the 1980s. Armed with a degree in communications/TV/film from the New York Institute of Technology, McDaniels took his role as host of *Video Music Box* very seriously. The show was shot on location in New York City and became a way to bring hip-hop straight from the moment to living rooms via local television.

Inspired by the microphone boxes used by network reporters, this one-of-a-kind object is an example of the many DIY stories from the early days of hip-hop. The mic box is lined with dark grey foam and has a circular cut-out through the center for the microphone. All four sides of the box read "VIDEO MUSIC BOX" so that when seen from any angle, the message is clear. The words were printed out at home just like flyers, then cut into pieces and glued onto the sides of the box. After a while, the pieces started to come apart, so tape was wrapped around the box to keep things in place.

As the impact of *Video Music Box* grew, so did interest in the program's signature shout-outs. The possibility of audience members giving shout-outs to family and friends on camera became so popular that McDaniels felt that the mic box was almost more important than him. If he walked in a room carrying it, everyone asked about shout-outs, and if he walked in without it, they asked where it was and if he would be taping a new show. The mic box and the show became fused with his identity, which he took on as an important responsibility rather than a burden. **TAB**

Michael and Janet Jackson's Scream

In the early 1990s, a new video from Michael Jackson (1958–2009) or Janet Jackson (see also p.30) was a significant event. Networks like MTV hyped up the premieres, and fans gathered in front of TV screens to see what the artists would do next. Michael Jackson's 1983 music video releases accompanying his hits "Billie Jean" and the epic "Thriller" transformed what music videos were and could be. Their popularity was critical to MTV putting videos by Black artists into regular rotation. Jackson's younger sister Janet also frequently had music videos circulating on MTV in the network's first decade. Between 1986 and 1990, she released twelve groundbreaking videos promoting her *Control* (1986) and *Janet Jackson's Rhythm Nation 1814* (1989) albums.

However, by the mid-1990s, Michael's presence had become shrouded in controversy as he faced public scrutiny for alleged misconduct and abuse. In this tumultuous time, Jackson turned to his family for support and music to express himself. Janet vehemently denied allegations directed toward her brother and made time to demonstrate solidarity and provide him with space to speak his mind. In 1995, the siblings came together to record their first duet, "Scream," which became the lead single on Michael's 1995 album, *HIStory: Past, Present and Future, Book I.* The music video was released that summer and premiered on MTV and BET. The video and the lyrical content received immediate acclaim and scrutiny.

The video opens with a large spacecraft traveling away from Earth. Michael and Janet appear alone, and then spend time together and apart in different rooms. They are filmed listening to music, watching anime, playing games, meditating, smashing guitars and vases, dancing, or thoughtfully lounging, as seen in the video storyboard above. Their coordinating outfits are either black or white and contribute to the futuristic and Afrofuturistic aesthetic of the video.

While the lyrics are precise in their reference to the feeling of permanence in Michael's public struggles, everything that makes up the video is fleeting, and at some point, it is clear the pair will have to return to Earth. Games are won or lost, objects get destroyed, and dance sequences end. And in the real world, their props and costumes were only meant to be worn or used for this sole purpose. In opposition to the message and legacy of the song and video, the material things were not created to be permanent.

During scenes in the Gallery room, Janet and Michael sit in a well-worn, off-white leather chair while they individually view paintings and sculptures

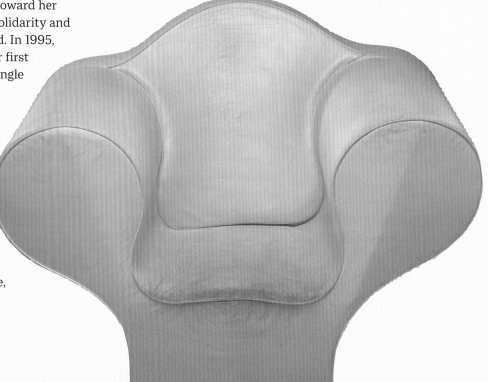

changing in front of them as though they are flipping through TV channels. The modern design of the chair is both inviting and potentially uncomfortable. Despite extensive conservation work by museum staff, it has visible wear and tear on the extended seat and rounded arms, presumably from multiple takes as Michael and Janet moved around on it during filming.

Janet's wardrobe for the video included a few different outfits. A white ensemble, worn briefly in the second half, is a mirror copy of the black outfits she and Michael wear throughout most of the video. The long-sleeved shirt is covered with circular gathered puckers of fabric that create a three-dimensional effect. Not intended to be worn more than necessary for the video shoot, the shirt has a shape and overall texture that are now deteriorated, almost delicate. Similarly, the pair of faux leather pants paired with the shirt cannot quite hug the legs and hips of the mannequin as they did Janet's. Textiles created for specific moments cannot always stand the test of time or even a museum exhibition. Still, this outfit demonstrates how objects can conjure or represent a mood.

The stark, futuristic setting of the "Scream" video has become iconic and continues to influence music videos of the twenty-first century. It received multiple awards and is still one of the most expensive music videos ever made. Janet performed to the song during an emotional tribute to her brother during the 2009 MTV Video Music Awards, less than four months after his death. Her image was removed from the video, and she danced their duet alongside him while the video was projected behind her.

Objects and the moments associated with them are often what we use to shape and hold on to memories. Costumes and props are usually only meant to be worn or used for a fleeting moment in time, but they are things that have a lasting impact on the way a song is remembered and felt. The era of blockbuster video premieres is long behind us. Individual, personalized small screens mean we can watch anything anytime, and we don't need MTV in order to watch music videos. For many artists, and Black artists in particular, music videos provided opportunities to craft visual identities for their music and continue telling the stories they wanted to tell in ways that were truly their own. Now, the things that were never meant to last—a weathered chair, a simple costume—are what is left of those moments. TAB

The Man Who Went to War

This photograph taken on February 20, 1944, features Josh White (1914–1969) playing his guitar alongside (from left to right) Paul Robeson, Ethel Waters, Canada Lee, and D.G. Bridson. (Not seen in this photo is Hall Johnson, who is standing to the proper right of Josh White.) White, along with Robeson and Lee, was part of a loose interracial network of entertainers, intellectuals, and activists advocating for racial equality, workers' rights, and anti-fascism during the World War II years. Others associated with this community included Langston Hughes, Billie Holiday, Lena Horne, Hazel Scott, Orson Welles, and John Hammond. Much of

this activist cabaret culture centered around the Café Society in Greenwich Village, an integrated nightclub that embraced the left-wing politics of the 1930s Popular Front. White was a regular there, often performing protest songs as a featured performer.

With the exception of Bridson, who produced the show, all of the people pictured here were cast members in the 1944 BBC Home Services broadcast of "The Man Who Went to War," a radio play by Langston Hughes (1901–1967) that highlighted the contributions of African American servicemen to the war effort. The narrative, interspersed with folk song selections picked by ethnographer Alan Lomax

and contributions from the Hall Johnson Choir and musical duo Sonny Terry and Brownie McGhee, communicated a story of how African Americans involved themselves in the fight to "win freedom for the world," as Robeson's opening speech states.

A surviving script for "The Man Who Went to War" further contextualizes the little-known show, which never aired in the US because of rights issues. Though recordings were long rumored to be lost, a copy is preserved at the Library of Congress, creating another opportunity to examine Langston Hughes's work. By the musical drama's premiere in 1944, Hughes had spent decades composing lyrics, librettos, and scripts for musicians working in jazz, concert music, and musical theater. In the 1930s, his participation in organizations like the Composers Collective and published pieces advocating for workers' rights, such as *The Worker's Song Book*, drew scrutiny. Hughes's leftist politics fed suspicions that he held Communist beliefs and endangered his career. By taking on commissions and projects like the BBC program in the 1940s that produced patriotic songs and scripts supporting the war effort, Hughes hoped to repair the damage to his reputation.

Josh White, Langston Hughes, Paul Robeson, Hazel Scott, and other Café Society regulars found themselves under serious pressure from government investigations in the late 1940s, as the rise of McCarthyism led to a crackdown on suspected Communist Party sympathizers. White was among the many artists and intellectuals called to testify before the House Un-American Activities Committee, or HUAC, and to disavow any alleged connections with "un-American" organizations. Targeted artists faced intense persecution from the FBI and other government agencies. Some of White's associates, like Alan Lomax and Hazel Scott, left the US in

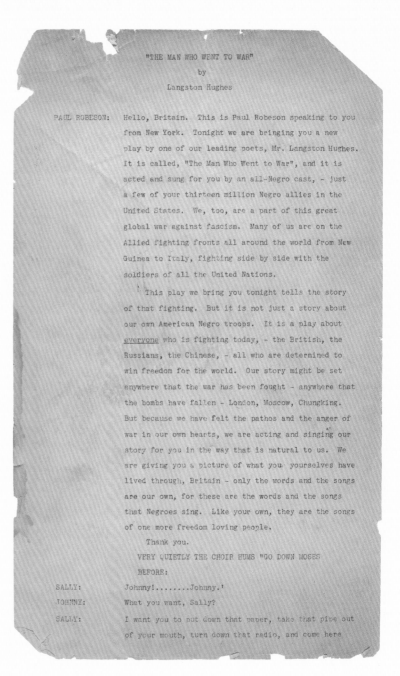

the early 1950s to find work in Europe after being blacklisted. In 1950, the State Department revoked Robeson's passport and forbade him from leaving the country until 1958.

White was able to weather this difficult period because of his voluntary, albeit limited, cooperation with HUAC. Other celebrities like Jackie Robinson also approached their testimony in this fashion. In multiple appearances before the committee, White disavowed "subversive" organizations and distanced himself from Robeson but refused to name Communist Party members. Although White's work with HUAC reflected his desire to protect his family and livelihood, some fellow activist-entertainers such as Harry Belafonte and Eartha Kitt would remain cool to him even after his death for his perceived "betrayal" of the leftist cause.

Following the Red Scare of the 1950s, Josh White received new attention during the Folk Revival of the 1960s that maintained his familiar national popularity. As an elder figure in the folk music community, White saw an increase in work, television engagements, and younger listeners during these years, as middle-America embraced folk music's storytelling and harmonizing voices accompanied by a guitar or banjo. In this stage of his career, White toured colleges and even partnered with the Kaman Corporation's Ovation Guitar division to design innovative new guitars for the new generation of folk musicians. In a 1967 Swedish television broadcast, White appeared with his right leg lifted—in a pose similar to the photograph taken years earlier in 1944 while working on "The Man Who Went to War"—so that this custom-made Josh White Acoustic Guitar model could rest on his thigh. The instrument, completed in 1966, resulted from years of interactions between White and engineers at Ovation to craft their Josh White model of guitars. The collaboration produced a distinctive semi-parabolic fiberglass back made from the company's patented Lyrachord material. The commercial venture anchored by White's public endorsement of a new guitar manufacturer revealed his enduring presence as a significant American musician and entertainer even after his travails in the 1950s. HG & SWL

THE STORY OF THE

JUBILEE

SINGERS

JUBILEE HALL, FISK UNIVERSITY, NASHVILLE, TENN.

WITH THEIR SONGS

Chapter 5

THE POWER(S) OF BLACK MUSIC

After emancipation, the formerly enslaved celebrated their newly found freedom with the hope of sharing in the same opportunities, rights, and privileges that were the legal right of all American citizens. This moment was short-lived. The quest for recognition of full citizenship soon became a freedom struggle of a different kind. The innovations, creativity, and sounds of African American music-making would not only transform the landscape of American culture and society but the global one as well.

The Fisk Jubilee Singers were reportedly the first ensemble to introduce African American music to Europe. This 1892 re-issue of *The Story of the Jubilee Singers: With Their Songs* (see opposite) recounts the story of the group's origins and their rise to international success and includes 139 spirituals fully notated in both open score and in a two-stave keyboard reduction that could be used for rehearsal or performance. Fisk was one of a number of historically Black colleges and universities that were established in the South to educate African Americans after the end of the Civil War. In 1871, when the University was experiencing financial difficulties, a professor formed a choral group of nine students to perform

concert versions of folk spirituals and earn money for the school.

After a successful run of performances in the country in 1872, including the World Peace Festival in Boston and a concert for President Ulysses S. Grant, in 1873 the group embarked on a European tour. The Fisk Jubilee Singers performed for Queen Victoria on behalf of the abolitionist movement and received a stamp of approval from German audiences, which cemented the group's reputation for excellence. Their enthusiastic reception overseas was not only a response to the group's skilled technique and artistic presentation, but also reflected the fascination with African American culture that dated back to the first international appearances of minstrel shows in the 1850s and has continued to the present day.

In the early decades of the twentieth century, as other HBCUs followed the Fisk model and formed their own ensembles to perform and raise money for their institutions, a period of intellectual and creative activity was brewing in Harlem and other urban metropolitan areas throughout the country.

Harlem, a neighborhood in upper Manhattan, was the unofficial capital of this New Negro Movement that began around 1920. It was a magnet for African Americans from the South and diasporic communities from the Caribbean, Africa, and other parts of the world. While the Harlem Renaissance put New York City at the center, the Renaissance was a community spirit of creativity, innovation, cultural affirmation,

During the 1870s, the Fisk Jubilee Singers toured the northern United States and Europe performing spirituals to raise money for the newly established and cash-strapped Fisk University. J.B.T. Marsh published the first edition of *The Story of the Jubilee Singers: With Their Songs* in 1883 to help raise funds for the University. Marsh's book includes text and music for many of the spirituals they popularized, including "Go Down, Moses" and "Down by the River."

Harlem Nightlife

Harlem was the preeminent center of African American culture during the interwar period. The New York City neighborhood attracted thousands of southern Black migrants who began a mass exodus to the North after World War I. From roughly the late 1910s through the mid-1930s, Harlem was the site of the Harlem Renaissance, a blossoming of Black culture that made a global impact. These factors made Harlem a symbolic capital of Black America, and the neighborhood developed a flourishing nightlife that attracted Black and white spectators.

Elmer Simms Campbell's elaborately illustrated 1933 map of Harlem is an affectionate parody of the neighborhood's club scene during this period. The Black cartoonist's illustrations feature major entertainers such as Cab Calloway and Bill "Bojangles" Robinson; restaurants like Tillie's; iconic venues including the Savoy Ballroom; and neighborhood characters like the "Reefer Man" and the "Crab Man." For all its vibrancy and lightheartedness, there is a wistful, nostalgic undertone to Campbell's map. By 1933, the effects of the Great Depression had led many of the great Harlem venues to close. Within a few months of the map's publication, the end of Prohibition put a stop to the lively speakeasy culture that was at the foundation of Harlem's nightlife in the 1920s and early 1930s.

Perhaps the most famous venue in Harlem was the Cotton Club, a nightclub that featured legendary Black artists such as Duke Ellington, Ethel Waters, and Cab Calloway, but admitted only white patrons. The club's dazzling floor shows and glamorous reputation made it a magnet for white tourists, who often left with souvenirs of their visits. This promotional Cotton Club clapper from 1933, for example, commemorates Ethel Waters's starring role with the Duke Ellington Orchestra in *The Cotton Club Parade of 1933*, when she introduced Harold Arlen's and Ted Koehler's new song, "Stormy Weather." Clappers and knockers were frequently used in nightclubs as noisemakers during audience applause and were nice keepsakes after a night on the town. SWL

intellectual engagement, strategizing, collective community-making, and a heightened sense of possibility and promise in achieving real social change, in the dawn of a new century, in Black communities and urban centers across the nation.

Memphis-born Alberta Hunter (1895–1984) started performing professionally at the age of 15 in low-rent venues in Chicago after running away from home. As her popularity grew, she eventually worked her way up to an engagement at Dreamland, the city's most prestigious club, with King Oliver and His Creole Jazz Band. The next stop for Hunter was New York City, where she found her niche as one of the classic blues singers and recorded her first song in 1921 for the short-lived but historically important Black Swan label. An opportunity to fill in for Bessie Smith in the stage show *How Come?* came soon after and her recording career took off. Hunter used her rich voice and precise diction to great effect, alternating between down-home earthiness and high sophistication. Hunter's vocal stylings, like Mamie Smith's and Ethel Waters's, fell into the theatrical or vaudeville blues camp, where the emphasis was on selling a lyric and not a big powerful sound. Hunter continued to record and perform as a solo artist and with numerous jazz musicians through the 1930s. She also contributed to the war effort during World War II, when she became the first African American to head a USO show, visiting twenty-five sites in Europe and the South Pacific.

Retiring from show business in the mid-1950s, Hunter worked as a nurse at Goldwater Memorial

Assembled by Rex Madsen in 1978 for his "dear friend" Alberta Hunter, this collage celebrates the decades-long career and impact of the blues vocalist. Hunter emerged to widespread awareness in 1923, following the release of her "Down Hearted Blues" with Paramount Records. She influenced generations of jazz listeners through her records, journalism, and late-in-life comeback at age 82.

Hospital in New York City for twenty years before she was "re-discovered" in 1977. A renewed interest in the blues led to a resurgence in Hunter's entertainment career and she continued to perform at venues like The Cookery in Greenwich Village and to record until her death in 1984. This collage (see opposite), part of the Museum's collection of materials relating to Jimmie Daniels (see p. 182) and his close friends, captures the journey of Hunter's career with newspaper clippings, photographs, and headlines highlighting her unique history and the joy and excitement that she and her audiences experienced together in connecting the past to the present.

Around the same time Alberta Hunter was launching her recording career, a Phi Beta Kappa graduate of Rutgers University and four-star athlete named Paul Robeson (1898–1976) had arrived in New York to attend Columbia Law School. Away from classes, Robeson was taken under the wing of W.E.B. Du Bois and found himself at the center of an artistic, social, and intellectual awakening. A key part of the Harlem Renaissance's legacy and of Robeson's own experience was a heightened awareness of the collective power of ideological, political, and cultural coming together to challenge and dismantle various manifestations of racial and social injustice, while affirming the humanity and inherent value of the African American experience.

The narrative arc of Robeson's career as an artist and activist began at this time and set the template for musicians and entertainers who chose to use their public platform to protest American racism, social injustice, and other forms of social oppression, in solidarity with freedom struggles around the world. In 1948 Columbia Records released Robeson's album, *Songs of Free Men*, a collection of folk songs from Russia, Spain, Germany, and the United States that he recorded in their native languages (see next page). The songs reflected Robeson's activism, pointing to his support for anti-fascist struggles in Spain (during

Paul Robeson's 1948 album *Songs of Free Men* is a set of four 78 RPM discs containing Robeson's performances of folk songs from Russia, Spain, Germany, and the United States. The album reflects Robeson's lifelong activism, with the repertoire pointing to his support for anti-fascist struggles during the Spanish Civil War and World War II.

the Spanish Civil War) and World War II (against the Nazi regime).

The album cover, designed by Columbia's first art director, Allen Steinweiss (1917–2011), draws upon the graphic artists of the Russian Revolution and the Avant-Garde Movement. The artwork also includes iconography that has historically been associated with the struggle for justice and liberation, such as the raised fist in broken shackles. While the symbolism behind the snake-like creature may be open to interpretation, the image of the swastika on its impaled body makes Robeson's message very clear. It connects the American civil rights struggle with international struggles against fascism and other forms of oppression.

While Robeson re-directed his professional career from American entertainment to concert and public-speaking engagements that addressed racism and social oppression on a global scale, African American men and women such as Willie Mae "Big Mama" Thornton were revolutionizing the field of popular music at a rapid pace.

My singing comes from my experience. I taught myself to sing and to blow harmonica and even to play drums by watchin' other people. I can't read music but I know what I'm singing. I don't sing like nobody but myself.
—Big Mama Thornton, quoted in *Black Diamond Queens*

Willie Mae "Big Mama" Thornton worked for decades to hone her impressive stage presence and sound before joining Peacock Records' roster. The multi-talented entertainer could hold her own on stage as a comedian but was most captivating when growling into the microphone or rapidly moving her way up and down a harmonica like the Hohner models she was known to use.

To Be Young, Gifted and Black

Norwegian popstar Webe Karlsen appears in a red-hued image on the disc sleeve for her first release with Triola Records in 1970. The 45 RPM single saw her pair "Et Smil og Noer Ord" with "Vær Slik Som Du Er." Written in a blue ink is the more precise original English title for the B-side of her single, "To Be Young Gifted and Black."

Written by Nina Simone, with lyrics by Weldon J. Irvine Jr., "To Be Young, Gifted and Black" celebrates young Black people whom Simone felt needed positive role models and messaging to counter the racism that frequently took their innocence at young ages. Within the contexts of her activism, and heavily influenced by the playwright Lorraine Hansberry (1930–1965), she wrote this anthemic addition to her 1969 album *Black Gold*. Simone dedicated the song in memory of her close friend, who had encouraged her for years. Simone's elegant piano playing on the original recording accompanies a choir proudly singing to young Black children. The lyrics are hopeful, imploring youth to seize the world of opportunity awaiting them.

Covering the song, Webe Karlsen curiously translated poet Irvine's words for her Scandinavian audiences. Karlsen's effort to cover the song shortly after Simone's initial release suggests the broader impact "To Be Young, Gifted and Black" had worldwide. This Norwegian single is one of four versions in the Museum's collection. The others include a French translation, "Bel Infant Noir," recorded by Christine Lebail (1971); a Japanese cover performed by Keiko Tsuru (1972); and an English-language version by Jamaican duo Bob and Marcia for Motown's Tamla label (1970). All four recordings were from the personal collection of Nina Simone. As a group, the different versions open lines of questioning for curious listeners. Did the translations successfully impart the song's message? Moreover, how did Nina Simone feel about these international covers of her music? HG

In her book *Black Diamond Queens* (2020),[58] Maureen Mahon identifies Willie Mae "Big Mama" Thornton (1926–1984) as an important precursor in the evolution of rock and roll. Born in Ariton, Alabama, Thornton was one of the R&B artists whose sound influenced rock and roll. Her deep voice was powerful but conveyed the nuances of feelings and emotions even as she belted out a lyric. Standing nearly six feet tall, her physical appearance amplified the strength of her voice. She upended gendered stereotypes in how she dressed and expanded expectations about female vocalists in her ability to play the harmonica (see p. 174) and the drums.

Thornton launched her recording career when she moved to Houston, Texas, and signed a contract with Don Robey's Peacock Records, a Black-owned label founded in 1949. After a couple of failed singles, she recorded "Hound Dog," which was especially written for her by songwriters Jerry Leiber and Mike Stoller. Thornton had moderate commercial success with the song, which sold more than half a million copies. Still, Elvis Presley's 1956 cover version sold ten million copies and led to his coronation as the innovator and the designated "King of Rock and Roll."

Photographer Anthony Barboza (b. 1944) was influential in changing the way Black and Brown women and men were represented in fashion and advertising in the US. His photograph of Stax recording artist Isaac Hayes (1942–2008) and model Pat Evans (b. 1944) honors the visual beauty of the Black body. It reflects the persona that was central to Hayes's public allure and musical sensibilities. Hayes initially joined Stax as a songwriter and producer, and his first effort as a recording artist received minimal attention. However, his second studio album, *Hot Buttered Soul* (1969), was a convention-breaking masterpiece that sold over a million copies and was the first Stax recording to go gold.

Photographer Anthony Barboza opened his New York City commercial photography studio in 1969 after being discharged from the Navy. Quickly, Barboza secured lucrative opportunities working with corporate clients and shooting magazine spreads for white and Black publications. In 1971, he photographed Isaac Hayes and Pat Evans clad in pan-African-inspired garments for *Essence* magazine.

Black Futures

A dynamic and evolving concept, Afrofuturism is the reimagining and reframing of the past, present, and future through a Black cultural lens. In music, Afrofuturism reaches the global masses, providing a sonic platform for the expression of futurist ideas in new musical sounds, languages, concepts, and genres. From the avant-garde jazz of Sun Ra to the present-day musical explorations of Janelle Monáe, musicians have created, adapted, and utilized new musical technologies to make new sounds and map out wider sonic landscapes that liberate music, and the artist, from the racialized constructions of genre and identity. Following Sun Ra's example, many musicians embraced the Afrofuturist concept he pioneered by employing costumes as an extension of their philosophical statements about liberation and futurist musings. Bernie Worrell (1944–2016) donned imaginative clothing like this custom-made cape over a purple shirt and pair of pants to support his role as the "Wizard of Woo" when stepping onstage with P-Funk (formerly Parliament-Funkadelic) during their 1996 Mothership Reconnection Tour.

Known primarily as a sideman, Bernie Worrell was a keyboardist, songwriter, and musical director whose work influenced the sound and artistic direction of 1970s funk. His visionary musical directions helped map out the sonic landscapes that gave Parliament-Funkadelic its cosmic and ethereal sound. Recognized at a young age as a prodigy, Worrell studied music at The Juilliard School and the New England Conservatory of Music. Artistically and consciously guided by his affinity for purple, the back of Worrell's cape, stitched with images of music notes and a grand piano placed among the stars above the flowing

length of fabric with waving lines of gold and purple, visually communicates his love-infused philosophy of "Woo." As the "Wizard of Woo," Worrell employed a futurist approach utilizing studio technology to create new musical effects, such as the synthesized, futuristic sounds heard on the song "Mothership Connection." KMS

The album—consisting of four tracks, with three of them running over nine minutes—changed the game for Black artists in the music industry, as Hayes demonstrated the commercial viability of concept albums by Black artists. Hayes's sensual sounds and public presentation on full display in the cover art for his albums, in photographs, and his stage performances exuded a form of masculine glamour. Through gold chains, furs, and bald head, Hayes shifted the racist trope of the Black man as a dangerous threat to a more sensual human being who instilled comfort over fear. This is clearly illustrated by Hayes's moniker, "Black Moses," the title of his fifth album.

Hayes's musical persona did not demand space to express his sense of selfhood but claimed it as an inalienable right. His legacy, from bold declarations and incisive social commentary to trends in fashion and adornment, is evident in hip-hop and rap of the 1980s and '90s.

Graffiti artist, music video, and film producer Fred Brathwaite (b. 1959), better known as Fab 5 Freddy, was the original host of *Yo! MTV Raps*, which ran on MTV from 1988 to 1995. At the time of the show's premiere, hip-hop jewelry styles included thick gold rope necklaces, crosses, heavy medallions, and Mercedes logos. However, Freddy wanted something unique and worked with Tito the Jeweler, aka "Manny," to design this gold and diamond ring. Fab 5 Freddy's "MTV" ring was one of his signature pieces. MTV played a critical role in making the style, sound, and voices of hip-hop available to millions of people across the globe, and Fab 5 Freddy's ring symbolized his status as hip-hop's most visible ambassador as he captured the voices and stories about hip-hop's origins and evolution within the communities of people and places that inspired it.

This chapter's title is informed by Samuel Floyd's groundbreaking book *The Power of Black Music* (1995), where he introduced a new way of listening to African American music.[59] As we have explored through the music-related objects in the Museum's collection, the power of Black music is extended in multiple ways and activated individually and collectively through different identity formations, community values, and historical movements.

In 2015, as the outrage that fueled the Black Lives Matter movement grew, Janelle Monáe (b. 1985) released a new protest anthem, "Hell You Talmbout," on her Wondaland Records label. The song was

Yo! MTV Raps was the first hip-hop program on mainstream television. The show ran from 1988 until 1995 and was originally hosted by artist, filmmaker, and video DJ, Fab 5 Freddy. To commemorate the achievement, Fab 5 Freddy donned this gleaming "MTV" ring, designed by Tito the Jeweler, on the middle finger of his right hand.

stark in its simplicity compared to Monáe's concept-based albums and performances, where she reclaims the historical narrative of oppression to create a universe through a Black feminist and Afrofuturist lens. Comprised of a repetitive chant and a drumline, each utterance of "Say His Name" or "Say Her Name" is preceded by the name of a Black man or woman who had been killed by the police or vigilantes. In the fall of 2021, Monáe released a follow-up to "Hell You Talmbout" titled "Say Her Name," a 17-minute single featuring fifteen other Black musical artists and activists. Through a material culture lens, this one photograph points to an overlapping network of narratives, histories, and experiences activated by individual and community actions connected by the past, present, and future.

Singer and actress Janelle Monáe participates in a Black Lives Matter rally in Atlanta, Georgia. Monáe and an unidentified woman hold a sign with the name Alexia Christian written on it. Christian was killed in a police shootout while sitting handcuffed in the backseat of a patrol car on April 30, 2015.

Happy Birthday to Ya!

Efforts to establish a national holiday honoring Martin Luther King Jr. began shortly after King's assassination in 1968. Congressman John Conyers introduced a bill for a federal holiday honoring King that year and continued to reintroduce the bill each year for fifteen years. His efforts received important support from the Southern Christian Leadership Conference and the Congressional Black Caucus. In 1979, fifty years after King's birth, Coretta Scott King and the staff of the King Center launched a nationwide effort to establish a King holiday and collected 300,000 signatures for a petition to do so. The bill failed to pass because of opposition from the Republican party.

After the defeat of the 1979 bill, Stevie Wonder (b. 1950) stepped in to become the holiday's most famous advocate. A 1965 meeting with King in Chicago had made an important impression on Wonder, and his music became increasingly socially and politically conscious after King's assassination. Many of his classic songs from the 1970s, including "Higher Ground," "Living for the City," and "You Haven't Done Nothin'," reflect Wonder's growing activist spirit. Wonder would eventually lend his voice to causes ranging from anti-racism to AIDS charities and humanitarian aid in Africa.

Wonder wrote a new song called "Happy Birthday," which became a hit single after its release in 1980, to advocate for the King holiday. He also made appearances at King birthday commemorations, as in this 1981 photograph by Milton Williams taken on the grounds of the Washington Monument. Pictured from left to right in the front row are LeBaron Taylor, vice president of CBS Records; Kenny Gamble, co-founder of Philadelphia International Records; Lula Hardaway, Stevie Wonder's mother; Samuel H. Jordan, a Washington, DC city government official, Washington, DC City Council Chairman Dave Clark (standing behind Hardaway and Jordan); Reverend Jesse Jackson; Stevie Wonder; US Representative John Conyers; singer Johnnie Taylor; and Philadelphia DJ Georgie Woods.

Wonder both funded lobbying efforts and worked with Coretta Scott King to collect six million signatures for a petition which was presented to the Speaker of the House in 1982. This time, the King holiday bill received significant bipartisan support, passed both houses of Congress, and was signed into law by President Reagan on November 2, 1983. "Happy Birthday" has remained prominent in Black culture, with birthday gatherings sometimes singing it as an alternative to the traditional song, "Happy Birthday to You." SWL

Jimmie Daniels, Renaissance Man

In the mid-1920s, a young Jimmie Daniels (1907-1984) arrived in New York City to attend classes at Bird's Business Institute in the Bronx. Over the course of the next decade, he would become a well-known entertainer, a prominent socialite, and an iconic figure in the city's gay community. Daniels was born in Laredo, Texas, in 1907 and raised in Little Rock, Arkansas. After completing his studies at Bird's Business Institute, he returned home to Little Rock, where he worked as an administrative assistant to the president of the Century Life Insurance Company. But Daniels, a talented singer and entertainer, found himself longing for the vibrant performing arts scene he had left behind.

He moved back to New York City in 1928 to pursue a career as a cabaret and theater performer. His first professional job was at Harlem's Hot-Cha nightclub. Daniels broke into the world of Harlem nightlife amidst the Harlem Renaissance. Fueled by the Great Migration of Black southerners to Harlem, the Renaissance helped to establish the Manhattan neighborhood's place as the cultural capital of twentieth-century Black America. Daniels developed close friendships with notable artists and intellectuals, including vocalist Alberta Hunter, sculptor Richmond Barthé, and philosopher Alain Locke.

This photograph from the early 1930s of Jimmie Daniels is likely by Harlem Renaissance-era photographer Carl Van Vechten. Although this rare photograph has not been definitively connected to Van Vechten, it has stylistic similarities to other photographs of Daniels that the famous patron took during the same period. In particular, Daniels appears shirtless in both this photo and a 1933 Van Vechten portrait where Daniels poses with a bust of himself by Richmond Barthé. The sensuality of this image, in which a shirtless Daniels peeks at the viewer through artfully placed vegetation, communicates Daniels's position as an icon of the vibrant gay nightlife that flourished in Harlem in the 1930s, '40s, and '50s. From the start of his professional singing career at Harlem's Hot-Cha nightclub in the 1930s, Daniels attracted a devoted following of gay fans with his sophisticated renditions of jazz standards and showtunes.

Daniels had two successful stints performing in Europe in the 1930s. From 1933 to 1934, he performed in Monte Carlo and London. He was back in Europe in 1935, only a year after he had returned home to New York City. This time, he spent four years performing in Paris. Daniels left France just before the outbreak of World War II and opened his own supper club in Harlem in November 1939. Daniels's eponymous nightclub developed a reputation as

a sophisticated establishment that hosted famous artists, actors, athletes, and socialites.

World War II continued to escalate, with the United States entering the conflict in December 1941 after the bombing of Pearl Harbor. Daniels enlisted in the military on October 17, 1942, as one of the many African Americans who joined the fight against the Axis powers. Although his honorable discharge record lists his military occupational specialty as "supply clerk," Daniels served primarily as an entertainer, giving regular performances to the troops to raise morale. As a record of his service, Daniels's honorable discharge points both to the support that Black musicians and entertainers provided for the war effort and to the ongoing contributions of gay men in the American military.

Jimmie Daniels' Nightclub closed during the war, and Daniels returned to a busy schedule of performances after his discharge in 1945. By 1950, he had begun the most famous professional engagement of his career as the MC of the Bon Soir supper club in Greenwich Village. The Bon Soir hosted up-and-coming artists, including a young Barbra Streisand, during Daniels's tenure.

Daniels may have owned this cane during this period. The top of the cane is carved in the image of an African American man's head. There is an ivory ring directly below the head and the bottom of the cane has a metal tip. Although it is impossible to know precisely when Daniels acquired and began using this cane, its unusual design reflects the showmanship that made him a popular entertainer and beloved nightclub host for decades. This object raises questions about Daniels's life and career that may be impossible to answer. Whose head is represented in the cane's carved handle—is it Daniels, or someone else? Did Daniels use this cane while he was hosting, or as part of his performance routine? These and other questions represent aspects of Daniels's story and Black LGBTQ history in need of exploration and documentation. SWL

183

Instrumental Women

NATIONAL ACADEMY OF RECORDING ARTS & SCIENCES
TERRI LYNE CARRINGTON
Artist/Producer
BEST JAZZ INSTRUMENTAL ALBUM – 2013
MONEY JUNGLE: PROVOCATIVE IN BLUE

I
n 2013, history was made off-camera at the National Academy of Recording Arts & Sciences' annual award ceremony when Terri Lyne Carrington (see also p. 52) became the first woman to win the Grammy Award for Best Jazz Instrumental Album. The text-heavy plaque with golden script beneath the gleaming gramophone recognizes her work as an "Artist/Producer" on her 2013 album *Money Jungle: Provocative in Blue*. This award documents a monumental achievement for women working in jazz and is an embodiment of Carrington's efforts to address gender inequalities through her music and recent role in founding the Berklee Institute of Jazz and Gender Justice at the Berklee College of Music in Boston. Carrington's Grammy joins a body of materials

in the NMAAHC collection challenging established histories of jazz that often canonize a long list of men.

Carrington has had a lifetime of music-making that informs her music and teaching style. Her father, Matt Carrington, noticed his daughter's musicality early on and fostered her talent by going to jam sessions with her, where she would sit on drums while he played his tenor saxophone. From those early days she went on to play with Clark Terry (1920–2015), completed studies at Berklee, and transitioned into a professional career that has kept her consistently working for decades. Her trajectory has been groundbreaking and revelatory of the obstacles women working in jazz encounter that impede them from regularly being recognized for their achievements.

For generations, women working in jazz have navigated an industry governed by men who dismissed their work as novelties or unsellable. Female instrumentalists were frequently criticized for being too physically weak to play jazz. Sometimes even fellow women like bandleader and vocalist Blanche Calloway (1902–1978), who greatly influenced male acts like her brother Cab, refused to hire women in her band, despite the limiting gendered obstacles they also faced. The societal consensus in jazz's early years was that it was undignified for women to perform jazz. These attitudes fed their erasure from the historical record and contributed to assumptions widely held in the jazz community that women could not and did not play. However, the material culture of jazz tells a different story and shows that women have led lively, successful jazz careers as instrumentalists and composers.

Calling folks near Springfield, Ohio, to "Dance to the Smooth Rhythm of [the] Harlem Playgirls," a 1937 poster captures a moment on the lengthy trail of one-nighters that introduced the Harlem Playgirls

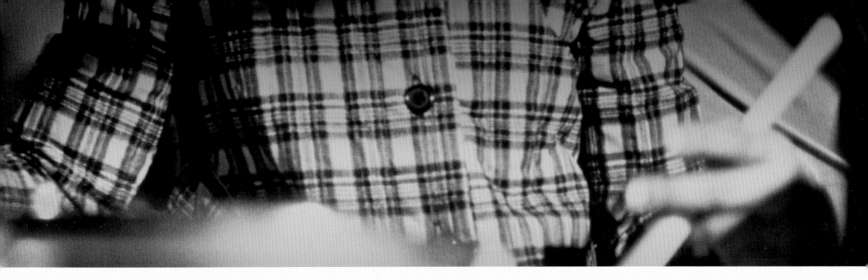

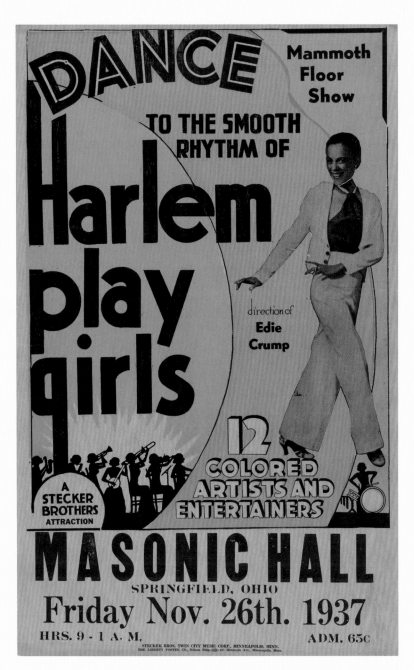

to audiences in vaudeville theaters and ballrooms nationwide. Just days prior to this engagement, their pictured bandleader, Edie Crump, had been hospitalized after she attempted to take her own life. Her bandmates postulated to reporters with the *Afro-American* that her so-called "jittery" behavior resulted from exhaustion caused by uninterrupted work and constant traveling since they first embarked from Minnesota in 1935. It is likely the difficult combination of isolating touring, sexism, and dangerous encounters with racism that the women experienced on the road, which dissuaded many Black women from this path, impacted Crump.

In the 1930s, Crump alongside her "Queens of Swing" projected a modern femininity and lifestyle. Experimenting with gender-bending wardrobes, perhaps most readily apparent in Crump's characteristic white suits, the group leaned into the freedom of expression available to them as musicians. The members' abilities to double on multiple instruments not typically associated with women, such as saxophones and brasswinds, while performing arrangements by the band's trombonist Lela Julius, impressed audiences and became a crucial component in disseminating jazz to areas within the United States outside of major urban centers.

Following the path that female musicians like the Harlem Playgirls opened, younger women trained in classical music or local churches made names for themselves working in jazz during the 1950s. During this period, pianist Alice McLeod Coltrane (1937–2007) emerged in Detroit as a second-generation bebop musician. An October 26, 1970, segment of *Black Journal* featured an interview with Coltrane at home in her music room, capturing an intimate look at her artistry and creative synergy with her late husband, John Coltrane.[60] While discussing

her perspectives on making music, Alice Coltrane is filmed skillfully running her hands along her harp's strings. She picked up the harp in 1965 and worked it into her compositions. She appreciated the instrument's connections to ancient Egypt and its harmonic setting that differed from the piano, which had been her primary instrument. Her harping style became a prominent voice in the music she and John collaborated on that brought spirituality and Eastern philosophies into jazz's musical vocabularies during the 1960s and '70s. The segment spotlights the multiple roles that she, like many female musicians, managed as performers, composers, bandleaders, spouses, and mothers. HG

Rock's True Colors

A red 1973 Cadillac Eldorado convertible is a beacon for visitors to the NMAAHC's *Musical Crossroads* exhibition. Donated by Chuck Berry (1926–2017), this Cadillac helps tell stories not only of transportation, movement, and youth culture, but also of personal freedom and agency.

During the star-studded performance that anchors the 1984 documentary film *Chuck Berry: Hail! Hail! Rock 'n' Roll*, Berry sits on top of the backseat as the car is driven onto the stage of the Fox Theatre in St. Louis, Missouri. This act is a moment of defiance and self-declaration. That same theater had turned Berry away many years prior because he was Black. At this moment, with this car, Berry is not hiding. He is commanding a moment that resulted from his many years of navigating the racially segregated music industry. With the car and his guitar, he proclaims

and demonstrates his undeniable contributions to American music as one of the foundational sonic architects of rock and roll.

The roots of rock and roll rest in African American music traditions, from gospel to the "race music" of rhythm and blues. One constant element has been the guitar. While early vital figures such as Sister Rosetta Tharpe and Muddy Waters favored semi-acoustic models, later legends such as Jimi Hendrix were known for their signature sounds on solid-body electric models. Hendrix was also known for his often-flamboyant style, as seen above in 1968, playing an electric guitar with his mouth. Years later, a multicolored ESP Mirage electric guitar was Vernon Reid's main instrument during a critical moment both for the band Living Colour and for Black representation in contemporary rock and roll. In 1988

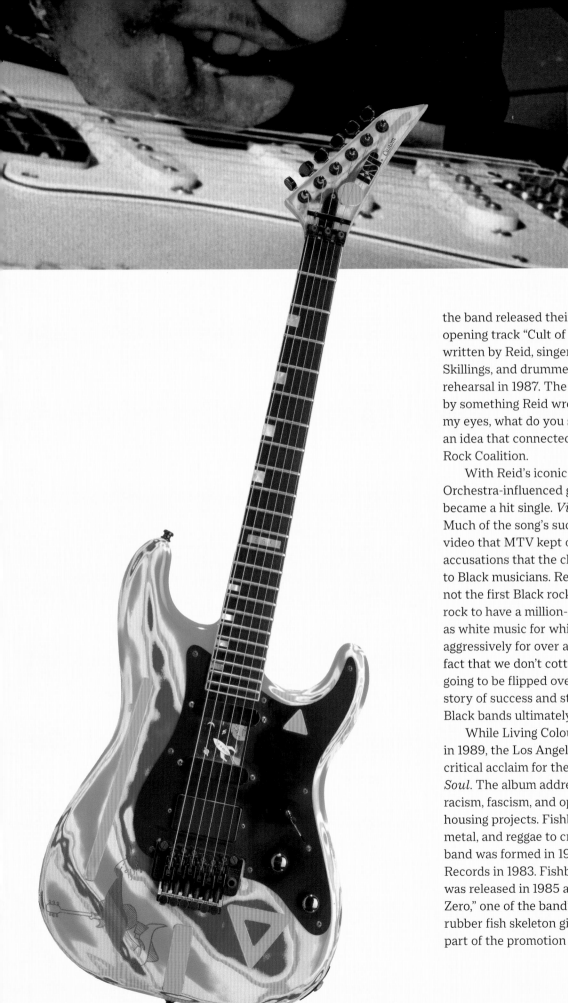

the band released their debut album, *Vivid*, with the opening track "Cult of Personality." The song was written by Reid, singer Corey Glover, bassist Muzz Skillings, and drummer Will Calhoun during a band rehearsal in 1987. The lyrical content was sparked by something Reid wrote in his notebook: "Look in my eyes, what do you see? The cult of personality," an idea that connected to Reid's work with the Black Rock Coalition.

With Reid's iconic Led Zeppelin- and Mahavishnu Orchestra-influenced guitar riff, "Cult of Personality" became a hit single. *Vivid* went platinum by July 1989. Much of the song's success was fueled by the music video that MTV kept on repeat, almost answering accusations that the channel was not paying attention to Black musicians. Reid stated that Living Colour was not the first Black rock band, "just the first in hard rock to have a million-selling record. The idea of rock as white music for white people has been promoted aggressively for over a quarter of a century, and the fact that we don't cotton to that doesn't mean it's going to be flipped over overnight."[61] Living Colour's story of success and struggle was not isolated, as other Black bands ultimately faced similar fates.

While Living Colour was climbing the charts in 1989, the Los Angeles band Fishbone celebrated critical acclaim for their 1988 album *Truth and Soul*. The album addressed topics such as families, racism, fascism, and oppression in lower-income housing projects. Fishbone combined punk, funk, ska, metal, and reggae to create their signature sound. The band was formed in 1979 and signed to Columbia Records in 1983. Fishbone's self-titled debut EP was released in 1985 and featured "Party at Ground Zero," one of the band's most well-known songs. This rubber fish skeleton given out on April Fool's Day was part of the promotion package for the EP. Even after

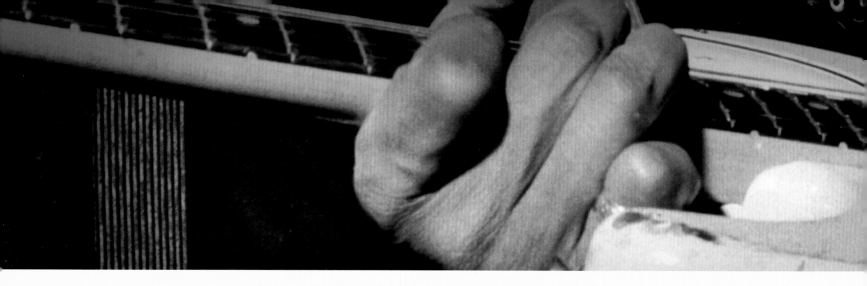

performing on the 1993 Lollapalooza tour, the band was dropped by their record label and never achieved the kind of commercial success their popularity and critical acclaim suggested. As with Living Colour, the music industry was unwilling to make room for a band in the white-dominated space that rock and roll had become.

Years before Fishbone and Living Colour tried to infiltrate a genre that Chuck Berry helped create, Atlanta-based band Mother's Finest were creating their own version of funk-infused rock and roll. Founded with both Black and white members, Mother's Finest's sound did not fit into pre-conceived ideas of style and genre. This jacket worn by bassist Jerry "Wyzard" Seay (b. 1952) features words that can be found in the band's lyrics and themes such as trust, hate, passion, war, peace, and freedom.

Mother's Finest formed in 1970, and the band's impact was felt almost immediately. Many bands that were also experimenting with blending genres covered their songs during performances in the 1970s and early 1980s. In 2007, Prince put Mother's Finest back into the spotlight when he performed "Baby Love," a song from the band's 1977 album, *Another Mother Further*. Prince's version can be heard on his live album *Indigo Nights*, featuring Shelby J. on lead vocals. However, despite acclaim and success within music communities, the band were not embraced nor given space of their own by the music industry, a representation of the continued complex and imbalanced narrative that has been placed upon rock and roll music. TAB

Women Fashioning Hip-Hop

Women have been part of hip-hop's evolution from the start. They scratched vinyl, grabbed mics, and pressed record on what would become one of African American culture's most dynamic and influential elements. Furthermore, women participated in and influenced one of the main pillars of hip-hop culture: fashion.

The 1970s witnessed the rise of streetwear, from denim to tennis shoes to casual dress, all in reaction to the Black Power Movement, which shunned the "respectability politics" woven into the previous generation's style. When hip-hop emerged in the late 1970s and early 1980s, the already present emphasis on the vernacular style of Black urban life was refined into the iconic looks we know today: tracksuits, ballcaps and Kangol hats, pristine sneakers, gold chains, and denim—and often in colorful, loud, eye-catching prints that reflected pan-African and African American pride.

Women in hip-hop were drawn to similar aesthetics. They, however, encountered a conundrum, wherein their style signaled their inclusion in hip-hop but they would risk being treated as mere eye candy if they fully leaned into broader feminine trends in fashion. In the 1980s, women in hip-hop navigated the emergence of a culture that set the trends. They also demanded respect for their prowess on the 1s and 2s or on the mic through their own adaptation of the hip-hop aesthetic.

Black women have historically contended with stereotypes and assumptions about their womanhood and sexuality. The earliest women in hip-hop adopted the swagger and baggy clothes of their male counterparts, not only for protection from harm but also to establish their equality on the mic. Lana Michele Moorer (b. 1970), better known as MC Lyte, is considered a pioneer in hip-hop. She expressed her authority in both her seminal single "Paper Thin"—about a philandering boyfriend—and her style in the music video—tracksuit, varsity jacket, sneakers, and turtleneck, with doorknocker earrings swinging as she confronts said boyfriend on the New York subway with his arms around big-haired, acrylic-wearing women.

These gold and blue satin Converse sneakers were customized for MC Lyte, a Sigma Gamma Rho sorority member. Text is embroidered in blue on the outside heel of each shoe. The left shoe reads "MC LYTE," and the right shoe reads "est. 1922" in reference to the Black sorority's founding year. Customizing shoes and clothing with personal elements has remained a popular trend in hip-hop fashion.

Though MC Lyte and other women rappers of her generation wore streetwear that was almost unisex in fashion, the addition of large earrings, neatly pressed or crimped hair (often dyed a bold shade of auburn), and pastel colors to their sartorial repertoire marked a striving towards a specific expression of womanhood in hip-hop. This is most present in the *Female*

Rappers, Class of '88 photograph taken by Janette Beckman. Seated in the center, MC Lyte is flanked by several other pioneers, including Sparky D, Sweet Tee, MC Peaches, Yvette Money, Ms. Melodie, Synquis, Roxanne Shante, and Finesse. In a nod to the soon-to-be ubiquitous melding of R&B and hip-hop, and the bold bombast of female rappers in the 1990s, the singer Millie Jackson, whose songs often featured talking/rapping sections, kneels in the center of the group with her arms raised.

Pioneering hip-hop group J. J. Fad was one of the original acts signed to Ruthless Records by Eazy-E. The original lineup included Dania Birks (Baby D), Juana Burns (MC J.B.), Anna Cash (Lady Anna), Fatima Shaheed (O.G. Rocker), and Juanita Lee (Crazy J). In 1987, J. J. Fad released the track "Anotha Ho," with "Supersonic" as the B-side to the album. All but Baby D and MC J.B. soon left the group and were replaced by Michelle Franklin (Sassy C) and

D.J. Train. The new lineup re-recorded "Supersonic" in 1988, re-releasing it as an A-side. The electro-charged single was certified gold by the Recording Industry Association of America and was nominated for a Grammy Award in 1988 for Best Rap Performance. This satin jacket represents J. J. Fad's early time in the spotlight and their connection to Los Angeles. The front is embroidered in white (see above) with "Ruthless/Atco Records. M.C.J.B." and the back with "J.J. Fad in Effect." The group had the custom jackets made at Slauson Swap Meet in Compton, a Los Angeles neighborhood that in 1988 was becoming well represented in hip-hop.

By the end of the 1980s, women had begun to make space for themselves in the still male-dominated genre. The impact of Black women not only controlling their image and status as rappers, but also their own fashion, was a culmination of the struggle for women to shape and develop their role in hip-hop culture. **TAB & AT**

Endnotes

1. Jules Prown quoted in Karen Harvey, ed., *History and Material Culture a Student's Guide to Approaching Alternative Sources*, 2nd ed. (New York: Routledge, 2018), 8.

2. Katrina Dyonne Thompson, *Ring Shout, Wheel About: The Racial Politics of Music and Dance in North American Slavery* (Urbana, IL: University of Illinois Press, 2014), 77.

3. Ibid., 73–4.

4. In 1982, Eubie Blake celebrated his "99th birthday." However, although Blake claimed to have been born in 1883, in 2003, almost twenty years after his death, historians confirmed through newly available records his birth year as 1887.

5. The Recording Academy introduced the Soul Gospel category in 1969 to acknowledge that gospel music influences contemporary popular music. The category was discontinued in 1991, and was eventually replaced by Best Gospel Album and Best Roots Gospel Album in the 2010s. The honor came to the Dixie Hummingbirds after recording and performing for close to forty years.

6. The House of God, Jewell Dominion, was established by Bishop Mattie Lou Jewell in the 1930s as The House of God, which is the Church of the Living God, Pillar and Ground of the Truth.

7. Pete Cosey and George Cole, "Interview: Pete Cosey," *The Last Miles*, n.d.: https://www.thelastmiles.com/interviews-pete-cosey/ (accessed July 5, 2022).

8. Steve Marzullo, personal communication with Dwandalyn R. Reece, February 10, 2022.

9. See Amiri Baraka, "Blind Tom: The Continuity of Americana," in Baraka, *Digging: The Afro-American Soul of American Classical Music* (Berkeley, CA: University of California Press, 2009).

10. Shanthy Nambiar, "Kennedy Center Picks 5 Live Ones," *Washington Post*, September 9, 1993.

11. Cynric R. Williams, *A Tour Through the Island of Jamaica, from the Western to the Eastern End, in the Year 1823* (London: Hunt and Clarke, 1826): facing page 100.

12. Tanisha C. Ford, *Liberated Threads: Black Women, Style, and the Global Politics of Soul* (Chapel Hill, NC: University of North Carolina Press, 2015), 29.

13. X Clan, "Funkin' Lesson," from the album *To the East, Blackwards*, released by 4th & Broadway, 1990.

14. bell hooks, "In Our Glory," in *Beyond The Frame: Women of Color and Visual Representations*, ed. Neferti X.M. Tadiar and Angela Y. Davis (New York: Palgrave Macmillan, 2005), 1–4.

15. Hall Johnson, "Notes on the Negro Spiritual," in *Readings in Black American Music*, ed. Eileen Southern (New York: W.W. Norton & Company, 1983), 272.

16. In 1955, Robert McFerrin Sr. became the first African American man to sing at the Metropolitan Opera.

17. See Jacqueline Cogdell DjeDje, "Context and Creativity: William Grant Still in Los Angeles," *Black Music Research Journal* 31, no. 1 (2011): 1–27.

18. *Afro-American Symphony*, composed by William Grant Still, was the first symphony written by an African American to be performed for a US audience by a leading orchestra. It was premiered in 1931 by the Rochester Philharmonic Orchestra, and was performed by over thirty orchestras around the United States—including the New York Philharmonic at Carnegie Hall—in the 1930s.

19. "National Capital Topics," *New York Age*, September 27, 1890.

20. See Olly Wilson, "The Heterogeneous Sound Ideal in African-American Music," in *New Perspectives on Music: Essays in Honor of Eileen Southern*, ed. Josephine Wright and Samuel A. Floyd Jr. (Warren, MI: Harmonie Park Press, 1992), 327–38.

21. Jinsol Jung, Jenny Wagnon Courts, Tonya Simpson, and Steve Osunsami, "The Gap Band's Charlie Wilson discusses hit song's connection to 1921 Tulsa massacre," ABC News, April 6, 2021, https://abcnews.go.com/US/gap-band-leader-discusses-hit-songs-connection-1921/story?id=76886953.

22. Ralph Ellison, *The Collected Essays of Ralph Ellison*, ed. John F. Callahan (New York: Modern Library, 2003), 440.

23. Regina Bradley, *Chronicling Stankonia: The Rise of the Hip-Hop South* (Chapel Hill, NC: University of North Carolina Press, 2021), 8–9.

24. Rob Kenner, *The Marathon Don't Stop: The Life and Times of Nipsey Hussle* (New York: Atria Books, 2020), 234.

25. This chapter draws its title—"I Wish I Knew How it Would Feel to be Free"—from the song composed by jazz pianist and educator Dr. Billy Taylor in 1952. Originally composed as an instrumental, the melody became one of the freedom songs of the Civil Rights Movement, when Nina Simone released a version with lyrics on her 1967 album, *Silk and Soul*.

26. Howard W. Odum and Guy B. Johnson, *Negro Workaday Songs* (Chapel Hill, NC: University of North Carolina Press, 1926), 78.

27. David C. Driskell, *Two Centuries of Black American Art* (Los Angeles, CA: Los Angeles County Museum of Art, 1976), 180.

28. bell hooks, *Art on My Mind: Visual Politics* (New York: The New Press, 1995).

29. Billie Holiday with William Dufty, *Lady Sings the Blues* (New York: Penguin Books, 1992), 61.

30. This ankle-length black lace cocktail gown worn by Billie Holiday was acquired by the Museum along with a signed agreement on Associated Booking Corp. letterhead dated April 30, 1954, in which Holiday agrees to have a certain amount deducted from each engagement to repay a debt to Wilma Gowns. One might assume that the purchase referenced on the signed agreement is directly related to this gown. A material culture study would require a closer examination of the gown and additional research on Wilma Gowns, Holiday's relationship with Joe Glaser and Associated Booking Corporation, photographs of Holiday during that period, and what was going on in her life at that time.

31. Richard Rogers wrote the part of Barbara Woodruff especially for Diahann Carroll. The story takes place in Paris and follows the love affair between fashion model Woodruff and the expatriate Pulitzer Prize-winning author David Jordan (co-star Richard Kiley), who meet, fall in love, but eventually end their relationship when David returns to the United States. The fact that David and Barbara were an interracial couple was quite daring, given the time period, but the topic of race was never raised in the plot.

32. In an interview with NPR shortly after Diahann Carroll's death in 2019, her daughter, Suzanne Kay, explained, "It became really clear to her by the reaction that everything she did was going in the history books. She carried that pretty elegantly throughout her life." The published article continues: "That elegance shocked white America...and it also provided Black women with an aspirational role model. The style and class may have been new to white people, but [Kay stated] 'we as Black people knew women like that....'" Kay also noted that her mother was "very aware" that her choice of roles "was changing the dialog. She was doing something different." https://www.npr.org/2020/07/14/891177902/remembering-the-divine-diahann-carroll (accessed July 7, 2022).

33. Juanita Hall was the first African American to receive a Tony Award. In 1950, she was

named Best Supporting Actress for her role as Bloody Mary in Rodgers and Hammerstein's *South Pacific*.

34. John H. Johnson, "Publisher's Statement," *Ebony* 31, no. 1 (November 1975): 30.

35. See Reebee Garofalo, "Industrializing African American Popular Music," in *Issues in African American Music: Power, Gender, Race, Representation*, ed. Portia K. Maultsby and Mellonee V. Burnim (New York: Routledge, 2017), 90.

36. Ibid., 95.

37. *Cashbox* (also known as *Cash Box*) was a trade magazine that published weekly editions, which included record charts, from 1942 to 1996.

38. Nadine Cohodas, *Princess Noire: The Tumultuous Reign of Nina Simone* (Chapel Hill, NC: University of North Carolina Press, 2010), 150.

39. Interview with John Storyk (this appears to be an outtake from an interview with Storyk for the film *Jimi Hendrix: Hear My Train A Comin'*), "Electric Lady Studios – Web Exclusives," American Masters, October 25, 2013: video on https://www.pbs.org (accessed July 6, 2022).

40. "John Storyk – Designing Electric Lady Studios for Jimi Hendrix," Recording Studio Rockstars, December 4, 2020: video on YouTube (accessed July 6, 2022).

41. Clarence Avant, in *The Black Godfather*, dir. Reginald Hudlin, 2019.

42. Cited in Jack Whatley, "Behind the Mic: The Story of Public Enemy's Anthem 'Fight the Power,'" *Hip Hop Hero*, March 16, 2022: https://hiphophero.com/behind-the-mic-the-story-of-public-enemys-anthem-fight-the-power/ (accessed July 5, 2022).

43. Cited in Kory Grow, "Public Enemy Reveal Origins of Name, Crosshairs Logo," *Rolling Stone*, August 18, 2014, http://www.rollingstone.com/music/news/public-enemy-reveal-origins-of-name-crosshairs-logo-20140818 (accessed November 12, 2015).

44. The prop shown on p. 131, which was one of several boomboxes used during filming, is intact.

45. In footage taken during the film's production, Spike Lee interviews Bill Nunn about his character, Radio Raheem, asking, "Why do you think young brothers like that walk around with that music blasting as if they're the only people in the world?" Nunn responded, "If there's something that you really like, you feel compelled to impose it on other people.... I just want everybody to hear it, and they're going to dig it like I do. It's not so much of a rudeness thing.... You see me through my music...and this is this power of music...[and it's] an extension of me.... This is my power of music that's right here with me all the time." "*Do the Right Thing* 1989 (Live Footage Behind the Scenes)," video on YouTube (accessed July 5, 2022).

46. Cited in Chris Richards, "In Maryland, George Clinton, Parliament-Funkadelic and a missing Mothership," *Washington Post*, April 12, 2010.

47. Grouchy Greg Watkins, "Bill Adler's Eyejammie Studio To Close," *AllHipHop*, January 14, 2008, https://allhiphop.com/news/bill-adlers-eyejammie-studio-to-close/ (accessed July 5, 2022).

48. Queen Latifah, *Yo! MTV Raps*, September 22, 1989.

49. The bones are a percussion instrument traditionally made from a pair of animal bones. They are played in a manner similar to castanets.

50. Judy Dearing, in "The Tailor's Daughter," *Essence* 20, no. 9 (January 1990): 17.

51. Daphne Brooks, "'A Woman Is a Sometime Thing': (Re)Covering Black Womanhood in *Porgy and Bess*," *Dædalus* 150, no. 1 (Winter 2021): 98–117.

52. While many of these vocalists used the surname Smith, Bessie, Mamie, and Clara were not related.

53. Angela Y. Davis, *Blues Legacies and Black Feminism* (New York: Pantheon Books, 1998), 23.

54. From the 1960s through the 1980s, Black jazz musicians, including Dr. Billy Taylor and Duke Ellington, advocated for the "America's classical music" label as a means of elevating jazz to levels of respect given to European art music. The label fell out of favor in the 1990s and early 2000s as its Eurocentrism came under sustained critique by musicians and scholars. For a more complete discussion of this history, see Tom Arnold-Forster, "Dr. Billy Taylor, 'America's Classical Music,' and the Role of the Jazz Ambassador," *Journal of American Studies* 51, no. 1 (2017): 117–39.

55. Daniel Villarreal, "Little Richard Was Anti-Gay When He Died, but His Queer Cultural Influence Overshadows Us All," *LGBTQ Nation*, May 11, 2020, https://www.lgbtqnation.com/2020/05/little-richard-anti-gay-died-queer-cultural-influence-overshadows-us/ (accessed July 7, 2022).

56. Between 1942 and 2019 Johnson Publishing Company published numerous magazines that highlighted Black musicians, including *Ebony*, *Jet*, *Negro Digest*, *Black World*, *Tan*, *Black Stars*, and *Hue*.

57. "Lena Horne: In her own words. Lena Horne Biography," American Masters, May 14, 2010: https://www.pbs.org/wnet/americanmasters/lena-horne-about-the-performer/487/ (accessed July 7, 2022).

58. Maureen Mahon, *Black Diamond Queens: African American Women and Rock and Roll* (Durham, NC: Duke University Press, 2020).

59. Samuel A Floyd Jr., *The Power of Black Music: Interpreting Its History from Africa to the United States* (New York: Oxford University Press, 1995).

60. *Black Journal* was an award-winning monthly one-hour program hosted on National Education Television from 1968 to 1977. The show dove into topics about Black communities, including politics, public perception, civil rights, and music.

61. Richard Harrington. "Rock's Changing Colour," *Washington Post*, July 9, 1989.

Appendix

State of Louisiana

EXECUTIVE DEPARTMENT

Baton Rouge

JIMMIE H. DAVIS
GOVERNOR

December 3, 1962

Mr. Charles Sullivan
Sullivan's Enterprises
919 Grove Street
San Francisco, California

Dear Mr. Sullivan:

   Of course, the Ray Charles version of "YOU ARE MY SUNSHINE"
is far different to my version; and, incidentally, my version is more or
less on the "cornfed" side. But, nevertheless, the tune itself is well
established and planted in the minds of the people throughout the world.

   But, now to the Ray Charles version -- I had a feeling when I
heard his recording that it would be a nation-wide hit and perhaps go to
the No. 1 position. I had always felt that if it got the right kind of what
I call the "wild treatment", by the right artist, it couldn't miss. And,
frankly, I do not know of a person who is in a better position to give it
this "wild treatment", or the modern touch, or whatever you want to call
it, than Ray Charles because he is a person that knows pretty much what
to do with any song that he records, and when he sings one, it's had the
works. "SUNSHINE" is one of the "naturals" that lends itself to various
background support, and this group that Ray Charles had on this number
really worked it over.

   I don't care how they sing it -- just so they sing it!

Very truly yours,

Jimmie Davis

JIMMIE DAVIS

JHD/A

Letter from Louisiana
governor Jimmie Davis to
Charles Sullivan about the
song "You Are My Sunshine,"
1962 (see p. 21).

May 19, 1983
Reno, Nev.

Dear Sir:

I received your album of "MAXINE" SULLIVAN WITH TED EASTON'S JAZZ BAND a couple of days ago. I enjoyed it very much. She has a very soft voice which I like not like a lot of the singers nowdays who seem to shout their voice and have no rythm in the music.

I also think Ted Easton's Jazz band is terrific. Maxine & Ted go well together like bread and butter. I taped this album on my reel to reel recorder and it even sounds better. In fact some of the tennants in the apt bldg. where I live think she wonderful for her age. "Keep up the good work". I'm ordering another album of Maxine Sullivan which you will see on my order.

I would like to know if she is a colored person? On the cover she looks colored but

Letter from John L. Lewis inquiring about Maxine Sullivan, 1983 (see p. 22).

Handwritten lyrics to Willie Dixon's song "You Need Love," ca. 1962 (see p. 31).

THE EIGHTH WONDER
OF THE WORLD.

THE GREAT
MUSICAL PRODIGY OF THE AGE.

THE MOST
MARVELLOUS GENIUS LIVING!

EMANCIPATION COMPLETE

The Last Slave Set Free by order of the Supreme Court of the United States.
Come and hear him play for himself and for your entertainment.
The Genuine, Original and Only

BLIND TOM

The son of ordinary Southern field hands, untutored and sightless from birth, is presented to a critically discriminating public as surpassing anything ever known to the world as a MUSICAL PHENOMENON. There is no art about him. Unlike the great masters, whose manipulations result from deep and unwearied study, his instructions come from a higher power, and this philosophers are pleased to term GENIUS, which enables him without a knowledge of either language to SING IN GERMAN, FRENCH and ENGLISH, without understanding a single rudiment of written music, to compose artistic gems,

Evincing Rare Natural Ability

and to perform the most difficult CLASSICAL COMPOSITIONS with all the correctness, purity of expression, skill and excellence of the most distinguished artists. He can execute

THREE AIRS SIMULTANEOUSLY,

each in a different key, and perform music correctly with HIS BACK TO THE INSTRUMENT. He will play SECOND or BASS to any piece of music that can be produced by any performer from the audience, and will afterwards change seats and play the PRIMO. His wonderful memory and remarkable faculty for analyzing and locating sounds enable him to imitate upon the piano-forte almost every known musical instrument, and to repeat, without understanding their meaning, the speeches of our greatest orators (to which he has listened at different times) with most faithful accuracy, and to reproduce upon the piano any piece played in his presence after once hearing it. This Great

NATURAL MUSICAL CURIOSITY

was born in Georgia, blind from his birth, and with his mind clouded from infancy, possesses musical ability such as has never been acquired by any individual but after years of laborious study. But when the veil of darkness was drawn over his eyes, as if to make amends for the affliction upon the POOR NEGRO BOY, a flood of light was poured into his brain, and his mind became an OPERA OF BEAUTY, written by the hand of God in syllables of music for the delight of the world.

=== For Particulars See Newspapers and Other Advertisements. ===

JACOB DUX & CO., Steam Printers, 350 West 42d Street, N. Y.

Broadside advertising musical prodigy Thomas Greene Wiggins, known as "Blind Tom," ca. 1887 (see p. 46).

5219 McKinley Avenue,
Los Angeles, California,
May 13th, 1938.

Dear Mr. Kosson,

Tonight I was cleaning out my desk and found the enclosed letters. One was written by a very inexpert typist because I didn't want my regular secretary to know the contents.— the other is a later condensed version.

After they were written I decided that it was not worth while to send them, but tonight, on re-reading them, I decided to send them anyhow. It occurred to me that any editor of any paper has the right, (and should have the desire) to know all the effects of any writings appearing in his paper.

The whole thing seems rather remote to you at this time and would seem the same way to me, but for the fact that I have had proofs that this bad publicity has affected the attitude of several other schools toward us. It would never occur to them to doubt the veracity of your paper. Even at this late date, it would be helpful if you would print something by way of explanation, if not of apology. Also, I still think I have the right to know the source of the "quotations" credited to me. Will you kindly drop me a line? Am enclosing air-mail stamps.

Sincerely
Hall Johnson

Letter from Hall Johnson addressed to a Mr. Kosson, 1938 (see p. 65).

JOSEPH H. DOUGLASS
Solo Violinist

ENGAGEMENTS ACCEPTED
FOR RECITALS
CONCERTS AND CHURCH
SERVICES

NOW TOURING
AMERICA

1644 Fla. ave n.w,
Wash. D.C, May 31ˢᵗ 1911

My dear Mrs Terrell:

Replying to your esteemed favor just received, will say that it is my pleasure to accept the invitation to be present and render a violin selection on the occasion of the one hundredth anniversary of Harriet Beecher Stowe.

I thank you for the opportunity and honor which enables me to add my little mite in the celebration of that noble woman's birth as well as to appear before such a body of honored women.

I am proud of the fact that among those mentioned in your letter, none will be more representative or distinguished among the speakers of the meeting, than your honored self.

Yours most sincerely
Joseph H. Douglass.

(P. S.
I have carefully noted the date June 14ᵗʰ)

Letter from Joseph Douglass to Mary Church Terrell, 1911 (see p. 73).

C. S. C. No. 67782

(May 1926)

NAME ADAMS, Alton Augustus

SHIP OR STATION	PLACE	CHANGE OF STATUS	DATE	RATING	TERM ENLIST O EXTEN
S/M BASE	ST.THOMAS,V.I.		12-31-42	Bmstr (PA)	
S/M BASE	ST.THOMAS,V.I.		6/30/43	"	
S/M BASE	ST.THOMAS,V.I.		12/31/43	"	
S/M BASE	ST.THOMAS,V.I.	C	11/1/43	Rating chang	
NOB	ST.THOMAS,V.I.	Rec.	4/25/44	CMus (PA)	
NAS	SAN JUAN,P.R.	Rec.	5/31/44	CMus (PA)	
NAS	SAN JUAN, P.R.		5/31/44	Completed 2	
NAS	SAN JUAN, P.R.		12/31/44	CMus (PA)	
NAS	SAN JUAN, P.R.	T.	4/10/45	"	
NAVAL STATION	ST.THOMAS,V.I.	Rec.	5/11/45	"	
NAVAL STATION	ST.THOMAS,V.I.		5/11/45	Released to	

(Revised May, 1926)

Alton Adams's Continuous Service Records documenting his service with the US Navy, 1942–45 (see p. 99).

SERVICE NUMBER 100-11-96.

J. C. WORK

F ENT ON	Proficiency in Rating	Seamanship	Mechanical Ability	Ability as Leader of Men		CONDUCT	CAUSE AND CHARACTER OF DISCHARGE	Recommended for Re-enlistment	SIGNATURE OF COMMANDING OFFICER
	40			40		40			
	40			40		40			H.C.F.
	40			40		40			H.W.L.
d from Bmstr to CMus(PA)									H.C.F.
	40			40		40			G.K.G. REILLY
						40			A.H. BALSLEY
years net service for pay purposes									FRANK E. WELD
	40		40	40		40			C.O. ALIRED
	40		40	40		40			ISM(hg)
									FEW(jm)
									WORK
Inactive Duty this date.									J. C. WORK

A-1 SOUND STUDIOS, INC.
234 WEST 56th STREET
NEW YORK 19, N. Y.

INVOICE NO. 3728

	Vee-Jay Records	INVOICE DATE 5-13-65
SOLD TO	att. Calvin Carter	
	1449 South Michigan Ave	SHIPPED TO
	Chicago, Ill.	

OUR ORDER NO.	YOUR ORDER NO.	SALESMAN	TERMS	SHIPPED VIA	PPD. OR COLL.

QUANTITY	DESCRIPTION	PRICE	AMOUNT
	LITTLE RICHARD RECORDINGS		
4 hrs	11:00 pm to 3:00 am 4 track recording	45.00	$ 180.00
1 1/2 hrs	3:00 am--4:30 am 4 tr overdubbing	35.00	52.50
1 hr	4 tr to mono remix	25.00	25.00
2400'	1/2 in low noise tape	20.00	20.00
1200'	1/4 in tape	5.00	5.00
2	45 rpm D.F. discs	3.50	7.00
2	" " S.F. "	2.50	5.00
	No tax tax shipped to Chicago		$294.50

"I Don't Know What You've got" Part 1 and Part 2
"You've Got To Stop It Now"

APPROVED

Little Richard Penniman

Little Richard Penniman

PRINTED BY GRAYARC CO., INC., BROOKLYN 32. N. Y.

Invoice from New York's A-1 Sound Studios to Vee-Jay Records, signed by Little Richard, 1965 (see p. 157).

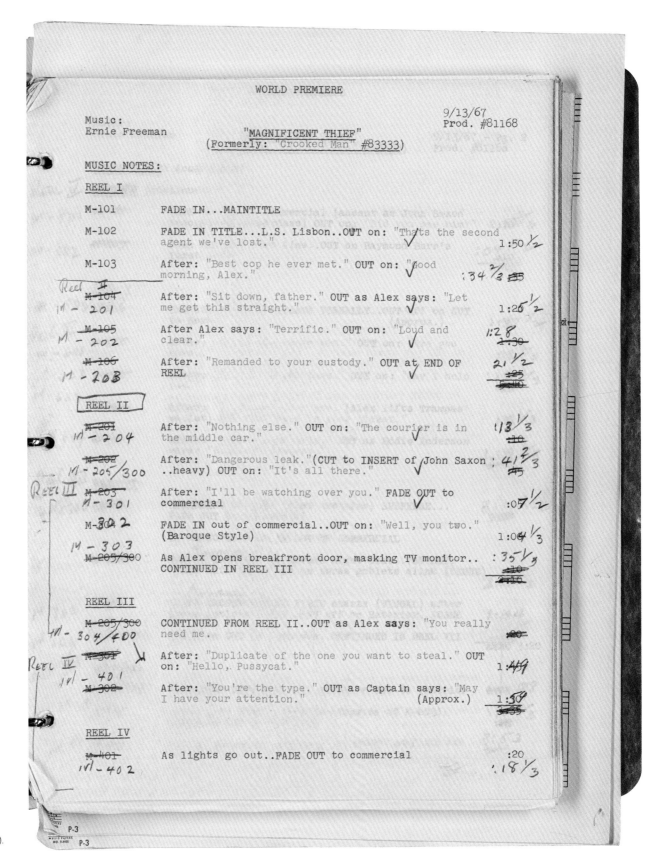

WORLD PREMIERE

Music:
Ernie Freeman

9/13/67
Prod. #81168

"MAGNIFICENT THIEF"
(Formerly: "Crooked Man" #83333)

MUSIC NOTES:

REEL I

M-101   FADE IN...MAINTITLE

M-102   FADE IN TITLE...L.S. Lisbon..OUT on: "That's the second
         agent we've lost."   1:50 ½

M-103   After: "Best cop he ever met." OUT on: "Good
         morning, Alex."   :34 ⅔

Reel II
~~M-104~~   After: "Sit down, father." OUT as Alex says: "Let
M-201   me get this straight."   1:25 ½

~~M-105~~   After Alex says: "Terrific." OUT on: "Loud and
M-202   clear."   1:28

~~M-106~~   After: "Remanded to your custody." OUT at END OF   21 ½
M-203   REEL

REEL II

~~M-201~~   After: "Nothing else." OUT on: "The courier is in   1:13 ⅓
M-204   the middle car."

~~M-202~~   After: "Dangerous leak."(CUT to INSERT of John Saxon :41 ⅔
M-205/300   ..heavy) OUT on: "It's all there."

Reel III ~~M-203~~   After: "I'll be watching over you." FADE OUT to
M-301   commercial   :07 ½

M-302   FADE IN out of commercial..OUT on: "Well, you two."
            (Baroque Style)   1:04 ⅓

M-303   ~~M-205/300~~   As Alex opens breakfront door, masking TV monitor.. :35 ⅓
            CONTINUED IN REEL III

REEL III

M-304/400   ~~M-205/300~~   CONTINUED FROM REEL II..OUT as Alex says: "You really
            need me.

Reel IV   ~~M-301~~   After: "Duplicate of the one you want to steal." OUT
M-401   on: "Hello, Pussycat."   1:49

~~M-302~~   After: "You're the type." OUT as Captain says: "May
            I have your attention."   (Approx.)   1:50

REEL IV

~~M-401~~   As lights go out..FADE OUT to commercial   :20
M-402   :18 ⅓

P-3
MUSIC PAPERS
NO. 9-6400   P-3

Bibliography

Abbott, Lynn, and Doug Seroff. "'They Cert'ly Sound Good to Me': Sheet Music, Southern Vaudeville, and the Commercial Ascendancy of the Blues." In *Ramblin' on My Mind: New Perspectives on the Blues*, edited by David Evans. Urbana, IL: University of Illinois Press, 2008.

Allen, Jeffery Renard. "Silence: On the History of Hearing and Seeing Blind Tom." *Black Scholar* 45, no. 1 (2015): 44–50.

Allen, William Francis. *Slave Songs of the United States*. New York: A. Simpson & Co., 1867.

André, Naomi. *Black Opera: History, Power, Engagement*. Urbana, IL: University of Illinois Press, 2018.

André, Naomi, Karen M. Bryan, and Eric Saylor (eds.). *Blackness in Opera*. Urbana, IL: University of Illinois Press, 2012.

Baraka, Amiri. *Digging: The Afro-American Soul of American Classical Music*. Berkeley, CA: University of California Press, 2009.

Baram, Marcus. "How Stevie Wonder Helped Create Martin Luther King Day." *San Francisco Bay View*, January 20, 2020.

Bastin, Bruce, and Kip Lornell. *The Melody Man: Joe Davis and the New York Music Scene, 1916–1978*. Jackson, MS: University Press of Mississippi, 2012.

Bell, Jennifer. "Shure Beta 58A Review." *OldTimeMusic*, updated 2022.

Berkman, Franya J. *Monument Eternal: The Music of Alice Coltrane*. Middletown, CT: Wesleyan University Press, 2010.

Biewen, John, and Alexa Dilworth (eds.). *Reality Radio: Telling True Stories in Sound*. Chapel Hill, NC: University of North Carolina Press, 2017.

Birch, Eugenie L., and Susan M. Wachter. *Rebuilding Urban Places after Disaster: Lessons from Hurricane Katrina*. Philadelphia, PA: University of Pennsylvania Press, 2006.

Bozanic, Andrew Durkota Augustine. "The Acoustic Guitar in American Culture, 1880–1980." University of Delaware, 2015.

Brackett, David. "Little Richard." *Grove Music Online*, 2020.

Bradley, Regina. *Chronicling Stankonia: The Rise of the Hip-Hop South*. Chapel Hill, NC: University of North Carolina Press, 2021.

Brooks, Daphne A. "'A Woman Is a Sometime Thing': (Re)Covering Black Womanhood in *Porgy and Bess*." *Dædalus* 150, no. 1 (2021): 98–117.

Brooks, Daphne A. *Liner Notes for the Revolution: The Intellectual Life of Black Feminist Sound*. Cambridge, MA: Harvard University Press, 2021.

Brown, Ernest D., Jr. "African American Instrument Construction and Music Making." In *African American Music: An Introduction*, edited by Mellonee V. Burnim and Portia K. Maultsby. New York: Routledge, 2015.

Bryant, Clora, Buddy Collette, William Green, Steve Isoardi, and Marl Young. *Central Avenue Sounds: Jazz in Los Angeles*. Oakland, CA: University of California Press, 1999.

Burnim, Mellonee V., and Portia K. Maultsby (eds.). *African American Music: An Introduction*. New York: Routledge, 2015.

Callahan, Mike. "The Vee-Jay Story." Both Sides Now Publications, December 19, 2006. http://www.bsnpubs.com/veejay/veejaystory1.html.

Carter, Marva Griffin. *Swing Along: The Musical Life of Will Marion Cook*. New York: Oxford University Press, 2008.

Chamberland, Carol P. "The House That Bop Built." *California History* 75, no. 3 (1996): 272–83.

Clark, Conrad. "As Much at Home in Slacks as Skirts Says Girl Swingster with Boy's Name." *Afro-American*, 1937.

Conway, Cecelia. *African Banjo Echoes in Appalachia: A Study of Folk Traditions*. Knoxville, TN: University of Tennessee Press, 1995.

Cordwell, Justine M., and Ronald A. Schwarz (eds.). *The Fabrics of Culture: The Anthropology of Clothing and Adornment*. In "World Anthropology" series, edited by Sol Tax. New York: Mouton Publishers, 1979.

Cottrell, Stephen. *The Saxophone*. New Haven, CT: Yale University Press, 2012.

Davis, Angela Y. *Blues Legacies and Black Feminism*. New York: Pantheon Books, 1998.

DeCosmo, Janet L. "Junkanoo: The African Cultural Connection in Nassau, Bahamas." *Western Journal of Black Studies* 27, no. 4 (2003): 246–57.

DeVeaux, Scott. *The Birth of Bebop: A Social and Musical History*. Berkeley, CA: University of California Press, 1997.

DjeDje, Jacqueline Cogdell. "Context and Creativity: William Grant Still in Los Angeles." *Black Music Research Journal* 31, no. 1 (2011): 1–27.

Duberman, Martin. *Paul Robeson*. New York: The New Press, 1989.

Dubois, Laurent. *The Banjo: America's African Instrument*. Cambridge, MA: Belknap Press, 2016.

Dyer, Richard, and Elizabeth Forbes. "Mattiwilda Dobbs." *Grove Music Online*, 2013.

Eidsheim, Nina Sun. "Marian Anderson and 'Sonic Blackness' in American Opera." *American Quarterly* 63, no. 3 (2011): 641–71.

Eidsheim, Nina Sun. *The Race of Sound: Listening, Timbre, and Vocality in African American Music*. Durham, NC: Duke University Press, 2019.

Epstein, Dena J. "The Folk Banjo: A Documentary History." *Ethnomusicology* 19, no. 3 (1975): 347–71.

Epstein, Dena J. *Sinful Tunes and Spirituals: Black Folk Music to the Civil War*. Urbana, IL: University of Illinois Press, 2003.

Feldstein, Ruth. *How It Feels to Be Free: Black Women Entertainers and the Civil Rights Movement*. New York: Oxford University Press, 2017.

Feman, Seth. "Marian Anderson's Presence." *American Art* 28, no. 1 (2014): 104–17.

Ferguson, Jordan. *J Dilla's Donuts*. New York: Bloomsbury Academic, 2014.

Fleming, E. McClung. "Artifact Study: A Proposed Model." *Winterthur Portfolio* 9, no. 1 (1974): 153–73.

Floyd, Samuel A., Jr. *The Power of Black Music: Interpreting Its History from Africa to the United States*. New York: Oxford University Press, 1995.

Ford, Tanisha C. *Liberated Threads: Black Women, Style, and the Global Politics of Soul*. Chapel Hill, NC: University of North Carolina Press, 2015.

Fulton, Will. "LL Cool J." *Grove Music Online*, 2014.

Fuster, John E. "Bill Hawkins Is New Disc Jockey Who Should Stay." *Cleveland Call and Post* (Cleveland, Ohio). 9B 1948.

Gaines, Caseen. *Footnotes: The Black Artists Who Rewrote the Rules of the Great White Way*. Naperville, IL: Sourcebooks, 2021.

Gannon, Bill. "Bill Hawkins Does Show from Workhouse." *Cleveland Call and Post* (Cleveland, Ohio). B 1955.

Gelder, Lawrence Van. "Papa Was a Rolling Stone, and a Famous Disc Jockey." *The New York Times*, June 14, 2008.

George, Marsha Washington. *Black Radio … Winner Takes All: America's 1st Black DJs*. Philadelphia, PA: Xlibris, 2001.

Goldman, Stuart A. (dir.). *Alberta Hunter: My Castle's Rockin'* (film). V.I.E.W., 2001. https://video.alexanderstreet.com/watch/alberta-hunter-my-castle-s-rockin.

Goslich, Siegfried, Rita H. Mead, Timothy Roberts, and Joanna C. Lee. "Radio." *Grove Music Online*, 2001.

Grace, Del. "Legends Talk Series – Felton W. Williams Jr." (video). YouTube. 2016.

Grace, Del. "Local Customs Presents Felton W. Williams" (video). YouTube. 2016.

Graham, Casey. "SNCC Freedom Singers (1962–1966)." Black Past, March 9, 2014.

Greene, Andy. "Flashback: David Bowie Rips into MTV for Not Spotlighting Black Artists." *Rolling Stone*, June 14, 2020.

Greene, Christina. "Black Women and Black Power: A Review Essay on New Directions in Black Power Studies." *The Journal of Southern History* 85, no. 3 (2019): 653–60.

Gussow, Adam. *Beyond the Crossroads: The Devil and the Blues Tradition*. Chapel Hill, NC: University of North Carolina Press, 2017.

Hall, Adriana. "Go-Go Music and Place Identity: The Perseverance of the Chocolate City." Rutgers University, 2021.

Hamilton, Marybeth. "Sexual Politics and African-American Music; or, Placing Little Richard in History." *History Workshop Journal* 46 (1998): 160–76.

Harold, Claudrena. "'Lord, Let Me Be an Instrument': The Artistry and Cultural Politics of Reverend James Cleveland and the Gospel Music Workshop of America, 1963–1991." *Journal of Africana Religions* 5, no. 2 (2017): 157–80.

Harris, Michael W. *The Rise of Gospel Blues: The Music of Thomas Andrew Dorsey in the Urban Church*. New York: Oxford University Press, 1992.

Harriss, M. Cooper. "Preacherly Texts: Zora Neale Hurston and the Homiletics of Literature." *Journal of Africana Religions* 4, no. 2 (2016): 278–90.

Harvey, Karen, ed. *History and Material Culture: A Student's Guide to Approaching Alternative Sources.* 2nd ed. The Routledge Guide to Using Historical Sources. New York and London: Routledge, 2018.

Hatfield, Edward A. "Bernice Johnson Reagon." *New Georgia Encyclopedia*, 2020.

Hatfield, Edward A. "Freedom Singers." *New Georgia Encyclopedia*, 2020.

Hazzard-Donald, Katrina. *Jookin': The Rise of Social Dance Formations in African-American Culture.* Philadelphia, PA: Temple University Press, 1990.

Henderson, Clayton W. "Minstrelsy." *Grove Music Online*, 2001.

Hobson, Maurice J. *The Legend of the Black Mecca: Politics and Class in the Making of Modern Atlanta.* Chapel Hill, NC: University of North Carolina Press, 2017.

Holden, Stephen. "Bell, Thom(as) Randolph." *Grove Music Online*, 2013.

Hopkinson, Natalie. *Go-Go Live: The Musical Life and Death of a Chocolate City.* Durham, NC: Duke University Press, 2012.

Horton, Luke. "Perry Bradford: The Man Who Sold the Blues." *Australasian Journal of American Studies* 32, no. 2 (2013): 13–26.

Hosiasson, José. "Calloway, Cab(ell)." *Grove Music Online*, 2001.

Jasen, David A., and Gene Jones. *Spreadin' Rhythm Around: Black Popular Songwriters, 1880–1930.* London: Taylor & Francis Group, 2005.

Jensen-Moulton, Stephanie. "'Specimens' and 'Peculiar Idiosyncrasies': Songs of 'Blind Tom' Wiggins." *American Music Review* 40, no. 2 (2011): 1–5.

Johnson, Birgitta J. "African Methodist Episcopal Church." *Grove Music Online*, 2012.

Jones, Jessica Janice. "DeFord Bailey." *Black Music Research Journal* 10, no. 1 (1990): 29–31.

Jones, LeRoi (Amiri Baraka). *Blues People: Negro Music in White America.* New York: Harper Perennial, 2002.

Jones, Rufus, Jr. *Dean Dixon: Negro at Home, Maestro Abroad.* Lanham, MD: Rowman & Littlefield, 2015.

Kelley, Robin D.G. *Thelonious Monk: The Life and Times of an American Original.* New York: Free Press, 2009.

Kemp, Mark Segal. "Wherefore Art Thou, Ovation?" *Acoustic Guitar*, 2014.

Kenner, Rob. *The Marathon Don't Stop: The Life and Times of Nipsey Hussle.* New York: Atria Books, 2020.

Kernodle, Tammy L. "Civil Rights Movement." *Grove Music Online*, 2012.

Kernodle, Tammy L. "Black Women Working Together: Jazz, Gender, and the Politics of Validation." *Black Music Research Journal* 34, no. 1 (2014): 27–55.

King, Jason. "Any Love: Silence, Theft, and Rumor in the Work of Luther Vandross." *Callaloo* 23, no. 1 (2000): 422–47.

Krigbaum, Ashleyanne. "The Spot: Walkin' Talkin' Bill Hawkins." *The Spot*, February 4, 2016.

Larson, Kate Clifford. *Bound for the Promised Land: Harriet Tubman, Portrait of an American Hero.* New York: One World Books, 2004.

Lee, Albert Rudolph. "The Poetic Voice of Langston Hughes in American Art Song." Florida State University, 2012.

Leonard, Marion. "Constructing Histories through Material Culture: Popular Music, Museums and Collecting." *Popular Music History* 2, no. 2 (2007): 147–167.

Lewis, David Levering. *When Harlem Was in Vogue.* New York: Penguin Books, 1997.

Lhamon, W.T., Jr. "Little Richard as a Folk Performer." *Studies in Popular Culture* 8, no. 2 (1985): 7–17.

Licht, Michael S. "Harmonica Magic: Virtuoso Display in American Folk Music." *Ethnomusicology* 24, no. 2 (1980): 211–21.

Lornell, Kip, and Charles C. Stephenson Jr. *The Beat! Go-Go Music from Washington, D.C.* Jackson, MS: University Press of Mississippi, 2009.

Lott, Eric. *Love and Theft: Blackface Minstrelsy and the American Working Class.* New York: Oxford University Press, 1993.

Mahon, Maureen. *Right to Rock: The Black Rock Coalition and the Cultural Politics of Race.* Durham, NC: Duke University Press, 2004.

Mahon, Maureen. *Black Diamond Queens: African American Women and Rock and Roll.* Durham, NC: Duke University Press, 2020.

Malone, Bill C., and Travis D. Stimeling. "Davis, Jimmie [James] H(ouston)." *Grove Music Online*, 2013.

Malone, Jacqui. "The FAMU Marching 100." *The Black Perspective in Music* 18, no. 1 of 2 (1990): 59–80.

Malone, Jacqui. *Steppin' on the Blues: The Visible Rhythms of African American Dance.* Urbana, IL: University of Illinois Press, 1996.

Matlin, Daniel. "'Lift Up Yr Self!' Reinterpreting Amiri Baraka (LeRoi Jones), Black Power, and the Uplift Tradition." *The Journal of American History* 93, no. 1 (2006): 91–116.

Matthews, Ralph. "Can Girl Musicians Take It? No! Says Blanche Calloway Yes! Says Edie Crump." *Afro-American*, 1937.

McDuffie, Candace. "Janet Jackson's Music Videos: A History." *Glamour*, January 28, 2022.

McGee, Kristin A. *Some Liked It Hot: Jazz Women in Film and Television, 1928–1959.* Middletown, CT: Wesleyan University Press, 2009.

McLarney, Ellen. "Beyoncé's Soft Power: Poetics and Politics of an Afro-Diasporic Aesthetics." *Camera Obscura* 34, no. 2 (2019): 1–39.

Miller, Matt. *The New Encyclopedia of Southern Culture.* Chapel Hill, NC: University of North Carolina Press, 2014.

Moran, Pat. "Fishing with Josh: Could This Ovation Be the Prototype of the Josh White Signature Model." *Acoustic Guitar*, 2014.

Mosbrook, Joe. "Part 67 – Evelyn Freeman Remembers Her Swing Band.' Jazzed in Cleveland. WMV Web News Cleveland, December 21, 2001.

Munro, Martin. "James Brown, Rhythm, and Black Power." In Munro, *Different Drummers: Rhythm and Race in the Americas.* Berkeley, CA: University of California Press, 2010.

Museum of Contemporary Art Denver. "An Evening with Rakim: Revelations on Creativity from the Lyrical Genius" (video). YouTube. 2020.

Narine, Dalton. "The Maestros: Black Symphony Conductors Are Making a Name for Themselves." *Ebony*, February 1989.

Neal, Mark Anthony. *What the Music Said: Black Popular Music and Black Public Culture.* London: Routledge, 1998.

Neal, Mark Anthony. "Race-Ing Katrina." *Transforming Anthropology* 14, no. 1 (2006): 22–3.

Neal, Mark Anthony. "Fear of a Queer Soul Man." In Neal, *Looking for Leroy: Illegible Black Masculinities.* New York: New York University Press, 2013.

Ogbar, Jeffrey O.G. *Black Power: Radical Politics and African American Identity.* Baltimore, MD: Johns Hopkins University Press, 2019.

Parler, Samuel. "DeFord Bailey in Country Music's Multiracial Canon." *Journal of the American Musicological Society* 73, no. 1 (2020): 53–94.

Perry, Imani. *May We Forever Stand: A History of the Black National Anthem.* Chapel Hill, NC: University of North Carolina Press, 2018.

Placksin, Sally. *American Women in Jazz, 1900 to the Present: Their Words, Lives, and Music.* New York: Seaview Books, 1982.

Porter, Lewis. *John Coltrane: His Life and Music.* Ann Arbor, MI: University of Michigan Press, 1997.

Price, Emmett George, Tammy L. Kernodle, and Horace J. Maxile Jr. (eds.). *Encyclopedia of African American Music.* Santa Barbara, CA: Greenwood, 2011.

Prown, Jules David. "Mind in Matter: An Introduction to Material Culture Theory and Method." *Winterthur Portfolio* 17, no. 1 (1982): 1–19.

Reagon, Bernice Johnson. *If You Don't Go, Don't Hinder Me: The African American Sacred Song Tradition.* Lincoln, NE: University of Nebraska Press, 2001.

Retman, Sonnet. "Between Rock and a Hard Place: Narrating Nona Hendryx's Inscrutable Career." *Women & Performance: A Journal of Feminist Theory* 16, no. 1 (2006): 107–18.

"'Ridin' 'n Jivin' and Talkin' with Bill Hawkins' Hits Airways Monday." *Cleveland Call and Post* (Cleveland, Ohio). 12B1949.

Riggs, Marlon T. (dir.). *Ethnic Notions* (film). California Newsreel, 1986.

Riis, Thomas L. "Musical Theater." In *African American Music: An Introduction*, edited by Portia K. Maultsby and Mellonee V. Burnim. New York: Routledge, 2015.

Roberts, Evelyn Freeman. "Biography." *The History Makers*, March 31, 2006.

Roberts, Les. "Talkin Bout my Generation: Popular Music and the Culture of Heritage." In *International Journal of Heritage Studies*. London: Taylor & Francis Group, 2012: 262–80.

Rosenthal, David H. *Hard Bop: Jazz and Black Music, 1955–1965*. New York: Oxford University Press, 1992.

Roy, Elodie A. *Media, Materiality and Memory: Grounding the Groove*. Farnham, Surrey: Ashgate Publishing, 2015.

Sakakeeny, Matt. "'Under the Bridge': An Orientation to Soundscapes in New Orleans." *Ethnomusicology* 54, no. 1 (2010): 1–27.

Sakakeeny, Matt. "New Orleans Music as a Circulatory System." *Black Music Research Journal* 31, no. 2 (2011): 291–325.

Samuels, David. "Rakim: 'We Need a Few More Kanyes'." *The Atlantic*, April 23, 2012.

Sarrouh, Adonees, and J. Mark Souther, "Cleveland's Second Downtown." Cleveland Historical. September 19, 2010. https://clevelandhistorical.org/items/show/49.

Scheller, Christine A. "Pentecostalism's Neglected Black History." Huffington Post, January 23, 2012.

Schenbeck, Lawrence. *Racial Uplift and American Music, 1878–1943*. Jackson, MS: University Press of Mississippi, 2012.

Schofield, A.J. "Never Mind the Relevance? Popular Culture for Archaeologists." In *Matter, Materiality and Modern Culture*, edited by P.M. Graves-Brown. New York: Routledge, 2000.

Seawright, John Ryan. "Blind Tom Wiggins: Slavery Onstage." In *The Oxford American Book of Great Music Writing*, edited by Marc Smirnoff. Fayetteville, AR: University of Arkansas Press, 2008.

Seymour, Craig A. "'Searching' for Luther Vandross: The Politics and Performance of Studying an African-American Icon." University of Maryland, 2005.

Simpson, Eugene Thamon. *Hall Johnson: His Life, His Spirit, and His Music*. New York: Scarecrow Press, 2008.

Slaughter, John Brooks, Yu Tao, and Willie Pearson (eds.). *Changing the Face of Engineering: The African American Experience*. Baltimore, MD: Johns Hopkins University Press, 2015.

Smith, Christopher J. *The Creolization of American Culture: William Sidney Mount and the Roots of Blackface Minstrelsy*. Urbana, IL: University of Illinois Press, 2014.

Smith, Suzanne E. *Dancing in the Street: Motown and the Cultural Politics of Detroit*. Cambridge, MA: Harvard University Press, 2001.

Southall, Geneva. "Blind Tom: A Misrepresented and Neglected Composer-Pianist." *The Black Perspective in Music* 3, no. 2 (1975): 141–59.

Southern, Eileen. "Francis Johnson (1792–1844)." *The Black Perspective in Music* 4, no. 2 (1976): 208–12.

Southern, Eileen. "The Philadelphia Afro-American School." *The Black Perspective in Music* 4, no. 2 (1976): 238–56.

Southern, Eileen. *The Music of Black Americans: A History*. 3rd ed. New York: W.W. Norton & Company, 1997.

Southern, Eileen, and John Graziano. "Blake, Eubie." *Grove Music Online*, 2001.

Staff. "Colored Performers Rights Society, a New Barney Young Venture." *Variety*, September 11, 1957.

Staff. "Conover." Antique Piano Shop. 2017. https://antiquepianoshop.com/online-museum/conover/.

Staff. "Ernest 'Ernie' Freeman." *Encyclopedia of Cleveland History*. Case Western Reserve University. https://case.edu/ech/articles/f/freeman-ernest-ernie.

Staff. "Jimmie Daniels." NYC LGBT Historic Sites Project. https://www.nyclgbtsites.org/site/jimmie-daniels/.

Staff. "New Music Licensing Society Seeks Contracts from Stations." *Broadcasting*, November 11, 1957.

Staff. "Stevie Wonder." International Civil Rights Walk of Fame. National Park Service. https://www.nps.gov/features/malu/feat0002/wof/stevie_wonder.htm.

Staff. "The Tailor's Daughter." *Essence*, January 1990.

Stephens, Randall J. "'Where else did they copy their styles but from church groups?': Rock 'n' Roll and Pentecostalism in the 1950s South." *Church History* 85, no. 1 (2016): 97–131.

Stockhouse, Janis. *Jazzwomen: Conversations with Twenty-One Musicians*. Bloomington, IN: Indiana University Press, 2004.

Stone, Robert L. *Sacred Steel: Inside an African American Steel Guitar Tradition*. In "Music in American Life" series. Urbana, IL: University of Illinois Press, 2010.

Suisman, David. "Black Swan." *Grove Music Online*, 2015.

Sullivan, Denise. *Keep on Pushing: Black Power Music from Blues to Hip-Hop*. Chicago, IL: Chicago Review Press, 2011.

Taylor, William Allen. "Walkin' Talkin' Bill Hawkins." *Lost & Found Sound*, NPR, December 17, 2005. https://www.npr.org/2005/12/17/3207138/walkin-talkin-bill-hawkins.

"The Great Migration." Cleveland Restoration Society, 2018.

Thomas, Veona. "Judy Dearing: Costume Designer Supreme." *Black Masks*, 1987.

Thompson, Katrina Dyonne. *Ring Shout, Wheel About: The Racial Politics of Music and Dance in North American Slavery*. Urbana, IL: University of Illinois Press, 2014.

Toll, Robert C. *Blacking Up: The Minstrel Show in Nineteenth-Century America*. New York: Oxford University Press, 1977.

Trotter, Joe W. "African American Fraternal Associations in American History: An Introduction." *Social Science History* 28, no. 3 (2004): 355–66.

Tucker, Sherrie. "Nobody's Sweethearts: Gender, Race, Jazz, and the Darlings of Rhythm." *American Music* 16, no. 3 (1998) 255–88.

Turner, Lorenzo Dow. *Africanisms in the Gullah Dialect*. Columbia, SC: University of South Carolina Press, 2002.

Villarreal, Daniel. "Little Richard Was Anti-Gay When He Died, but His Queer Cultural Influence Overshadows Us All." *LGBTQ Nation*, May 11, 2020. https://www.lgbtqnation.com/2020/05/little-richard-anti-gay-died-queer-cultural-influence-overshadows-us/.

Wald, Elijah. *Josh White: Society Blues*. London: Taylor & Francis Group, 2002.

Wall, Bennett H. *Louisiana: A History*. 4th ed. Wheeling, IL: Harlan Davidson, Inc., 2002.

Walsh, Jason. "Fender Shutters Ovation's Us Factory." *Acoustic Guitar*, 2014.

Waltzer, Jim, and Tom Wilk. *Tales of South Jersey: Profiles and Personalities*. New Brunswick, NJ: Rutgers University Press, 2001.

Ward, Brian. *Just My Soul Responding: Rhythm and Blues, Black Consciousness and Race Relations*. London: University College of London Press, 1998.

Washburne, Christopher. "The Clave of Jazz: A Caribbean Contribution to the Rhythmic Foundation of an African-American Music." *Black Music Research Journal* 17, no. 1 (1997): 59–80.

Washburne, Christopher. "Latin Jazz, Afro-Latin Jazz, Afro-Cuban Jazz, Cubop, Caribbean Jazz, Jazz Latin, or Just…Jazz: The Politics of Locating an Intercultural Music." In *Jazz/Not Jazz: The Music and Its Boundaries*, edited by David Ake, Charles Hiroshi Garrett, and Daniel Goldmark. Berkeley, CA: University of California Press, 2012.

Watts, Jerry Gafio. *Amiri Baraka: The Politics and Art of a Black Intellectual*. New York: New York University Press, 2001.

Weisenfeld, Judith. "'The Secret at the Root': Performing African American Religious Modernity in Hall Johnson's *Run, Little Chillun*." *Religion and American Culture: A Journal of Interpretation* 21, no. 1 (2011): 39–80.

Winans, Robert B. (ed.). *Banjo Roots and Branches*. Urbana, IL: University of Illinois Press, 2018.

Wolfensberger, Don. "The Martin Luther King, Jr. Holiday: The Long Struggle in Congress, An Introductory Essay." Paper presented at "The Martin Luther King, Jr. Holiday: How Did It Happen?" seminar, Woodrow Wilson International Center for Scholars, January 14, 2008. wilsoncenter.org/sites/default/files/media/documents/event/King%20Holiday-essay-drw.pdf.

Woodard, Komozi. *A Nation within a Nation: Amiri Baraka (LeRoi Jones) and Black Power Politics*. Chapel Hill, NC: University of North Carolina Press, 1999.

York, Elizabeth. "Barney and Gloria: Revisiting Tin Pan Alley." *Notes* 73, no. 3 (2017): 473–501.

Acknowledgments

Musical Crossroads: Stories Behind the Objects of African American Music is a book about music, material culture, and the African American experience. Like music, it is a collaborative endeavor that was shaped and guided by the knowledge, skills, and unique talents of many people. First, I want to thank Lonnie G. Bunch III, Smithsonian Secretary and Founding Director of the National Museum of African American History and Culture, and Rex M. Ellis, NMAAHC Associate Director Emeritus, for providing the support to launch this project, as well as Kevin Young, NMAAHC's current Andrew W. Mellon Director, for supporting the book's completion and writing the Foreword for the publication.

A close second is our fantastic core team: Timothy Anne Burnside, a museum specialist who has brought her talent and expertise to bear and worked with me over the last twelve years in building the Museum's music and performing arts collection, permanent exhibitions, programs, and recordings, among other things; Dr. Steven W. Lewis, who has taken over my position as Curator of Music and Performing Arts; Hannah Grantham, a former intern and current curatorial assistant, with superb research and organizational skills; and Douglas T. Remley, Publications and Rights Specialist, who coordinated all aspects of the production of this book. This core team kept everything afloat and advised on all stages of the process. In addition, my assistant, Fatima Elgarch, brought her unique skills and collegiality in coordinating all our meetings, facilitating correspondence, and anything else that came across the transom.

I am also grateful to my colleagues for graciously taking time from their busy schedules to offer their points of view and write on a topic of interest. Thank you, Timothy Anne Burnside, Tuliza Fleming, Hannah Grantham, Steven W. Lewis, Vanessa L. Moorer, Kelly Elaine Navies, Douglas T. Remley, Deborah Tulani Salahu-Din, Kevin M. Strait, Angela Tate, and Eric Lewis Williams. A special thanks goes to my colleague, Aaron Bryant, who listened to my ideas in the earliest stages of this project and made the connection to Fleming's Model of Artifact Study.

Finally, our second core team, comprised of my colleagues who worked on acquisitions, archives, collections management, conservation, cataloging, and digitization, brought their skills, knowledge, and enthusiasm to make this book possible. I'd specifically like to thank Alana Donocoff, former Archives Technician, and Candace Oubre, Museum Specialist, for making the collection accessible for research; Antje Neumann and her conservation team, Cait Shaffer, Laura Mina, and Nick Pedemonti, for providing conservation assessments, recommendations, and treatments; Pauline Lopez, for her work obtaining permissions and licenses for the image reproductions; Emily Houf, who coordinated the object cataloging and documentation; and Walter Larrimore and his team of photographers, who created the beautiful object images reproduced throughout the book.

It's been a pleasure to work with the staff at D Giles Limited, specifically Dan Giles, Managing Director; Alfonso Iacurci, designer; Allison McCormick, Managing Editor; Louise Ramsay, Production Manager; Jenny Wilson, copyeditor and proofreader; and Liz Japes, Sales and Marketing Manager. Thanks for your enthusiasm about the topic and support during the long journey towards completion.

I am indebted to the object donors, musicians, Smithsonian Institution colleagues, curators, scholars, museum visitors and supporters, and music lovers for all the great conversations we've had about music and culture, music and performance, music and creativity, music and race, music and social justice, and music in the human experience. Your generosity, talent, creativity, and passion continually humbled and inspired me. Through the Museum's collections, your stories—those of the past and those that remain to be told—will be available for generations to come.

I hope this journey through the Museum's collection encourages readers to engage with music collections through a material culture framework. By posing questions that invite a more expansive conception of the meaning of music and the extensive networks it creates, we can more easily understand the culture of African American music-making and the foundation it has built in the United States— and globally—in the quest to live and make music in a world where freedom of expression, devoid of the oppressive structures, practices, values, and beliefs that stand in its way, is an experience available to us all.

Dwandalyn R. Reece
Associate Director for Curatorial Affairs
Curator of Music and Performing Arts 2009-21
National Museum of African American
History and Culture

Contributors

Dwandalyn R. Reece (DRR)

Dwandalyn R. Reece PhD is Associate Director for Curatorial Affairs at the National Museum of African American History and Culture and has more than thirty years of experience as a scholar, performer, grantmaker, and curator, including twelve years as the NMAAHC's Curator of Music and Performing Arts from 2009 to 2021. Reece curated the Museum's *Musical Crossroads* exhibition, which won the Secretary's Research Prize in 2017; co-curated the Museum's grand opening music festival, *Freedom Sounds: A Community Celebration* (2016), the Smithsonian Year of Music (2019), and the Smithsonian Folklife Festival Program, *Rhythm and Blues: Tell It Like It Is* (2011); served as contributing producer on the *Smithsonian Anthology of Hip-Hop and Rap* (2021); and co-hosted the first season of the award-winning NMAAHC and SiriusXM podcast series, *All Music is Black Music* (2021). As chair of Smithsonian Music, she leads a pan-institutional effort to raise the profile of the Smithsonian's music collections and is frequently called upon to talk about a variety of issues, including such topics as performing arts collections, exhibitions and museums, African American music history and performance, gender and vocal performance, musical theater, the Harlem Renaissance, blackface minstrelsy and stereotypes, and American popular entertainment.

Timothy Anne Burnside (TAB)

Timothy Anne Burnside is a public historian and museum professional with almost twenty years of experience at the Smithsonian. Her work explores intersections between history and culture through the lenses of music and performing arts by building collections inclusive of unique objects that center the experiences of those whose stories are captured. At the NMAAHC, Burnside develops exhibitions and programs that create engaging and educational experiences for visitors to the Museum and worldwide audiences online.

Tuliza Fleming (TF)

Tuliza Fleming PhD is the interim Chief Curator of Visual Arts at the NMAAHC. She played a critical role in building the Museum's art collection and served as lead curator for *Reckoning: Protest. Defiance. Resilience* (2021) and the inaugural exhibition *Visual Art and the American Experience* (2016). She also curated *Clementine Hunter: Life on Melrose Plantation* (2018), and co-curated *Ain't Nothing Like the Real Thing: How the Apollo Theater Shaped American Entertainment* (2010).

Hannah Grantham (HG)

Hannah Grantham is a curatorial research assistant at the NMAAHC with a background in musicology. The North Carolina native began her love affair with music at a young age, singing with different community groups in the Durham and Raleigh area. Grantham stumbled upon the fascinating world of museum work when she was a jazz studies student at the University of North Texas. She has spent the last several years happily working with music collections at the Smithsonian Institution and other museums across the United States.

Steven W. Lewis (SWL)

Steven W. Lewis PhD is Curator of Music and Performing Arts at the NMAAHC. Prior to joining the staff, he served as the founding curator of the National Museum of African American Music in Nashville, Tennessee. Lewis has also worked as historian and curator for the Ed Johnson Memorial Project and as an advisory scholar for the Carnegie Hall Corporation.

Vanessa L. Moorer (VLM)

Vanessa L. Moorer PhD is a scholar at the NMAAHC focusing on collection acquisitions, and on curatorial projects involving social justice, the Johnson Publishing Company collection, web-based content, and exhibitions. She started as the first Andrew

W. Mellon Curatorial Fellow, and subsequently worked on the inaugural exhibition, *A Changing America*. Moorer has earned degrees from the University of South Florida, Wake Forest University, and Howard University.

Kelly Elaine Navies (KEN)

Kelly Elaine Navies is the museum specialist in oral history at the NMAAHC. She coordinates the Museum's oral history initiative. Navies's oral history projects and interviews are located at the Southern Oral History Program, The Reginald F. Lewis Maryland Museum of African American History and Culture, The People's Archive at the Washington, DC Public Library, and the NMAAHC. She is also a writer, poet, and avid Prince fan.

Douglas T. Remley (DTR)

Douglas T. Remley is the publications and rights specialist at the NMAAHC. He joined the NMAAHC team in 2014 to assist in coordinating the Museum's slate of inaugural publications. Since then, he has coordinated the publication of numerous books and online features highlighting the Museum's collection and exhibitions, while also managing all copyright clearances and the distribution of images and information relating to objects in the NMAAHC collection.

Deborah Tulani Salahu-Din (DTS)

Deborah Tulani Salahu-Din is a museum specialist at the NMAAHC. Since 2010, she has developed content and collected artifacts for the Museum's exhibitions and publications. As a language and literature specialist, she focuses on the written and oral tradition in African American poetry. A goal of her work is to promote the unique value of poetry of the academy and Spoken Word.

Kevin M. Strait (KMS)

Kevin M. Strait PhD is a museum curator at the NMAAHC. Since 2010, he has worked on the research, development, and acquisition of objects for several of the Museum's permanent exhibitions. He is currently curating a temporary exhibition, entitled *Afrofuturism—A History of Black Futures*, which will open at the NMAAHC in 2023, and is co-authoring a book to accompany the exhibition.

Angela Tate (AT)

Angela Tate is Curator of Women's History at the NMAAHC. She collects and interprets the stories of women and non-binary persons of African descent, and tells the story of gender, race, and sexuality through the lens of African American history. Her academic background looks at Black women's radio and film history through the lens of pan-Africanism and diplomacy to uncover "hidden herstories" of diasporic civil rights activism.

Eric Lewis Williams (ELW)

Eric Lewis Williams PhD is Curator of Religion at the NMAAHC. Williams holds a Bachelor of Arts degree in Communications and Sociology from the University of Illinois at Chicago, a Master of Arts degree in Theological Studies from the McCormick Theological Seminary, a Master of Divinity degree from Duke University, and a PhD in Religious Studies from the University of Edinburgh in the United Kingdom.

Author initials appear at the end of each entry profile and story.

Image credits

Unless otherwise noted all objects are from the collection of the Smithsonian National Museum of African American History and Culture.

Key: top (*t*), bottom (*b*), left (*l*), right (*r*), center (*c*)

Page 4
Helen Rose
Green velvet dress worn by Lena Horne
in the film *Stormy Weather*
1943
2011.90

Foreword
Pages 6–7
General Motors Corporation
Red Cadillac Eldorado
owned by Chuck Berry
1973
Donation of Charles E. Berry
2011.137.1

Page 9
The Angela Davis Legal Defense Fund
Flyer Advertising an Evening
with Angela Davis
July 1972
2015.97.27.135

Introduction
Page 10
Yamaha Corporation
Flugelhorn used by Ronnie Wilson
of The Gap Band
before 1974
Gift of Ronnie Wilson
2013.31.1.1ab

Page 11
Clemens Kalischer
Photograph of John Lee Hooker with
diagram of the evolution of the blues
1951
© Clemens Kalischer Photos
2013.46.21

Page 12
Jean Gleason
Pinback button for Dizzy Gillespie
1964
Gift of Jeff Gold and Jody Uttal Gold
2012.15.3

Page 13
José Enrique Arteaga
Dress worn by Celia Cruz
1970s
Gift of the Celia Cruz Knight Estate
2013.8

Chapter 1
Page 14
Shirley Verrett
Page from a music manuscript book
belonging to Shirley Verrett
1960
Gift of Francesca LoMonaco in memory
of Shirley Verrett
TA2019.88.3.1

Page 16 (*tr*)
Henry Horenstein
DeFord Bailey
1974
National Museum of American History,
© Henry Horenstein
2003.0169.043

Page 16 (*bl*)
Hohner
Musikinstrumente GmbH & Co. KG
Harmonica played by DeFord Bailey
ca. 1976
Gift of Christine Bailey Craig
2022.3

Page 17
Country Music Association
CMA Award for Male Vocalist of the
Year awarded to Charley Pride
1971
Gift of Charley Pride
2012.125.67

Page 18
Photograp of Cab Calloway and his
band in a sleeper car
1933
Gift of Cabella Calloway Langsam
2013.237.14

Page 19
Herkert and Meisel
Travel wardrobe trunk used
by Cab Calloway
after 1927
Gift of Cabella Calloway Langsam
A2015.273.1.1

Page 20
Hall Johnson
Photograph of Paul Robeson, Jester
Hairston, and three unidentified men
mid-20th century
Gift of Dr. Eugene Thamon Simpson,
Representative, Hall Johnson Estate,
© Hall Johnson Estate
TA2013.166.2.1

Page 21 (*tl*)
Bill Gillohm
Photograph of Ray Charles
1965
© Johnson Publishing Company
Archive. Courtesy J. Paul Getty Trust
and Smithsonian National Museum of
African American History and Culture

Page 21 (*tr*)
Jimmie Davis
Letter from Jimmie Davis to Charles
Sullivan about Ray Charles's version of
the song "You Are My Sunshine"

December 3, 1962
2011.68.1.2

Page 22
John L. Lewis
Letter from John L. Lewis to
Maxine Sullivan
May 19, 1983
2013.46.29.98ab

Page 23
Philip Paul Bliss and Ira D. Sankey
Gospel Hymns No. 2
Personal hymnal of Harriet Tubman
1876
Gift of Charles L. Blockson
2009.50.25

Page 24
Lena Horne
Letter to Edouard Plummer
from Lena Horne
May 31, 1967
Gift of Edouard E. Plummer
TA2010.104.5.1a

Page 25
Gilbert Pictorial Enterprise
Photograph of Lena Horne and Edouard
Plummer at the Harlem YMCA
1960s
Gift of Edouard E. Plummer
TA2011.1.2.1

Pages 26–27
Gretsch
Gretsch G6138 "Bo Diddley" model
rectangular guitar owned by Bo Diddley
2005
2013.177.3.1a

Page 28
Bob Mackie
Costume worn by Diana Ross as Billie
Holiday in *Lady Sings the Blues*
1972
2012.64.4

Page 29
Clock worn by Flavor Flav
mid-1980s
Gift of Flavor Flav
2018.49

Page 30
Hoop and key earring worn
by Janet Jackson
1987–90
2021.28.2

Page 31
Willie Dixon
Handwritten lyrics to "You Need Love"
by Willie Dixon, signed by Ron Wood

ca. 1962
© Willie Dixon
2013.75.2

Page 32
Poster for an Ernie Fields performance
in Tulsa, Oklahoma
mid-20th century
Gift of Ernie Fields Jr. and Carmen
Fields; Ernie Fields Sr. Estate
TA2021.110.6.1

Page 33 (*tr*)
Barbara Walker
Color photograph of Eubie Blake
and artist Bob Walker during a
modeling session
1981
Gift of Bobbiegita Walker,
© Bobbiegita Walker
2011.128.3.2

Page 33 (*bl*)
Bobbiegita Walker
Eubie Blake
1981
Gift of Bobbiegita Walker,
© Bobbiegita Walker
2011.128.1ab

Chapter 2
Page 34
Jason Miccolo Johnson
*Liturgical Dancers Leap into
"Sanctified Air" during the Ceremonial
Groundbreaking Service for the New
Metropolitan Baptist Church, Largo,
Maryland, 2004* (detail)
2004; printed 2012
From the series *Soul Sanctuary*
© Jason Miccolo Johnson
2012.141.9

Page 36
The National Academy of Recording
Arts & Sciences
Grammy Award for Best Soul
Gospel Performance awarded to the
Dixie Hummingbirds
1974
Gift from Ira Tucker Jr. of the Dixie
Hummingbirds, © The National
Academy of Recording Arts & Sciences
2013.13.17

Page 37
Globe Poster Printing Company
Poster advertising the 1973 Memphis
Gospel Festival
1973
2013.46.24

Page 38
Heirloom Saxon violin and bow
1820–70
Gift of Clarence P. Cameron
2020.28.1ab

Page 39
Mattel, Inc.
"How to Breakdance" Reels for
Mattel View-Master featuring the
New York City Breakers
1984
© 1984 Hip Hop International, Inc.
2016.31.2.2

Page 40
National Washboard Company
Washboard owned by Bo Diddley
1950s–60s
2013.177.7

Page 41 (*tr*)
Photograph of Felton W. Williams Jr.
and another man playing guitar
1963
Gift of Felton W. Williams Jr.
2011.64.6.1

Page 41 (*b*)
Felton W. Williams Jr.
Electric console steel guitar built by
Felton W. Williams Jr.
ca. 1963
Gift of Felton W. Williams Jr.
2011.64.1a-f

Page 42
African Musical Instrument Company
Mbira owned by Pete Cosey
late 20th century
Gift of Karumah, Dunni, Ishmak,
Aribania and Mariama Cosey in memory
of Baba Pete Cosey
2021.105.4a-g

Page 43 (*tr*)
Ricky Powell
Chromogenic print of Rakim performing
at the Apollo Theatre in Harlem
1988
© Ricky Powell
2015.132.361

Page 43 (*b*)
Shure
Cordless microphone used by Rakim to
record *The 18th Letter*
1997
Gift of Rakim
2016.10.1

Page 44
James Baldwin
Some Days
Poem written to Paula Baldwin
by James Baldwin
mid-20th century
Gift of The Baldwin Family,
© James Baldwin Estate
2011.99.18

Page 45
Francis Johnson

General La Fayette Bugle Waltz
1824
2019.28.33

Page 46 (*bl*)
William R. Meinell
Flute made for Thomas Greene "Blind
Tom" Wiggins by William R. Meinell
1879–84
2014.138.1a-f

Page 46 (*br*)
Jacob Dux & Co.
Broadside for Thomas Greene
"Blind Tom" Wiggins
ca. 1887
2021.89

Page 47
H. C. Miner Lithographing Company
Poster for a Mattie Wilkes performance
at Holliday Street Theater
1899–1905
Gift of Stephen and Catherine Markardt
2013.137

Page 49
Domenic Serio
Lavender satin ensemble
worn by Prince
ca. 1998
2020.27.3.1-.2

Page 49
Andre Rostomyan
Lavender heeled boots worn by Prince
1993–2000
2020.27.2ab

Page 50 (*tr*)
Photograph of William "Ju Ju" House
playing the drums
1990s
Gift of William "Ju Ju" House
2013.106.11

Page 50 (*bl*)
Painted bass drumhead owned by
William "Ju Ju" House
ca. 1988
Gift of William "Ju Ju" House
2013.106.1

Page 51
Fela Anikulapo Kuti and Roy Ayers
Music of Many Colors
1980; published 1986
© 1986 Celuloid Records
2015.195.2ab

Pages 52–53 (*t*) and Page 53 (*tr*)
Mapex
Custom Mapex hanging 16-inch tom
drum owned by Will Calhoun
2005
Gift of Will Calhoun
2015.14.3

Page 52 (*bl*)
Windsor Shoe Company
Tap shoes used by Sammy Davis Jr.
1938
2013.118.302ab

Page 53 (*b*)
Avedis Zildjian Company
Drumsticks owned by Terri
Lyne Carrington
1970s
Gift of Terri Lyne Carrington
2021.101.2ab

Pages 54–57 (*t*)
Anthony Barboza
Dance Theatre of Harlem #2 (detail)
1983
Gift of Anthony Barboza,
© Anthony Barboza
2016.96.3

Page 55 (*c*)
Jack Mitchell
Alvin Ailey and Carmen de Lavallade in
Roots of the Blues
1964
© Alvin Ailey Dance Foundation,
Inc. and Smithsonian Institution, all
rights reserved.
A2013.245.1.1.2.22

Page 56 (*c*)
Charles Rudolph Davis
Page from a spiral notebook belonging
to Dr. Baba Chuck Davis
Gift of Ngoma & Normadien
Woolbright in memory of
Dr. Chuck Davis
TA2018.98.4.1

Page 57 (*r*)
Capezio
Custom-colored toe shoes worn by
Emiko Flanagan, Alexandra Jacob, and
Ingrid Silva of Dance Theatre of Harlem
2013–14
Gift of the Dance Theatre of Harlem
2015.19.1.1, .2.1, .3.2

Page 58 (*l*)
Gourd head banjo
ca. 1859
2017.108.19

Page 58 (*r*)
Wooden drum used on the Sea
Islands, South Carolina
19th century
2014.122.2

Pages 58–59 (*t*) and Page 59 (*bl*)
Moog Music Inc.
Minimoog Voyager synthesizer
used by J Dilla
2002–05
Gift of Maureen Yancy
2014.139.2a

Page 59 (*br*)
Akai Professional
MIDI Production Center 3000 Limited
Edition used by J Dilla
2000
Gift of Maureen Yancy
2014.139.1

Pages 60–63 (*t*) and Page 63 (*c*)
Wilshire Dames

Costume for Bahamas Junkanoo Revue,
a junkanoo troupe in Miami
2015
2015.140

Page 60 (*br*)
Gold necklace with Africa pendant
to promote Nina Simone's
Black Gold album
1970
2011.132.11ab

Page 61
Platon (*c*)
Maison Dorcas Women's Singing Group
2016; printed 2019
Gift of Platon, © Platon
2021.33.72

Page 62 (*b*)
Ernie Paniccioli
Chromogenic color print of
X Clan and Isis
1990
© Ernie Paniccioli
2021.65

Pages 64–65 (*t*) and Page 65 (*tl*)
Hall Johnson
Sheet music for "Ain't Got Time to Die"
inscribed for Robert McFerrin
mid-20th century
Gift of Dr. Eugene Thamon Simpson,
Representative, Hall Johnson Estate
TA2013.166.4.1

Page 64 (*tl*)
Sidney Cowell
Hall Johnson
1960
National Portrait Gallery,
Smithsonian Institution
NPG84.128

Page 64 (*tr*)
Franke & Heidecke
Rolleiflex Automat Model 1 camera
owned by Hall Johnson
1937–39
Gift of Dr. Eugene Thamon Simpson,
Representative, Hall Johnson Estate
A2013.166.1.9

Page 65 (*br*)
Hall Johnson
Letter to Mr. Kosson from Hall Johnson
May 13, 1938
Gift of Dr. Eugene Thamon Simpson,
Representative, Hall Johnson Estate
TA2013.166.4.1

Pages 66-67 (*t*)
Lloyd W. Yearwood
Photograph of Leontyne Price at
Carnegie Hall (detail)
ca. 1984
© Estate of Lloyd W. Yearwood
2014.150.10.9

Page 66 (*tl*)
Ensemble associated with
Marian Anderson's 1939 Lincoln
Memorial concert

1939; modified 1993
Gift of Ginette DePreist in memory
of James DePreist
2014.27.2

Page 67 (*tl*)
Holiday card from William Grant Still
1937
2015.97.38.3

Page 67 (*br*)
Arthur Leipzig
Dean Dixon, American Youth Orchestra
1944–49
Gift of Judith Leipzig in memory of
Arthur Leipzig, © Arthur Leipzig
2017.69.2

Pages 68–69 (*t*) and Page 68 (*bl*)
H. N. White Company
Alto saxophone owned and played
by Charlie Parker
ca. 1947
2019.10.1a-g

Page 69 (*tl*)
John Coltrane
Sheet music for "Nothing Beats a
Trial but a Failure"
1950s
2011.57.30

Page 69 (*br*)
Steve Jackson Jr.
Swinging Horn Section, c. mid 1950s
ca. 1955
Gift of Mary E. Jackson,
Posthumously and Linda A. Jackson,
© Linda A. Jackson/Steven Jackson Jr.
Archives/CTS Images
2016.117.16

Chapter 3
Page 70
Gaylord Oscar Herron
Untitled
Photograph of Robert Wilson of
The Gap Band at Cain's Ballroom in
Tulsa, Oklahoma
1973
Gift of Gaylord Oscar Herron,
© Gaylord Oscar Herron
2012.67.44

Page 73 (*tr*)
Denis Bourdon
Cabinet card of Frederick Douglass with
his grandson, Joseph Douglass
May 10, 1894
Gift of Dr. Charlene Hodges Byrd
A2010.26.29.8.1

Page 73 (*bl*)
Joseph Henry Douglass
Letter to Mary Church Terrell from
Joseph Douglass
May 31, 1911
2013.46.22

Page 74
The National Academy of Recording
Arts & Sciences

Grammy Lifetime Achievement Award
issued to Ella Jenkins
2004
Gift of Ella Jenkins, © The National
Academy of Recording Arts & Sciences
2018.7.1ab

Page 75
Lewis Wickes Hine
Photograph of men being led in an
orchestra at the Bordentown School
ca. 1935
Gift of Howard and Ellen Greenberg
2011.165.5

Page 76
Slade's Studio Photography
William Patrick Foster
1968
National Portrait Gallery, Smithsonian
Institution; gift of the Dr. William P. and
Mary Ann Foster Foundation, Anthony
F. Foster, son of Dr. William P. and
Mrs. Mary Foster
NPG.2017.86

Page 77 (*t*)
Shako used by Florida A&M
University Marching Band
1970s
Gift from Anthony Foster in memory of
William P. Foster
2019.94.3ab

Page 77 (*b*)
Sol Frank Uniforms, Inc.
Florida A&M University
Marching Band jacket
1970s
Gift from Anthony Foster in memory of
William P. Foster
2019.94.5.2

Page 79 (*t*)
Lloyd W. Yearwood
Photograph of Rabbi David
Matthew Doré blowing the shofar
on Rosh Hashanah
September 1983
© Estate of Lloyd W. Yearwood
2014.150.3.70

Page 79 (*b*)
Shofar from Beth Shalom B'nai Zaken
Ethiopian Hebrew Congregation
1998
Gift of Rabbi Capers Funnye and the
Beth Shalom B'nai Zaken Ethiopian
Hebrew Congregation
2011.88.6ab

Page 80
Steve Jackson Jr.
*Popular Bop City waitress poses with
military men, c. 1952*
ca. 1952
Gift of Mary E. Jackson,
Posthumously and Linda A. Jackson,
© Linda A. Jackson/Steven Jackson Jr.
Archives/CTS Images
2016.117.22

Page 81 (*bl*)
Photograph of Ray Barretto
and Celia Cruz
1980s
Gift of Brandy and Chris Barretto, in
memory of Ray Barretto
TA2020.52.3.1

Page 81 (*br*)
Conga played by Ray Barretto
late 20th century
Gift of Brandy and Chris Barretto, in
memory of Ray Barretto
A2020.52.1.2

Page 82
Philco
Radio owned by Herman and
Minnie Roundtree
1948
Gift of the Lyles Station Historic
Preservation Corporation
2012.155.9

Page 83
International Artists Corporation
Page from a promotional booklet
for the Wings Over Jordan Choir
announcing the winners of the Wings
Over Jordan Scholarships
1948
2019.22.6.1

Page 84
Promotional card for a piano recital
given by Eunice Waymon (Nina Simone)
1954
2011.132.2

Page 85 (*tr*)
NMAAHC
Pressed seal for the Colored
Performing Rights Society of America
2022

Page 85 (*bl*)
Seal embosser for the Colored
Performing Rights Society of America
ca. 1957
Gift of Charles Young and
Cheryl Deknatel
A2021.106.1.3

Page 86
Black Rock Coalition
Poster for a Black Rock festival in Italy
ca. 1991
Gift of the Black Rock Coalition -
LaRonda Davis, President
2015.42.12

Page 88
Motown Record Corporation
Gold Record Award for "I Heard it
Through the Grapevine"
ca. 1967
Gift of Merald "Bubba" Knight, William
Guest and the Estate of Edward Patten
of Gladys Knight & the Pips
2014.288.22

Page 89
Ira Rosenberg
Photograph of a man carrying a
contrabass and lantern during the
Detroit Rebellion
July 1967
© Ira Rosenberg
2011.57.11.14

Page 90 (*bl*)
Robert Houston
Photographic transparency of Rev.
Frederick Douglass Kirkpatrick playing
the guitar at Resurrection City during
the Poor People's Campaign
May 21–June 23, 1968
© Robert Houston
2015.245.277

Pages 90–91 (*t*)
Plywood panel mural, "Hunger's Wall,"
from Resurrection City
1968
Gift of Vincent DeForest
2012.110

Pages 92–93 (*t*)
E. F. Joseph
Photograph of the Fannie Wall
Home for Children in Oakland,
California (detail)
1943
Gift of Jackie Bryant Smith
2010.66.5

Page 92 (*tl*)
Photograph of Ernie Freeman at age 4
ca. 1926
Gift of Janis M. Freeman in memory
of Ernie Freeman
TA2021.12.7.1

Page 92 (*br*)
E.P. Carpenter & Company
Organ owned by Henry Long and family
ca. 1898
Gift from the Family of Henry L. Long
2012.7.1ab

Page 93 (*br*)
Doree Fromberg
Pale blue chiffon dress worn by Janet
Jackson at her first piano recital
1974–75
A2021.28.7.1.2

Pages 94–95 (*t*)
Jason Miccolo Johnson
*Rev. Dr. Grainger Browning (center),
Senior Pastor of Ebenezer AME Church,
Kneels Down in Prayer upon Entering
the Pulpit. Pastor Browning and
Co-pastor Jo Ann Browning (center,
right) are in the Vanguard of Husband/
Wife Pastorships in America, Fort
Washington, Maryland, 1997*
1997; printed 2012
From the series *Soul Sanctuary*
© Jason Miccolo Johnson
2012.141.5

Page 94 (bc)
The Cable Piano Company
Piano from Pilgrim Baptist Church used
by Thomas Dorsey
1930s
Gift of Rev. Richard C. Keller, Jr.,
Mr. Edward G. Keller, and Ms.
Paulene Austin Keller
2015.134.1a-g

Page 95 (bl)
Dirr Street Methodist Episcopal Church
Lyric sheet for James Weldon Johnson
and John Rosamond Johnson's "Lift
Every Voice and Sing"
Gift of Barry Greenstein
TA2014.304.4.5

Page 95 (tr)
Harry Pedler and Sons
Trumpet belonging to Roosevelt Hunter
ca. 1945
Gift of Ralph Hunter
2013.173.4

Pages 96–97 (t)
Wincraft, Inc.
HBCU Pennants
late 20th century–early 21st century
2013.183.7.1-.9

Page 96 (bc)
Photograph of William L. Dawson and
the Tuskegee Choir
October 1937
Gift of Dr. Eugene Thamon Simpson,
Representative, Hall Johnson Estate,
© Hall Johnson Estate
TA2013.166.2.2

Page 97 (tl)
Miraphone
Left-handed baritone used by the
Florida A&M University marching band
mid to late 20th century
Gift from Anthony Foster in memory of
William P. Foster
2019.94.2.1

Page 97 (br)
Globe Poster Printing Company
Poster advertising a James Brown
concert at Florida A&M University
1969
2011.96

Pages 98–99 (t)
Harry C. Ellis
Photograph of James Reese Europe's
369th Infantry Harlem Hellfighters
Brass Band at the American Red Cross
Hospital Number 5, in Paris, France
ca. 1918
2011.57.39

Page 98 (tl)
Bass drum from the 25th
US Infantry Band
ca. 1930
In memory of George M. Langellier Sr.
2012.171.15.8

Page 98 (br)
Handy Brothers Music Co. Inc.
Sheet music for "We Are Americans
Too" written and composed by Andy
Razaf, Eubie Blake, and Charles L. Cooke
Gift of Barry Greenstein
TA2014.304.4.6

Page 99 (tr)
United States Navy
Continuous service records for Alton
Augustus Adams Sr.
1917–45
Gift of Alton A. Adams Jr. Trustee
2014.263.5

Pages 100–103 (t)
Elmer Simms Campbell
Manhattan, Vol. 1, No. 1: A Night-Club
Map of Harlem (detail)
January 18, 1933
2020.26.34a-e

Page 100 (bl)
Ash tray from Club Harlem
mid-20th century
Gift of Vicki Gold Levi
2013.223.65

Page 101 (c)
Steve Jackson Jr.
Bop City proprietor, Jimbo (wearing
beret) with guests, c. mid 1950s
ca. 1955
Gift of Mary E. Jackson,
Posthumously and Linda A. Jackson,
© Linda A. Jackson/Steven Jackson Jr.
Archives/CTS Images
2016.117.17

Page 103 (c)
Harry Allen
LL Cool J Assault, Def Jam
label introductory showcase,
Benjamin Franklin H.S.
1984
© Harry Allen
2015.132.44.3

Pages 104–105 (t)
James A. Joyce
Photograph of Disc Jockey Bill Hawkins
and Bill Bailey
1950–58
Gift of W. Allen Taylor, son of "Walkin'
Talkin' Bill Hawkins" The First Black Disc
Jockey of Cleveland, Ohio
2018.91.2.15

Page 104 (bl)
James A. Joyce
Photograph of Bill Hawkins, Mary Lou
Williams, and Paul Breckenridge
ca. 1951
Gift of W. Allen Taylor, son of "Walkin'
Talkin' Bill Hawkins" The First Black Disc
Jockey of Cleveland, Ohio
2018.91.2.31

Pages 104–105 (bl)
Hawk Record Co.

"Blowing My Horn" by Allen
Thomas and Orchestra
1953
Gift of W. Allen Taylor, son of "Walkin'
Talkin' Bill Hawkins" The First Black Disc
Jockey of Cleveland, Ohio
2018.91.4.1ab

Page 105 (tr)
James A. Joyce
Photograph of Earl Bostic
signing autographs inside Bill
Hawkins' Record Studio
ca. 1952
Gift of W. Allen Taylor, son of "Walkin'
Talkin' Bill Hawkins" The First Black Disc
Jockey of Cleveland, Ohio
2018.91.2.11

Pages 106–107 (t)
Horace C. Henry
Atlanta Skyline (taken from the
Jackson Street Bridge) (detail)
From the series One Day in January: A
Collection of Images Taken at Dr. King's
First Memorial Service
January 15, 1969; printed 2011
Gift of Horace C. Henry,
© Horace Henry
2011.94.40

Page 106 (bl)
Tabu Productions
S.O.S.III
1981
Gift of Dwandalyn R. Reece,
© 1982 CBS Inc.
2015.197.4ab

Page 107 (bl)
New Era Cap Company
Purple Atlanta Braves baseball cap
owned by Big Boi
2013
Gift of Antwan Patton
2016.121.3

Page 107 (br)
Rainbow feather boa and shoulder pads
cape worn by André 3000
2000
Gift of André Benjamin
2016.120.1

Pages 108–109 (t)
Frank L. Stewart
Clouds and Railroad Tracks (detail)
2005
Gift of the Frank Stewart Estate,
© Frank Stewart, Courtesy of Frank
Stewart and Gallery Neptune and
Brown, Washington, DC
2016.158.6

Page 108 (br)
Pierre Cardin
Red and cream loafers designed by
Pierre Cardin and worn by Fats Domino
late 20th Century
Gift of Antoine "Fats" Domino
2013.59.3ab

Pages 108–109 (b)
Don Moser
Voodoo Guitar "Marie" made
by Don Moser with debris from
Hurricane Katrina
2005
Gift of Musician/Artist Don Louis Moser
2015.119.1-.2

Page 109 (tr)
Charles Gillam Sr.
Ain't That a Shame
2005-12
© Charles Gillam Sr.
2013.207.3

Pages 110–113 (t) and Page 110 (br)
Mercury Records
We Shall Overcome
1963
Gift of Dwandalyn R. Reece
2015.197.12ab

Page 111 (c)
E. J. Warner Poster Corp.
Poster for a concert to aid sit-in
movements and the Martin
Luther King Defense
1960
2019.28.22

Page 113 (c)
Tommy Oliver
Photograph of YG with a picture of
Nipsey Hussle at a Black Lives Matter
protest in Los Angeles
June 7, 2020
Gift of Tommy and Codie Oliver,
© Tommy Oliver
2021.31.60

Pages 114–115 (t)
Jermaine Gibbs
Photograph of a crowd of protesters at
Baltimore War Memorial (detail)
April 25, 2015
Gift of Jermaine Gibbs,
© Jermaine Gibbs
2016.61.12

Page 114 (br)
3rdEyeGirl.com
T-shirt from the Prince Rally 4 Peace
concert in Baltimore
2015
Gift from Dorothy and Eugene Bryant,
© Estate of Prince Rogers Nelson
2015.154.1

Page 115 (c)
Devin Allen
Untitled
Photograph of children at a Black Lives
Matter rally in Baltimore
2015
Gift of Devin Allen, © Devin Allen
2016.98.43

Chapter 4
Page 116
Bert Williams and Edward Furber

Sheet music for "He's Up Against the Real Thing Now"
1898
Gift of Sylvia Alden Roberts
2014.275.15

Page 118
Claude Clark Sr.
The Poet II
1946
Gift of Robert Booker, © Estate of Claude Clark
2018.92

Page 119
Hand-painted drum depicting caricatures of nine male faces
ca. 1925
Gift of the Collection of James M. Caselli and Jonathan Mark Scharer
2007.7.444

Page 121
Andora
Cocktail dress worn by Billie Holiday
early 1950s
2021.59.3.1

Page 122
American Theatre Wing, Inc.
Tony Award® won by Diahann Carroll for Leading Actress in a Musical
1962
© American Theatre Wing, Inc.
2020.15.3

Page 123
Johnson Publishing Company
Ebony
October 1967
Gift of Portsmouth Black Heritage Trail, Inc., © Ebony Media Group LLC
2011.12.53.6

Page 125
East Publications Inc.
Contract signed by Otis Redding for "Mr. Pitiful"
1965
2010.50.1

Page 126 (*tr*)
Bernard Gotfryd
Photograph of Nina Simone recording the song "Don't Let Me Be Misunderstood"
1964
2011.132.6.1

Page 126 (*bl*)
Sam Fox Publishing Company
Album sleeve for the single, "Mississippi Goddam," recorded by Nina Simone
1964
2011.132.9ab

Page 126 (*br*)
Ten shards of stained glass collected after the 16th Street Baptist Church bombing in Montgomery, Alabama
September 1963
Gift from the

Trumpauer-Mulholland Collection
2010.71.1.1-.10

Page 127
Jimi Hendrix
Recording made by Jimi Hendrix at Electric Lady Studios
1970
2020.53.9ab

Pages 128–129
Sussex Records, Inc.
Interior of album jacket for *Still Bill* recorded by Bill Withers
1972
Gift of Dwandalyn R. Reece, © 1972 Sussex Records Inc., courtesy of Sony Music Entertainment
2015.197.7abc

Page 130
Recording Industry Association of America
Gold record award presented to Ernie Freeman to commemorate more than one million dollars in sales for the album *Strangers in the Night*
1966
Gift of Janis M. Freeman in memory of Ernie Freeman
TA2021.12.1.1

Page 131
Promax
Boombox carried by Radio Raheem in the film *Do the Right Thing*
1989
2014.270.2

Page 132
Winterland Productions
Public Enemy crosshairs logo necklace owned by Chuck D
ca. 1990
Gift of Public Enemy
2013.149.2

Page 133
George Clinton, Jules Fisher, and Peter Larkin
The Mothership
1990s
Gift of Love to the planet
2011.83.1.1-.9

Page 135
Al Pereira
Photographic print of Queen Latifah on the set of the "Fly Girl" video
June 23, 1991
© Al Pereira
2015.132.302

Page 136
Luther Vandross
Lyrics for "Dance with My Father" handwritten by Luther Vandross
2003
Gift of Fonzi Thornton in Memory of Luther Vandross, © Estate of Luther Vandross

2018.87

Page 137
Tony Chase
Outfits worn by Luther Vandross and backup singers Kevin Owens, Ava Cherry, and Lisa Fischer
1980s
Gift of Seveda Williams in Celebration of the Musical Legacy of her Uncle, Luther Vandross
2018.86.2-.5

Pages 138–139 (*t*)
Five figurines in the form of caricatured male musicians
1930s–40s
Gift of the Collection of James M. Caselli and Jonathan Mark Scharer
2007.7.141.1-.5

Page 138 (*bl*)
A. T. B. De Witt
Tambo: His Jokes & Funny Sayings
1882
2015.97.26.13

Page 138 (*tr*) and Page 139 (*bl*)
John H. Buckbee
Banjo created for Charles P. Stinson
late 19th century
Gift of the Clark and Sarah Case Family
2018.83.1

Page 139 (*br*)
Film still of Louis Armstrong on the set of "Going Places"
1938
2013.46.25.85

Pages 140–141 (*t*)
RCA Records
Photographs from the interior of the album jacket for *Ain't Misbehavin': The New Fats Waller Musical Show* (detail)
1978
© 1978 RCA Records, courtesy of Masterworks Broadway, a label of Sony Music Entertainment
2015.189.13abc

Page 140 (*tl*)
Eubie Blake, Noble Sissle, Flournoy Miller, and Aubrey Lyle
Sheet music for "Love Will Find a Way" from the musical *Shuffle Along*
1921
2013.118.288

Page 141 (*br*)
Geoffrey Holder
Costume for The Wiz worn by André De Shields in the original Broadway production of *The Wiz*
1975
Gift of André De Shields
2018.1.3.3, .4ab, .5, .6ab, .7.1

Page 142 (*br*)
Judy Dearing
Costume design drawing by Judy Dearing for Porgy and Bess

1995
2014.128.12

Pages 142–145 (*t*) and Page 142 (*c*)
Columbia Records
Ledger page for Clara Smith listing contracted recordings for Columbia's Race Records Division
1928–29
Gift of Jerry and Jane Williams
TA2019.98.2.1.1

Page 143 (*r*)
Larry LeGaspi
Costume worn by Nona Hendryx of Labelle
1975
Gift of Nona Hendryx of Labelle
2014.246.3.1-.4ab

Page 145 (*c*)
Sign from the 2017 Women's March on Washington with lyrics from Beyonce's duet with Jack White, "Don't Hurt Yourself"
2017
2017.85.18

Pages 146–149 (*t*)
Sign for Minton's Playhouse
after 1984
Gift of Harlem Community Development Corporation, a subsidiary of the New York State Urban Development Corporation, d/b/a/ Empire State Development
2015.1

Page 147 (*c*)
Charles "Teenie" Harris
Photograph of Billy Eckstine conducting his band at the Aragon Ballroom in Pittsburgh, Pennsylvania
August 1944
Gift from Charles A. Harris and Beatrice Harris in memory of Charles "Teenie" Harris, © Carnegie Museum of Art, Charles "Teenie" Harris Archive
2014.302.49

Page 148 (*r*)
Minton's Playhouse
Invitation to the Gala Opening of the Music Room at Minton's Playhouse
August 29, 1940
Gift from grandaughters Michelle Redmond and Lisa Baskett
TA2019.87.5.1

Page 149 (*c*)
Baldwin Piano Company
Grand piano owned and used by Thelonious Monk
1962
Gift of T.S. and Gale Monk in memory of Thelonious Monk
2018.89.1

Pages 150 and 152 (*t*)
G. Marshall Wilson
Photograph of Little Richard outside a

church in Brooklyn, New York
1957
© Johnson Publishing Company
Archive. Courtesy J. Paul Getty Trust
and Smithsonian National Museum of
African American History and Culture

Page 150 (*tr*)
Photograph of Little Richard and three
men outside Jack's Barber Shop
late 1950s
TA2020.53.18.3.1

Pages 151 and 153 (*t*)
Maurice Sorrell
Little Richard and His Royal Order of
Bodyguards Leave the Ambassador
Hotel in Washington, D.C.
1978
© Johnson Publishing Company
Archive. Courtesy J. Paul Getty Trust
and Smithsonian National Museum of
African American History and Culture

Page 151 (*c*)
William Collins, Sons
King James Bible belonging
to Little Richard
ca. 1959
A2020.53.17.7.1

Page 153 (*c*)
Melvin James
Pink, green, and gold floral brocade
costume worn by Little Richard
late 1960s
2020.53.1ab

Page 153 (*c*)
Rino Orsato
Platform boots worn by Little Richard
1970s
2020.53.3ab

Page 154 (*tl*)
Johnson Publishing Company
Ebony (detail)
July 1978
© Ebony Media Group LLC
2016.69.1

Pages 154–155 (*tc*)
Johnson Publishing Company
Jet vol. 1 no. 9 (detail)
December 27, 1951
Courtesy of Johnson Publishing
Company, LLC, © Ebony
Media Group LLC
2015.122.12

Page 154 (*br*)
Printing plate with an image of
Marian Anderson
ca. 1950
Gift of the Chicago Defender Publishing
Company, © Chicago Defender
Publishing Company
2012.18.5.49

Page 155 (*tr, tl*)
Johnson Publishing Company
Black Stars, Vol. 28, No. 4 (detail)

February 1979
© Black Stars
2011.166.16.3

Page 155 (*tr*)
Miller Publishing Group, LLC
Vibe
July 2006
Gift of Rhea L. Combs, © Vibe
Magazine and © Matthais Clamer
2018.3

Pages 156–157 (*t*) and Page 156 (*br*)
Black Swan Records
LP recording of "Long Lost Mama"
by Ethel Waters
1921–23
Gift of Dwandalyn R. Reece
2015.197.1

Page 157 (*bl*)
A-1 Sound Studios, Inc.
Invoice to Vee-Jay Records for Little
Richard recordings
May 13, 1965
A2020.53.17.5.1

Page 157 (*tr*)
Steinway & Sons
Upright piano used by Thom Bell at
Philadelphia International Records
ca. 1900
Gift of Legendary producer Thom Bell
2015.203

Pages 158–159 (*t*)
Loew's Incorporated
Lobby card for *Cabin in the Sky* (detail)
1943
2013.118.97

Page 158 (*br*)
Helen Rose
Green velvet dress worn by Lena Horne
in the film *Stormy Weather* (detail)
1943
2011.90

Page 159 (*tl*)
Ernie Freeman
Page from the production score for the
pilot episode of *It Takes a Thief*
1967
Gift of Janis M. Freeman in memory
of Ernie Freeman
TA2021.12.4.2

Page 159 (*tr*)
Ampex
Gold Tape Award for the album
Superfly given to Curtis Mayfield
June 1973
Gift of the Mayfield Family Trust
2014.236.3

Pages 160–161 (*t*)
Applause sign from the set of *Soul Train*
1970s
Gift of Soul Train Holdings, LLC
2011.50.3.2

Page 160 (*bl*)

Bob Frazier, CBS Television
Photograph of Una Mae Carlisle with
Roy Sneed Jr. and the Southern Sons
Quartet on set at CBS studios
1944
Gift of Charles Young and
Cheryl Deknatel
TA2021.106.3.1

Page 161 (*bl*)
Soul Train
Soul Train Award for Artist of
the Decade – Female given to
Whitney Houston
2000
Gift of the Estate of Whitney Houston
2014.161.5

Page 161 (*tr*)
Ralph McDaniels
Microphone box used by Ralph
McDaniels on the television show
Video Music Box
ca. 1988
Gift of Ralph McDaniels, Founder of
Video Music Box
2015.188

Pages 162–163 (*t*)
Tom Foden
Storyboard page for the "Scream"
music video (detail)
1995
© Tom Foden
2021.28.5.23

Page 162 (*br*)
Chair used in the music video "Scream"
by Michael Jackson and Janet Jackson
1995
2014.97.1

Page 163 (*tr*)
Dexter Wong
White long-sleeved shirt worn by Janet
Jackson in "Scream" music video
1995
2021.28.4.1

Page 163 (*tr*)
Imitation leather pants worn by Janet
Jackson in "Scream" music video
1995
2021.28.4.3

Pages 164–167 (*t*) and Page 166 (*c*)
Ovation Guitar Company
Josh White Model Guitar
owned by Josh White
ca. 1966
Gift of Gene C. Feldman
2021.107ab

Page 164 (*b*)
Photograph of Paul Robeson, Ethel
Waters, Josh White, Canada Lee, and
D.G. Bridson on the set of "The Man
Who Went to War"
February 20, 1944
© BBC Photo Archive
2016.91

Page 165 (*r*)
Langston Hughes
First page of a script for the radio show
"The Man Who Went to War"
1944
© Estate of Langston Hughes
2019.28.30a-v

Chapter 5
Page 168
J. B. T. Marsh
*The Story of the Jubilee Singers:
With Their Songs*
1883
2010.34.1

Pages 170–171 (*c*)
Elmer Simms Campbell
Manhattan, Vol. 1, No. 1: A Night-
Club Map of Harlem
January 18, 1933
2020.26.34a-e

Page 171 (*br*)
Wooden clapper from the Cotton Club
promoting Ethel Waters
ca. 1933
Gift of Dwandalyn R. Reece in memory
of Pauline Watkins Reece
2015.45.3

Page 173
Rex Madsen
Collage of Alberta Hunter news
clippings by Rex Madsen
1978
Gift of Paul Bodden in memory of Thad
McGar and James "Jimmie" Daniels
A2020.19.1.2

Page 174 (*t*)
Columbia Records
Songs of Free Men recorded
by Paul Robeson
1948
Gift of Edward L. Bell in memory
of Ruth G. Bell
2019.70a-e

Page 174 (*b*)
Hohner
Musikinstrumente GmbH & Co. KG
Harmonica owned by
Big Mama Thornton
ca. 1950
2021.59.1

Page 175
Triola
"Et Smil Og Noen Ord / Vaer Slik Som
Du Er" 45 rpm cover of Nina Simone's
"To Be Young, Gifted and Black"
by Webe Karlsen
1970
© 1970 Triola Records
2011.132.8.4ab

Page 176
Anthony Barboza
Pat Evans and Isaac Hayes
1971; printed 2021

© Anthony Barboza
2021.21

Page 177
Jacki Robinson
"The Wizard of Woo" cape worn by
Bernie Worrell of Parliament-Funkadelic
ca. 1996
Gift of Judie Worrell and Bassl Worrell
2021.43.1-.3

Page 178
Tito D. Caicedo
Ring with gold and diamond "MTV"
design owned by Fab 5 Freddy
ca. 1988
2020.38.6

Page 179
Sheila Pree Bright
*"Say Her Name" Protest, Artist Janelle
Monae and Wondaland Records
Members Perform "Hell You Talmbout"
Protest Song, Atlanta, GA*
From the series *#1960Now*
2016
Gift of Sheila Pree Bright,
© Sheila Pree Bright
2021.56.1

Page 181
Milton Williams
Untitled
Photograph of Stevie Wonder singing
"Happy Birthday" to advocate for the
Martin Luther King Jr. Holiday on the
grounds of the Washington Monument
January 15, 1981
Gift of Milton Williams Archives,
© Milton Williams
2011.15.100

Pages 182–183 (*t*) Page 183 (*br*)
Walking stick used by Jimmie Daniels
mid-20th century
Gift of Paul Bodden in memory of Thad
McGar and James "Jimmie" Daniels
A2020.19.1.1

Page 182 (*tr*)
Carl Van Vechten (likely)
Photograph of Jimmie Daniels
early 1930s
Gift of Paul Bodden in memory of Thad
McGar and James "Jimmie" Daniels
TA2020.19.3.1

Page 183 (*bl*)
United States Army
Honorable discharge papers for Jimmie
Daniels (detail)
November 11, 1945
Gift of Paul Bodden in memory of Thad
McGar and James "Jimmie" Daniels
TA2020.19.2.1

Pages 184–185 (*t*) and Page 185 (*c*)
G. Marshall Wilson
Photograph of Matt and Terri Lyne
Carrington performing together
1977

Gift of Terri Lyne Carrington, © Johnson
Publishing Company Archive. Courtesy
J. Paul Getty Trust and Smithsonian
National Museum of African American
History and Culture
2021.101.5

Page 184 (*tl*)
The National Academy of Recording
Arts & Sciences
Grammy Award for Best Jazz
Instrumental Album received by Terri
Lyne Carrington
2013
Gift of Terri Lyne Carrington, © The
National Academy of Recording
Arts & Sciences
2021.101.1

Page 186 (*l*)
Stecker Brothers Agency
Poster for Edie Crump and the
Harlem Playgirls
1937
2012.46.61

Page 187 (*r*)
National Educational Television
Frames depicting Alice Coltrane at a
harp from *Black Journal: 26*
1970
Gift of Pearl Bowser, © National
Educational Television
2012.79.1.16.1a

Pages 188–191 (*t*)
G. Marshall Wilson
Photograph of Jimi Hendrix (detail)
1968
© Johnson Publishing Company
Archive. Courtesy J. Paul Getty Trust
and Smithsonian National Museum of
African American History and Culture

Page 188 (*b*)
General Motors Corporation
Red Cadillac Eldorado
owned by Chuck Berry
1973
Donation of Charles E. Berry
2011.137.1

Page 189 (*l*)
ESP Guitars
Custom ESP guitar owned and
played by Vernon Reid on Living
Colour's album *Vivid*
1985-86
Donated by Vernon Reid
2021.92.2a-f

Page 190 (*b*)
Columbia Records
Rubber Fishbone toy
1985
Gift of the documentary "Everyday
Sunshine: The Story of Fishbone"
2012.95.52

Page 191 (*c*)
Jeff Hamilton

Leather jacket owned by Jerry "Wyzard"
Seay of Mother's Finest
ca. 1992
Gift of Mother's Finest
2014.145.20

Pages 192–193 (*t*) and Page 193 (*tr*)
Hartwell
Pink satin "J.J. Fad in Effect" jacket
worn by MC J.B.
ca. 1988
2020.38.9

Page 192 (*tl*)
Converse
Customized Sigma Gamma Rho
Converse sneakers for member MC Lyte
2005-10
Gift of MC Lyte
2011.118.3ab

Page 193 (*bl*)
Janette Beckman
Female Rappers, Class of '88
1988; printed 2004
© Janette Beckman
2015.132.65

Index

Page numbers in *italics* refer to the illustrations and their captions

ABC Records (prev. ABC-Paramount Records) 21, 124
Academy Awards *28*, 29, 134
activism 60, 84, 90–91, 94, 95, 106, 112, 114–15, 119, 123, 164, 173–74, *174*, 175, 180
Adams, Alton A., Snr. 99
    Continuous Service Certificate 99, *99*, *202–3*
Adler, Bill 102, 134 *see also* Eyejammie Fine Arts Gallery
African and African-inspired clothing 60, *61*, 62–63, *62–63*, 134, *135*, 176
African diaspora 20, 48, *51*, 57, 60, 63, 169
African influences on Black music 11–12, 16, 20, 35, *36*, 43, 48, *51*, 52, 59, 71, 74, 94 *see also* African musical instruments
African musical instruments 40, 42, *42*, 48, 54, 58, 59, 74, 139
Afrobeat 48, *51*
Afrofuturism 107, 133, 140–41, *141*, 162, 177, 179
Aghayan, Ray *28*, 29
Ailey, Alvin 54, *55*
Ain't Misbehavin' (musical, 1978) 140, *140–41*
Akai MPCs 59, *59*
Allen, Devin 114–15, *115*
Allen, Harry 102, *103*
American Federation of Musicians strike (1942–44) 156
Anderson, Marian 66, 78, *154*
    clothing for concert at the Lincoln Memorial 66, *66*
Angela Davis Legal Defense Fund poster *9*
Aragon Ballroom, Pittsburgh 146, *147*
Armstrong, Louis 129, 139, *139*
Atlanta, Georgia ("Black Mecca") 50, 106–7, *106–7*, 155
Avant, Clarence 129, 131
Ayers, Roy
    Music of Many Colors (album, 1980) 48, *51*
        "2000 Blacks Got To Be Free" 48, 51

B-Boy dance crews 39, *39*, *132*
Bahamas Junkanoo Revue 63, *63*
    costumes *62–63*
Bailey, DeFord 16, *16*
    Hohner harmonica 16, *16*
Baldwin, James 24, 42, *44*, 45
    Jimmy's Blues and other Poems
        "Some Days" 42, *44*, 45
Baldwin, Paula *44*
Baldwin Piano Company 146, 148, *149*
Baltimore 33, 50, 114, 115
banjos 39, *138*, 138–39, *139*, 167 *see also* gourd banjos
Barboza, Anthony 176, *176*
    photographs
        Dance Theater of Harlem *54–55*, *56–57*, 57
        Isaac Hayes and Pat Evans for *Essence* magazine *176*
Barretto, Ray 81
    conga drum 81, *81*
Barton, Willene 69, *69*
beatboxing 52
Beatles 84, 152, 157
bebop *12*, 80, 146, 148
Beckman, Janette 192–93, *193*
Belafonte, Harry 112, 167
Bell, Thom (PIR) 157
    turquoise-blue Steinway upright piano 157, *157*
Benjamin, André "André 3000" (OutKast) 107
    cape 107, *107*
Berry, Chuck 84, 188, 190

Cadillac Eldorado convertible *6–7*, 188, *188*
    Chuck Berry: Hail! Hail! Rock (film, 1984) 188
Beth Shalom B'nai Zaken Ethiopian Hebrew Congregation, Chicago 78, *79*
Beyoncé (Beyoncé Knowles-Carter) 144
    Lemonade (album, 2016)
        "Don't Hurt Yourself" (with Jack White) 144, *145*
Billboard charts 37, 124, 141, 160
Billy Eckstine Orchestra 146, *147*
Black Journal (television program) 186–87, 195n.60
Black Lives Matter protests 112, *113*, 114, 178, *179*
Black Power Movement *42*, 144, 192
Black Rock Coalition (BRC) 84, *86*, 189
    Festival poster *86*, 87
Black Stars magazine 154–55, *155*
Black Swan Records 156, *156–57*, 173
blackface performances *see under* minstrels and minstrelsy
Blackwatch Movement 60, 62
Blake, James Hubert "Eubie" 33, *33*, 194n.4
    portrait bust by Walker 33, *33*
    music
        "Charleston Rag" 33
        Shuffle Along musical (music) 33, 140
            "I'm Just Wild About Harry" 33
            "Love Will Find a Way" 33, 140, *140*
            "We Are Americans Too" (with Razaf and Cooke) *98*, 99
Blockson, Charles L. 22
blues 16, 19, 21, 31, 32, 37, 40, *40*, 42, 53, 54, 68, 82, 94, 99, 120, 139, 143, 173 *see also* Chicago blues; Mississippi Delta blues
Bon Soir supper club, Greenwich Village 183
bones 138, 195n.49
boomboxes 131, *131*, 132, 195n.44
Bop City *see* Jimbo's Bop City
Bordentown School, New Jersey 74–75
    school band 75, *75*
Bradford, Perry 85
brass bands 45, 98
breakdancing 39, *39*
Bridson, D.G. 164, *164*
Broadcast Music, Inc. (BMI) 124
Brother J the Grand Verbalizer (X Clan) 62, *62*
Brown, Chuck (The Soul Searchers) 50
Brown, Ernest (FAMU Marching "100") 77
Brown, James 132
    concert at FAMU (1969) 97, *97*
    concert in Boston (1968) 114
Brown v. Board of Education case (1954) 74, 75
Buckbee, J H. 138
Buffalo Soldiers 98–99
Bunch, Lonnie G., III, Smithsonian Institution 11
Bush, George W. 11

Café Society, Greenwich Village 164, 165
Cain's Ballroom, Tulsa 32, *70*, 71
Calhoun, Will (Living Colour) 53, 189
    Mapex floor tom drum *52–53*, 53
call-and-response singing 54, 71, 74, 118
Calloway, Blanche 184
Calloway, Cab 18, *18*, 184
    steamer trunk 18, 19, *19*
Cameron, Clarence P.: violin 38, *38*

Campbell, Elmer Simms: *A Night-club Map of Harlem 2*, 100, *100–101*, *102–3*, 170, *170–71*
Carlisle, Una Mae 160, *160*
Carnegie Hall, New York 66, 126, 194n.18
E.P. Carpenter & Company 92, *92*
Carrington, Matt 184, *185*
Carrington, Terri Lyne 52, 53, 184, *185*
    Best Jazz Instrumental Album award (Grammy) 184, *184*
    drumsticks 52, *53*
    Money Jungle: Provocative in Blue (album, 2013) 184
Carroll, Diahann (Carol Diann Johnson) *28*, 112, 122, 124, 194n.32
    awards 122
        Tony Award for Best Leading Actress in a Musical 122, *122*
    roles
        Carmen Jones (film, 1954) 122
        Chance of a Lifetime (television program) 122
        House of Flowers (musical, 1954) 122
        No Strings (musical, 1962) 122, 194n.31
        Paris Blues (film, 1961) 122
        Porgy and Bess (film, 1959) 122
Cashbox magazine 124, 195n.37
CBS radio station 83, *83*
Charles, Ray 21, *21*, 124
    letter from Jimmie Davis to Charles Sullivan 21, *21*, *196*
    music
        "You Are My Sunshine" 21
Cherry, Ava (Luther Vandross back-up singer) 137
Chess Records 31
Chicago 31, 41, 73, 78, 94
Chicago Blues 31, 71
The Chicago Defender 154, 155
    photographic plate of Marian Anderson 154, *154*
Chicago Symphony Orchestra 67, 94, 96
Chuck D. (Carlton Douglas Ridenhour, Public Enemy) 29, 132, *132*
Civil Rights Movement *12*, 66, 90, 110, *110–11*, 112, *112–13*, 126, 159, 194n.25
Civil War 72, 98, 99, 138, 169
Clark, Claude, Sr. 118
    The Poet II (painting) 118, *118*
Clark, Dave (City Council Chairman, Washington, DC) 180, *181*
classical music 45, 47, 64, 66, 67, 73, 96, 97, 154, 156, 186, 194n.16, 194n.18
Cleveland 68, *83*, 93, 104–5
Cleveland, Rev. James 37
    "You're the Best Thing That Ever Happened to Me" 37
Clinton, George (Parliament-Funkadelic) 107, 133
clothing *see* costume and clothing
Club Harlem, Atlantic City 100
    glass ashtray 100, *100*
clubs 73, 78, 83, 102, 160 *see also* nightclubs
Colored Performing Rights Society of America (CPRSA) 85
    embosser and seal 85, *85*
Coltrane, Alice McLeod 186–87, *187*
Coltrane, John 68–69, 80, 186
    "Nothing Beats A Trial But A Failure" 69, *69*
Columbia Records 173, 174, 189 *see also* Race Records
The Commandment Keepers 78

Communism and the Communist Party 165, 167
community bands 115, *115*
community, importance of music and dance 11, 15, 36,
    54, 57, 59, 63, 71, 72, 73, 78, 80, 82, 83, 87–88,
    96–97, 102, 104–5, 115
concerts *20*, 33, 54, 66–67, 68, *73*, 96, 97, *97*, 110, 114,
    156, 160, 169, 174
Conover Cable Company 41, 94, *94*
Conyers, John 180, *181*
Cooke, Charles L.: "We Are Americans Too" (with Blake
    and Razaf) *98*, 99
Cooke, Sam 37, 78, 124
Cooper, Jack 104
Cornelius, Don 131, 160, *161*
Cosey, Pete 40, 42, *42*
costume and clothing 47–48, 133, 141, 144, 152, 163, 177
    African-inspired clothing 60, *61*, 62–63, *62–63*,
        134, *135*, *176*
    André 3000's cape 107, *107*
    André De Shield's jumpsuit from *The Wiz*
        140, 140–41
    Bernie Worrell's cape 177, *177*
    Billie Holiday's lace dress *121*, 194n.30
    Celia Cruz's dress *13*
    Diana Ross's costume from *Lady Sings the*
        Blues 28, *28*
    FAMU marching band uniform *76*, 77, *77*
    hip-hop fashion 192–93, *192–93*
    Janet Jackson
        child's dress 93, *93*
        white ensemble from "Scream" music
            video 163, *163*
    Jerry Seay's leather jacket 190, *191*
    Lena Horne's dress from *Stormy Weather 4*, 158, *158*
    Little Richard's floral brocade two-piece 152, *153*
    Luther Vandross costumes 137, *137*
    Marian Anderson's concert costume 66, *66*
    Nona Hendryx's silver costume *143*, 144
    parade costumes *62–63*, 63
    Prince's lavender suit 48, *49*
    statement T-shirts 114, *114*
    see also shoes and boots
Cotton Club, Harlem 158, 170
    clapper 170, *171*
Count Basie Orchestra 32, 120
country music 16, *17*, 21, 71
Country Music Association award *17*
Cropper, Steve 124
    "Mr. Pitiful" (with Redding) 124, *125*
Crump, Edie (Harlem Playgirls) 186, *186*
Cruz, Celia ("Queen of Salsa") *13*, 81
    dress *13*

dance *34*, 35, 36, 39, 52, 54–57
Dance Theater of Harlem (DTH) *54–55*, *56–57*, 57
    dyed tights and ballet shoes 57, *57*
Daniels, Jimmie 173, *182*, 182–83
    cane 183, *183*
    honorable discharge record 183, *183*
Davis, Dr. Chuck "Baba Chuck" 54, 57
    notebook *56*, 57
Davis, Jimmie 21
    letter to Ray Charles 21, *21*, *196*
    "You Are My Sunshine" 21
Davis, Miles 40, 42, *42*, 78
Davis, Sammy, Jr. 52, 100, 130, 159
    tap shoes 52, *52*
Dawson, William Levi 96, *96*
De Lavallade, Carmen 54, *54*
De Shields, André 141
Dearing, Judy 141
    costume design for *Porgy and Bess* 141, *141*

Def Jam Recordings 102, 134
Detroit 41, 87, 88, 186 *see also* Detroit Riots
Detroit Free Press 88, *89*
Detroit Riots (1967) 87, 88, *89*, 123
Diddley, Bo (Ellas Otha Bates) 28
    instruments 40
        "Brass King" washboard 40, *40*
        Gretsch G6138 rectangular guitar *26–27*, 27–28
Dilla, J. (James Yancey) 59
    Akai MPC 59, *59*
    Moog synthesizer *58–59*, 59
disc jockeys *see* DJs
Dixie Hummingbirds 35–36, 194n.5
    Best Soul Gospel Performance award (Grammy) 35,
        36, 194n.5
    "Loves Me Like a Rock" (Paul Simon) 35, *36*
Dixon, Dean 67, *67*
Dixon, Willie: "You Need Love" lyrics 31, *31*, *198*
DJs 60, 82, 104, 105, 124, *178*, 180
Domino, Antoine "Fats" 108–9, 124
    loafers (Pierre Cardin) 108, *108*
    "Ain't That a Shame" painting *109*
Doré, Rabbi David Matthew *79*
Dorsey, Thomas A.: Conover "Fairy Grand" piano 94, *94*
Douglass, Frederick 73, *73*
Douglass, Joseph 73, *73*
    letter to Mary Church Terrell 73, *73*, *200*
Dreamland, Chicago 173
drums and drumming 39, 50, *50*, 52, 53, *58*, 59, 63, 81,
    98, *98*, 100, 184
    conga drum (Ray Barretto) 81, *81*
    drum with blackface caricatures 119–20
    Mapex floor tom drums (Will Calhoun) *52–53*, 53
Du Bois, W.E.B. 173
Dunham, Katherine 54

E U. (Experience Unlimited) 50
    "Da Butt" 50
East Publications Incorporated *125 see also*
    Stax Records
Ebenezer AME Church choir, Fort Washington,
    Maryland 94, *94–95*
Ebony magazine 104, 122, 123, *123*, *154*, 195n.56
Eckstine, Billy 146, *147*
Edwards, John "Jimbo" 78, 102
Electric Lady Studios, Greenwich Village 124, 127, *127*
    magnetic tape 124, 127, *127*
Elliot, Gregory "Sugar Bear" 50
Ellison, Ralph 96
emancipation of enslaved people 46, *46*, 59, 169, *201*
enslaved people and slavery 7, 11–12, *34*, 35, 38, 39, 45,
    46, 58, 64, 68, 110, 117, 139 *see also* emancipation;
    freed enslaved people
Ernie Fields Orchestra 32
    "In the Mood" *32*
    poster 31–32, *32*
ESP Guitars 188, *189*
Essence magazine 141, *176*
Europe, James Reese 99, *98–99*
Evans, Pat *176*, 176
"An Evening of Music and Drama for Freedom Now"
    (1960) poster *111*, 112
Eyejammie Fine Arts Gallery and Hip-Hop Photography
    Collection 102, 134

Fab 5 Freddy (Fred Brathwaite) 134, *178*, *178*
    diamond ring (Tito the Jeweler) *178*, *178*
female performers 41, *61*, 69, *69*, 120, 142–44, 174
    Blues Queens *143*, 144
    hip-hop and rap 192–93, *193*
    instrumentalists 53, 184–87
    see also named performers

Female Rappers, Class of '88 photograph 192–93, *193*
feminism 134, 143, 144, 179
Fields, Ernie 32, *32*, 130
The Fifth Dimension 123, *123*
Fillmore District, San Francisco ("Harlem of the West")
    78, *80*, 102
film industry *see* Hollywood
First Class, Inc. 106
Fischer, Lisa (Luther Vandross back-up singer) 137
Fishbone 189–90
    rubber fish skeleton (promotional material) 189, *190*
    music
        Fishbone (EP, 1985) 189
        Truth and Soul (album, 1988) 189
Fisher, Jules 133
Fisk Jubilee Singers 19, 96, *168*, 169
    The Story of the Jubilee Singers ... (songbook,
        1883) *168*, 169
Fisk University, Memphis *168*, 169
Flav, Flavor (William Drayton Jr., Public Enemy) 29
    clock 29, *29*, 31
Fleming, Dr. E. McClung 15, 17, 20, 29
Florida A&M University (FAMU)
    James Brown concert poster 97, *97*
    marching band 76–77
        baritone horn 96–97, *97*
        Marching "100" *76*, 97
        uniform *76*, 77, *77*
Floyd, George 112, 114
folk music *11*, *16*, *40*, 74, 138, 167
Foster, Dr. William P. 76, *76*, 77, 97
freed enslaved people 45, *45*, 46, 47, 169 *see also*
    emancipation
Freedom Singers 110, *110*
    We Shall Overcome (album, 1963) 110, *110*
Freeman, Ernest "Ernie" *92*, 130, 158
    awards
        gold records 130, *130*
        Grammys 130, 159
    music
        arrangements for albums
            Bridge Over Troubled Water (1970) 130, 159
            Strangers in the Night (1966) 130, 159
        band music 93, 130
        film music 93, 158–59
        television music
            It Takes a Thief 159, *159*, *205*
funk 42, 48, 50, 52, *70*, 71, 106, 107, 114, 133, 144, 157,
    177, 189, 190
Funnye, Rabbi Capers 78

Gamble, Kenny (PIR) 157, 180, *181*
Gershwin, George 18, 141
Gillam, Charles: "Ain't That a Shame" painting *109*, 109
Gillespie, John Birks "Dizzy" *12*, 80, 90, 146, *147*
    "Dizzy Gillespie for President" button *12*
Gladys Knight and The Pips 87–88, *88*
    "I Heard it through the Grapevine" 88, *88*
    "You're the Best Thing That Ever
        Happened To Me" 37
Glaser, Joe (ABC) 129
Globe Poster Printing Corporation 37, *37*, 97, *97*
go-go music 50
Gober, Bertha (Freedom Singers) 110, *110*
Gold Tape Awards 159, *159*
Gordy, Berry (Motown Records) 28, 41, 87, 157
Gospel Hymns No. 2 (P.P. Bliss and Ira D. Sankey)
    22, *23*, 27
gospel music 35, *36*, 37, 40, 42, 54, 94, 104, 150, 188
gourd banjos 58, *58*
Grammys (National Academy of Recording Arts &
    Sciences) 35, *36*, 53, 74, *74*, 130, 184, *184*,

193, 194n.5
Grand Ole Opry, Nashville 16, *16*
Grandmaster Flash and the Furious Five 107
    "The Message" 159
Gray, Freddie 114
Great Migration 94, 95, 104, 182
Greenfield, Elizabeth Taylor 156
Greenwich Village, New York 124, 127, 164, 165, 173, 183
Greenwood district, Tulsa ("Black Wall
    Street") *10*, 71–72
Gretsch Guitars *26–27*, 27–28
guitars *26–27*, 27–28, 41, 109, *109*, 139, 188, 189
    acoustic 188
        Josh White Acoustic Guitar *164–65*, *166*, 167
    electric *27*, 41, 188, *188–89*, *190–91*
        ESP Mirage electric guitar (Vernon Reid) 188, *189*
        Gretsch G6138 rectangular guitar (Bo Diddley)
        26–27, 27–28
    steel guitars 41, *41*

Hairston, Jester *20*
Hall, Adelaide 140
Hall Johnson Choir *20*, 64, 65, 165
Hall, Juanita 195n.33
Handy Brothers Music Co. Inc. 99
Hansberry, Lorraine 112, 175
Harambee Singers 110
Hardaway, Lula 180, *181*
Harlem 64, 67, 78, *79*, 114, 169, 170, 182
    nightclubs 100, 148, 170, 182
        map *2*, *100–101*, *102–3*, 170, *170–71*
    see also Dance Theater of Harlem; Harlem
        Renaissance
Harlem Playgirls 184, 186
    poster 184, *186*
Harlem Renaissance 54, 140, 156, 169, 170, 173, 182
harmonicas 16, 68, 174, 178
    Hohner 16, *16*, *174*
Harris, Charles "Teenie" 146, *147*
Harris, Rutha Mae (Freedom Singers) 110, *110*
Hawk Records 105, *105*
Hawkins, Bill *104*, 104–5
Hawkins, Edwin 95
    "Oh Happy Day" 37
Hayes, Isaac 159, 176, *176*, 178
    Black Moses (album, 1971) 178
    Hot Buttered Soul (album, 1969) 176, 178
HBCUs (historically Black colleges and universities) 77,
    96–97, *96–97*, 169
Hebb, Bobby *40*
Hendrix, Jimi 50, *50*, 84, *86*, 87, 124, 127, *127*, 128
    electric guitar 188, *188–89*, *190–91*
    Rainbow Bridge (album, 1971) 127, *127*
        "Bleeding Heart" 127
        "Earth Blues" *127*
Hendryx, Nona (Labelle) 144
    silver costume for *The Midnight Special*
        (LeGaspi) *143*, 144
Herkert & Meisel steamer trunk (Cab Calloway)
    18, 19, *19*
Hine, Lewis Wickes *75*
hip-hop 19, 21, 28–29, 33, 39, *39*, 43, 50, 53, 59, 60,
    63, 71, 102, 106–7, 112, 131, 132, 134, 155, 159, 161,
    178, 192–93
Hohner harmonicas 16, *16*, *174*
Holder, Geoffrey 141
Holiday, Billie (Eleanora Fagan) 100, 120, 122, 129, 164
    fashion and elegance *28*, 120, *121*
        Chantilly lace dress (Andora) *121*, 194n.30
Hollywood film industry 130, 139, 158–59, 160
Holman, Michael (New York City Breakers) 39
homosexuality 134, 136–37, 150, 182, 183

Hooker, John Lee: photograph by Kalischer *11*
Horne, Lena *25*, 158, 164
    friendship with Edouard Plummer 24–25
        letter to Plummer *24*, 25
    films 158
        Cabin in the Sky (1949) 158, *158–59*
        Stormy Weather (1943) 158
        dress *4*, 158, *158*
Hot-Cha nightclub, Harlem 182
The House of God, Jewell Dominion 41, 194n.6
House Un-American Activities Committee
    (HUAC) 165, 167
House, William Julius "Ju Ju" 50, *50*
Houston, Robert 90, *90*
Houston, Whitney *28*, 160–61
    Soul Train Awards 160, 161
Hughes, Langston 83, 164, 165
    "The Man Who Went to War" (play, 1944) 164–65
        script 165, *165*
    The Worker's Song Book 165
"Hunger's Wall," Many Races Soul Center, Washington,
    DC *90–91*, 91
Hunter, Alberta *172*, 173, 182
Hunter, Elder Roosevelt T. 95
    trumpet 95, *95*
Hurricane Katrina 108, *108–9*

Irvine, Weldon J., Jr. "To Be Young, Gifted and Black"
    (with Simone) 175
Isis (X Clan) 62, *62*

Jackson, Janet 30, 93, 162, 163
    dress 93, *93*
    earring with key 30, *30*
    music videos 162
        Control (album, 1986) 162
        Janet Jackson's Rhythm Nation 1814
            (album, 1989) 162
        "Scream" 162–63, *162–63*
            white ensemble 163, *163*
            white leather chair 162, *162*, 163
    music
        Control (album, 1986) 30, 162
        Janet Jackson (album, 1982) 30
        Janet Jackson's Rhythm Nation 1814 (album,
            1989) 30, 162
        "Scream" (with Michael Jackson) 162
Jackson, Michael 162, 163
    Bad Tour (1987) 131
    HIStory: Past, Present and Future, Book 1
        (album, 1995) 162
        "Scream" (with Janet Jackson) 162
    music videos
        "Billie Jean" 162
        "Scream" 162, *162–63*
            white leather chair 162, *162*, 163
        "Thriller" 162
Jackson, Millie 193, *193*
Jackson-Ransom, Burnella "Bunnie" 106
Jackson, Rev. Jesse 180, *181*
Jackson, Steve, Jr. 78, 80, *80*, 102
Jacobs, "Little" Walter 68
jazz 19, 21, 37, 40, 41, 42, 43, 50, 52, 53, 67, 68, 69, 71,
    93, 100, 102, 104, 106, 140, 146, 184, 186, 195n.54
Jenkins, Ella 54, 74, *74*
    Grammy Lifetime Achievement Award 74, *74*
Jewell, Bishop Mattie Lou 41, 194n.6
jewelry 30, *30*, 60, *60*, *62*, 63, 108, 178, *178*, 192
Jewish congregations 78, *79*
Jim Crow segregation laws 16, 19, 80, 96, 154
Jimbo's Bop City, San Francisco 69, *69*, 78, 80,
    80, *101*, 102

Jimmie Daniels' Nightclub, Harlem 182–83
J.J. Fad 193
    satin jacket *192–93*, 193
Johnson, Francis 45
    "General La Fayette Bugle Waltz" sheet music
        45, *45*, 47
Johnson, Hall *20*, 54, *64*, 64–65, 164
    camera 64, *64*
    letter to "Mr. Kosson" 65, *65*, *199*
    music
        "Ain't Got Time to Die" *64–65*, 65
Johnson, James Weldon and John Rosamond: "Lift
    Every Voice and Sing" 95, *95*
Johnson, Jason Miccolo 36
    Liturgical Dance Ministry dancers *34*, 36
    Ebenezer AME Church choir *94–95*
Johnson Publishing Company 123, 154, 195n.56
Jordan, Samuel H. (city government official,
    Washington, DC) 180, *181*
The Juilliard School, New York *14*, 67, 177
Julius, Lela (Harlem Playgirls) 186
Junkanoo Revue 63

Kalischer, Clemens *11*
Karlsen, Webe: "To Be Young, Gifted and Black" (single,
    1970) 175, *175*
Kay, Suzanne 122, 194n.32
King, Coretta Scott 180
King, Dr. Martin Luther, Jr. 90, 112, 114, 180
    "An Evening of Music and Drama for Freedom Now"
        (1960) poster *111*
    birthday commemorations 180, *181*
    national holiday campaign 180
King Super saxophones 68, *68–69*
Kirkpatrick, Rev. Frederick Douglass 90, *90*
Knight, Gladys *88 see also* Gladys Knight and The Pips
Koch, Norma *28*, 29
Kuti, Fela 48
    Music of Many Colors (album, 1980) 48, *51*
        "2000 Blacks Got To Be Free" 48, 51

Labelle 144
lamellophones (thumb pianos) 40, *42*
Larkin, Peter 133
Led Zeppelin: "Whole Lotta of Love" *31*
Lee, Bill 132
Lee, Canada 164, *164*
Lee, Spike (Shelton Jackson Lee) 131, *131*, 195n.45
    Do the Right Thing (film, 1989) *131*, 131–32, 195n.45
    School Daze (1988) 50
LeGaspi, Larry *143*, 144
Leipzig, Arthur 67, *67*
Liston, Melba 53, 69
Little Richard (Richard Wayne Penniman) 84, *150*, 152
    King James Bible 150, *151*
    religious conversion 150, 153
    sexuality 150, 152
    stage costumes *150–51*, *152–53*
        floral brocade two-piece (Melvin James) 152, *153*
    Vee-Jay Records invoice 157, *157*, *204*
Liturgical Dance Ministry, Metropolitan Baptist Church,
    Largo, Maryland *34*
Living Colour 53, *86*, *188–89*, 190
    Best Hard Rock Performance award (Grammy) 53
    Vivid (album, 1988) 188–89
        "Cult of Personality" 189
LL Cool J (James Todd Smith) 102, *103*
    "I Need a Beat" 102, *103*
Lomax, Alan 164, 165, 167
Long, Henry, L. 92, 93
    Carpenter & Company parlor-style pump
        organ 92, *92*

Lyle, Aubrey: *Shuffle Along* musical (book, with Miller) 140

Mackie, Bob *28*, 29
Madsen, Rex: Alberta Hunter collage *172*
Maison Dorcas Women's Singing Group 60, *61*
Many Races Soul Center, Washington, DC 90–91
Mapex Drums *52–53*, 53
marching bands 76–77, 96–97
J.B.T. Marsh: *The Story of the Jubilee Singers: With Their Songs* (1883) *168*, 169
Marzullo, Steve 42, 45
material culture, study and interpretation 12, 14, 15, 17, 20, 27–28, 31–32, 45, 66, 119, 126, 131, 194n.30
    music and musical instruments 12, 15, 20, 22, 32, 35, 51, 52, 58, 69, 71, 87, 156, 179, 184
Matthew, Rabbi Wentworth Arthur 78, *79*
Mayfield, Curtis 159
    awards *159*
    Super Fly (film soundtrack, 1972) 159
MC Lyte (Lana Michele Moorer) 192
    Converse sneakers 192, *192*
    "Paper Thin" single 192
McCarthyism 165, 167
McDaniels, Ralph 161
McDonald, Audra: *Go Back Home* (album, 2013) 45
McFerrin, Robert, Sr. 65, 194n.16
Meinell, William R. 46
Memphis Gospel Festival (1973) 37
    poster 37, *37*
Memphis, Tennessee 37, 82, 95, 124, 129, 169, 176
microphones 43, *43*, 68, 161, *161*
The Midnight Special (television program) 144
Miley, James "Bubber" 68
military bands 45, 98–99, *98–99*
military service 45, 80, 98–99, 183
Miller, Flournoy: *Shuffle Along* musical (book, with Lyle) 140
minstrels and minstrelsy 47, 54, *116*, 117, *119*, 119–20, 138, 139
    blackface 47, 68, 117, 119, *119*, 120, 138–39, *138–39*
Minton's Playhouse, Harlem 146, 148
    gala night opening invitation 146, *148*
    neon sign 146, *146–47*, 148, *148–49*
Mirafone 96–97, *97*
Mississippi Delta Blues 53, 71
Mitchell, Arthur 54, 57
Mitchell, Jack 54, *55*
Monáe, Janelle 177, 179, *179*
    "Hell You Talmbout" 178–79
    "Say Her Name" 179
Monk, Thelonious: grand piano (Baldwin) 146, 148, *149*
Moog synthesizers *58–59*, 59
Moser, Don: Voodoo guitar ("Marie") 109, *109*
Mother's Finest 190
    Another Mother Further (album, 1977) 190
Mothership 133, *133*, 177
Motown Records, Detroit 28, 87–88, 131, 156, 157
    Soul Records label 88, *88*
    Tamla label 175
MTV 134, 162, 178, *178*, 189
    Video Music Awards 163
Mulholland, Joan Trumpauer 126
music education, importance of 72, 73, 74, *74*, 75, 77, 78, 87, 169 *see also* HBCUs
Music Inn, Lenox, Massachusetts *11*
music press 104, 122, 123, *123*, *154*, 154–55, *155*, 195n.56
music videos 131, 134, *135*, 161, 162–63, 178, 189, 192
musical instruments 28, 35, 38, 58–59, 76, 78, 95
    homemade 39–40, 41, 58
    see also specific instruments

musicals and musical theater 47, 119, 140–41, 165, 182
    see also named musicals

NAACP 66, 95
National Academy of Recording Arts & Sciences 74 *see also* Grammys
National Association of Negro Musicians (NANM) 83
National Museum of African American History and Culture, Smithsonian Institution *see* NMAAHC
Neblett, Charles (Freedom Singers) 110, *110*
New Era Cap Company 106
New Orleans 71, *108–9*, *108–9*
New York City 33, 65, 67, 96, 112, 146, 148, 155, 161, 169, 173, 182 *see also* Greenwich Village; Harlem
New York City Breakers 39, *39*
New York Philharmonic Orchestra 67, 194n.18
Newcomb, Bobby: *Tambo* (jokebook and instruction manual) 138, *138*
nightclubs 37, 80, 93, 100, *101*, 102–3, 182
    map 2, *100–101*, *102–3*, 170, *170–71*
    see also named nightclubs
Nipsey Hussle (Ermias Asghedom) 112, *113*
    "FDT" (with YG) 112
NMAAHC 7, 11, 15, 20, 31, 38, 50, 54, 57, 64, 98, 102, 134, 150, 188
Nunn, Bill *131*, 195n.45

Oliver, Tommy 112, *113*
oral traditions 42, 43, 78, 104
organs 92–93
    Carpenter & Co. parlor-style pump organ 92, *92*
    organ music *116*
Oscars *see* Academy Awards
OutKast (André 3000 and Big Boi) 106, 107, 155, *155*
    ATLiens (album) 106–7
    Idlewild (album and film) 155
    Southernplayalisticadillacmuzik (album) 107
    Stankonia (album)
        "B.O.B." 107
    see also Benjamin, André; Patton, Antwan
Ovation Guitar Division, Kaman Corporation 167
Owens, Kevin (Luther Vandross back-up singer) 137

P-Funk *see* Parliament-Funkadelic
Pace, Harry (Black Swan Records) 156
Paniccioli, Ernie *62*, 62–63
Paradise the Architect (X Clan) 62, *62*
Paramount Records *172* see also ABC Records
Parker, Charlie 68, 69, 146, *147*
    King Super 20 saxophone (H. N. White) 68, *68–69*
Parliament-Funkadelic (later P-Funk) 133, 177
    "Mothership Connection" 177
    Mothership stage prop *see under* Mothership
    T.A.P.O.A.F.O.M. (album, 1996) 133
Patton, Antwan "Big Boi" 106
    Atlanta Braves baseball cap 106–7, *107*
    Vicious Lies and Dangerous Rumors (album) 106
    see also OutKast
Peacock Records *174*, 176
Penniman, Richard Wayne *see* Little Richard
Philadelphia 45, 69, 83–84, *84*
Philadelphia International Records (PIR) 157, 180
Philco model 48-482 radio 82, *82*
photography and photographers 12, *20*, 24, 54, 63, 64, 66, 69, 78, 88, *89*, 90, 100, 102, 132, 134, 146, 173
    see also named photographers
pianos 45, 66, 72, 82, *92*, 92–93, 108–9, *109*
    Baldwin grand piano (Thelonious Monk) 146, 148, *149*
    Conover "Fairy Grand" piano (Thomas Dorsey) 41, 94, *94*
    Steinway upright piano (Thom Bell) 157, *157*

Pierre Cardin label 108, *108*
Pilgrim Baptist Church, Chicago 41, 94
Pittsburgh 138, 146
Pittsburgh Courier 99, 146
Plummer, Edouard 24, *25*
    friendship with Lena Horne 24–25
    letter from Horne *24*, 25
politics and music relationship 21, 45, 50, 60, 62, 82, 95, 110, 112, 114, *120*, 131, 132, 144, 156, 164–65, 173, 180
pop music 32, 88, 130, 160
Porgy and Bess (musical and film, Gershwin) 18, 122, 141
    costume design (Dearing) *141*
posters *9*, 24, 31–32, *32*, 37, *37*, 47, *47*, *86*, 87, 97, *97*, *111*, 112, 184, *186*
Presley, Elvis 84, 176
Price, Leontyne 66, *66–67*
Pride, Charley 16, *17*
    Country Music Association award *17*
Primus, Pearl 54
Prince (Prince Rogers Nelson) 48, 114, 190
    costumes 48
        boots with "Love Symbol" 48, *49*
        lavender suit (Serio) 48, *49*
    image on *Rally 4 Peace* T-shirt 114, *114*
    music
        "Baltimore" 114
        Indigo Nights (album, 2007)
        "Baby Love" 190
Professor X the Overseer (X Clan) 62, *62*
Public Enemy 29, *29*, 132
    "Fight the Power" *131*, 132
    necklace with cross hairs logo 132, *132*

Queen Latifah (Dana Owens) 134, *135*
    awards 134
    Nature of a Sista (album, 1991) *135*
    "Fly Girl" single and music video 134, *135*
queer *see* homosexuality

Race Records Division (Columbia) 85, 142–43, *142–43*, 143
    ledger 142, *142–43*, *144–45*
racism 12, 15, 29, 45, 54, 65, 66, 84, *87*, 99, 117, 119, 120, 122, 124, 132, 134, 138, 139, 146, 160, 173, 174, 175, 178, *186* see also stereotypes and caricatures
radio and radio stations 16, 66, 67, 80, *82*, 82–83, 85, 104
    Philco model 48-482 radio 82, *82*
    see also named radio stations
"Radio Raheem" (Bill Nunn) in *Do the Right Thing* (Lee) 132, 195n.45
    Promax Super Jumbo boombox 131, *131*, 132, 195n.44
ragtime 19, 21, 33, 68, 99, 140
Rakim (William Michael Griffin Jr.) 43, *43*
    The 18th Letter (album, 1997) 43
    Shure Beta 58A microphone 43, *43*
Rally 4 Peace concert, Baltimore (2015) 114
rap 21, 42, 43, 71, 178, 192–93
Razaf, Andy: "We Are Americans Too" (with Blake and Cooke) *98*, 99
R&B 21, 36, 37, 41, 43, 48, 53, *70*, 71, 93, 104, 106, 108, 124, 128, 146, 176, 188, 193
Reagon, Bernice Johnson (Freedom Singers, Harambee Singers, Sweet Honey in the Rock) 110, *110*
Reagon, Cordell (SNCC and Freedom Singers) 110, *110*
record labels 31, 110, 124, *125*, 129, 130, 131, 134, *135*, 156–57, 178, 180, 193 *see* named labels
record stores *104–5*, 105
recording studios 124, 127, 128–29
Redding, Otis 124
    "Mr. Pitiful" (with Cropper) 124, *125*